FROM LAWYER

TO

LAW FIRM

HOW TO MANAGE
A SUCCESSFUL LAW BUSINESS

BY ELIZABETH MILLER
AND JORYN JENKINS

This work is based, in part, on actual clients of the authors. Names and identifying details have been changed to protect the privacy of the persons involved. This publication is designed to provide accurate and authoritative information with regard to its subject matter. It is sold with the understanding that the publisher is not engaged in rendering legal, accounting, or other advice. If legal advice or other expert assistance is required, seek the services of a competent professional. The opinions expressed by this book's authors are not endorsed by Open Palm Press and are the sole responsibility of the authors. Because of the Internet's dynamic nature, any Web addresses or links referenced herein may have changed since publication and may no longer be valid.

Although the authors and publisher have made every effort to ensure that the information in this book was correct at press time, they do not assume and hereby disclaim any liability to any party for any loss, damage, or disruption caused by errors or omissions, whether such errors or omissions result from negligence, accident, or any other cause.

This title is available at special quantity discounts for bulk purchases for sales promotions, premiums, fundraising, and educational use. Special versions or excerpts can also be created to fit specific needs. Visit us online at www.OpenPalmPress.com.

FROM LAWYER TO LAW FIRM: HOW TO MANAGE A SUCCESSFUL LAW BUSINESS

Published by Open Palm Press
Copyright © 2017 by Joryn Jenkins
Cover art by 4EDGE, LLC

First Printing: May 2017
Printed in the United States of America

First Edition: May 2017

DEDICATIONS

I dedicate this book to my husband of 34 years, Richard Miller. Although his own career ended tragically more than 20 years ago due to an automobile accident, he has always encouraged my aspirations and pushed me to follow my dreams. His support has never wavered; he has always insisted that I could achieve my goals, no matter how far reaching they were. Getting this book published is as much an accomplishment of his as it is of mine because, without his constant support, this book never would have happened. You, Richie, are my rock.

—Liz Miller

***

I dedicate this book to my husband, Todd Jones, who has always been my biggest fan. I also dedicate it to my daughter, Alexis Jones, who motivates me to set a good example for her as a strong, ethical businesswoman. Finally, I dedicate this book to a few members of my staff who have shown me endless support throughout the years. Sheila Fickes, Bill Parsons, and Lori Skipper have each stood by me through the ups and downs and are a major reason why my firm is a success. I am eternally thankful for their support.

—Joryn Jenkins

Give me six hours to chop down a tree and I will spend the first four sharpening the axe.

— Abraham Lincoln

Prior Planning Prevents Piss Poor Performance.

— U.S. Army

ACKNOWLEDGEMENTS

I have always had an independent streak. I was an "out of the box" thinker before that phrase became a cliché. I do not believe that you can run down a checklist of what to do to run a law firm the same way you can run down a checklist for opening a file or filing a lawsuit. Summons, check; complaint, check; filing fee, check. The business of managing a law firm, with its particular protocols and policies and its various relationships and responsibilities, does not work this way.

I often read articles and advice columns written by HR people or accountants giving counsel on how to address issues in a law firm, and I sit here and scratch my head. You simply cannot run a law firm the same way you run a large corporation. The entire atmosphere of a law firm that sells services, coupled with the rules of bar associations governing what is and is not allowed, changes the entire dynamics of *managing the business of practicing law.*

What I have written in this book is the culmination of 38 years of working with the legal profession. In addition to writing about managing the business of practicing law, I detail real-life situations that have occurred throughout my career which have helped form the practices and guides shared in this book.

So, I first acknowledge and thank everyone with whom I have worked, engaged, and interacted during the course of my career. I am even thankful for the bad experiences that I have suffered over the course of my career. It is all of those experiences that have enabled me to write this book.

I must also acknowledge my good friend of over 40 years, Mike Fass. Mike made me realize that it is more important to follow your dreams than to follow the money. At the end of your career, you might not still have the money, but you will always be able to say that you did what you were passionate about.

I owe a debt of gratitude to my friend, attorney Chris Ragano. Chris is the attorney I interviewed with in December, 2015 for a position that I thought was full-time. He was very insistent that I accept the part-time position with his firm. He offered to refer other attorneys to me so that I could build a business as an independent firm administrator. Chris has been openly supportive of my work in the legal community and the publication of this book. I believe that everything in life happens for a reason. I am grateful to Chris Ragano for his friendship, support, and encouragement.

—Liz Miller

***

For decades, I have owned my own private law practice, and I have learned that a loyal staff is a firm's most valuable asset. Surround yourself with hardworking, reliable people, and you will have a much greater chance of success. I would like to acknowledge certain staff members who regularly surpass my expectations with their hard work and devotion.

Sheila Fickes has been my paralegal/legal assistant for many years. It is hard to recall a time when she did not work for my firm. The compassion that she shows to our clients, as well as her knowledge of both family legal and collaborative practice, make her invaluable to my firm.

My dear friend Bill Parsons has been my one-man IT department for decades. But to say that he is just "the IT guy" would not give credit where credit is due. Aside from his extraordinary IT skills, Bill does everything in my firm, from battling with service providers to finding the lowest rates possible to walking the office dogs (who all love him, and *not* just because he always carries dog treats in his pockets).

Lori Skipper began working as an attorney for my firm over ten years ago, fresh out of law school. She remained at my firm until she had her son two years ago. She now continues to support my firm by working from home, as well as in her new role as COO of *Open Palm Press*.

Your staff is a reflection of you. So surround yourself with diligent, dependable people. Treat them right, and they will do the same for you.

—Joryn Jenkins

WHAT OTHERS ARE SAYING ABOUT THIS BOOK

This is a wonderfully informative, remarkably thorough, and entirely engaging guide to the business side of law practice. The authors generously share a wealth of experience on subjects – ranging from ethics and client relations to the nitty-gritty of budgets – that will benefit both newly minted lawyers and those who are reevaluating their practices.

David A. Hoffman, Lecturer on Law
Harvard Law School
TEDx Talk *Lawyers as Peacemakers*
Founder, Boston Law Collaborative, LLC

This is a much-needed manual. Thank you for doing it. From time to time, I have represented a lawyer who came out of a big firm to open his or her own office and then got in trouble – inadvertently. Particularly on how to set up a trust account and keep the trust account and the business account separate. I succeeded each time in getting the attorney off with a requirement of taking a course in the subjects you explore. Your book does a fine job of explaining it all. Put it together with a good CLE course and a first-rate teacher to take the neophyte through, and there is some real hope. I wish there were a way for the bar to register every law office and insist that, before a lawyer opens his or her own law office, he or she take a course like the one you've written this for.

Sherman Cohn, Professor
Legal Profession and Professional Ethics
Georgetown University Law Center

Thanks to Jenkins and Miller, new lawyers now have Google Maps to all the major issues facing them when they opt to hang out their shingles: staffing, accountability, management, process improvement, outsourcing, technology, knowledge management and analytics, along with insightful comments on billing, ethics, and use of social media. The authors do a great job of summarizing the rules, objectives, and dangers of running a solo or small law firm, but they also offer easy fixes. This manual is an excellent resource for learning the practical approach to running your own law practice and should be required reading for law students, especially as the authors have supplemented their material with Review Questions aimed at both lawyers and law students. Understanding procedure, substantive law, and local practices of the courts is important, but the business of the law is essential to ethical operation of a successful practice. This manual nicely fills in the gap between law school and the professional arena.

Dorothea Beane, Professor
Co-Director Stetson Institute of Caribbean Law and Policy
Stetson University College of Law

Liz worked with me for many months during one of the most difficult times of transition that my former firm had ever experienced. Her insight into both the financial and people part of the practice was like a breath of fresh air. She negotiated every bit of funds we needed as often as she could, while still being practical about diminishing returns. She worked tirelessly in all aspects of the firm because she genuinely wanted to see the firm succeed and because she knew how to address problems in each area. This book is like a written version of Liz's helpful input and advice that she doled out to us daily—clearly written, simple to understand, and on point in every way. Just like Liz!

Dorothy V. DiFiore, Partner
Quintairos, Prieto, Wood & Boyer Law

From Lawyer to Law Firm *is a smart, practical reference guide that you will return to time and time again as you build your own law practice. Over the last 22 years I have twice hung my own shingle and I've learned that the practice of law is a business and must be treated as such to be successful. The insights in this book come from two women who have been in the trenches and are giving you a roadmap; there is no need to learn the hard way when they've given you this gift of hindsight.*

Sheryl Hunter, Owner
Hunter Business Law – The Entrepreneur's Law Firm®

Managing a law firm can be overwhelming. In fact, it's a lot like herding cats: unpredictable and chaotic. In this book, Elizabeth Miller, an experienced, no-nonsense professional law firm administrator, and Joryn Jenkins, with many years of practice in every possible size and type of law business, clearly and concisely guide their readers on how to run a profitable and efficient law practice. So read it and keep it handy the next time the cats and confusion threaten to take over your law firm.

Catherine Jones, Editor
Law Office Manager

I worked with Liz Miller for almost a year. I was a new paralegal at an old law firm where everyone had been there for many years. Liz was the only person I could turn to for help with everything. She ran the business of the law firm and had the knowledge to help each staff member with their day-to-day tasks, including personal issues. She is one of the smartest women I know and very charismatic. Her way of dealing with people at every level makes her one of the best administrators on the planet.

Shawn Neeley
Paralegal

Drawing on her years of experience assisting lawyers with firm administration and management, Liz Miller has written a useful, practical book about law firm administration and its best practices. This book will help the new lawyer just starting out in practice, as well as the successful lawyer overwhelmed by the demands of running a practice.

Ursula Furi-Perry, Director of Academic Excellence
Massachusetts School of Law

Liz Miller has been in the law firm game for over 38 years. Joryn Jenkins has been in the trenches, practicing law, for over 37. This book is a must read for any attorney in private practice, whether just starting out or with decades of experience. From day-to-day operations to how to get referrals and market a practice, Liz packs this book with info that's definitely important to know. I would recommend this book whole-heartedly.

Darrin T. Mish, Esquire
Nationally Recognized Tax Attorney

Liz Miller has been my firm administrator since December 2015. The one word I use to describe Liz's professionalism and administrator abilities is "amazing." Liz is, by far, the best administrator I have ever worked with in over 20 years of practicing law. Through working with Liz, I have realized the significant impact made by having a firm administrator who was a paralegal or legal assistant and who has a strong understanding of the concept of service to the client. Liz's perspective on every aspect of managing my firm is enhanced not only by her managerial talents and experience but her legal experience. She has impacted every aspect of the business of practicing law for this firm.
Liz and Joryn have really written the book on managing the business of practicing law. Her advice can help you whether you are just venturing out on your own, or whether you have been practicing for many years.

Chris E. Ragano, CEO and Founding Partner
The Law Firm of Chris E. Ragano, P.A.

Liz Miller joined this firm as an administrator shortly after I was hired as an administrative assistant. I had been at the firm for a few months by the time Liz came on board. Liz was exactly the breath of fresh air that we needed. She initiated office morale, as there was none. Through her efforts, the atmosphere of the office changed entirely. Liz saw the potential in every employee at this firm and worked hard to bring out the best in everyone to the extent that she was able and implemented procedures at every level. She made working fun and built a cohesive team, as well as trust in our administrative staff that was previously non-existent. She is one of the very best administrators I have ever worked with and I do miss her.

Belinda Trimble. Administrative Assistant
Holland & Hart, LLP

Liz was the administrator of a firm that I joined back in 2015. I have been in the legal field for 40 years and have worked with many office administrators, but . . . Liz is at the top of my list as the best office administrator. Liz is always pleasant, helpful, insightful, full of words of encouragement, and supportive. She has an open-door policy with any questions on office procedures or any obstacle that may arise on any given day. Every day, she would send positive emails to the staff so no matter what obstacle came before us, we had a "can do" attitude. If given the opportunity, I would go anywhere Liz is employed because I know that she cares for her staff and gives 100%. From the moment I was hired, we developed a great working relationship [and I found] a friend for life.

Cheryl D. Boyce, Paralegal
Quintairos, Prieto, Wood & Boyer Law

For the past year, it has been my absolute pleasure to work with Liz Miller, our firm administrator. She is always the first one to offer her extensive years of experience and knowledge of the legal profession to help me advance in my current career as a paralegal with the Law Firm of Chris E. Ragano, P.A. She is very knowledgeable with a practical approach to law office administration. As my boss has said, and I agree, Liz really knows her stuff. I am very proud to call her my colleague and friend.

Wendy L. Hammond, Florida Registered Paralegal
The Law Firm of Chris E. Ragano, P.A.

There's a lot that can be learned from someone who has "been there and done that." Liz Miller and Joryn Jenkins have the experience to give you an insider's look at how to best manage your law firm's business operations, whether you're just starting out or been around the block a few times like me. When I started my own law practice over 25 years ago, I wish I had had resources like Liz and Joryn's book available to me.
Read it, use it, and have fun practicing law.

Dale Appell, Personal Injury Attorney
Law Offices of Dale Appell

Running a small firm has a unique set of challenges. One of the most important is finding the right people to help manage your office and caseload. Our firm grew very fast over the last few years and bringing on Liz to help manage our cases has been invaluable. Her extensive knowledge of both personal injury cases and the management of the office has been an incredible help to our practice. She has helped me return to being a lawyer instead of being an office manager. This book provides insights that law school and CLEs do not teach you. Great read!

Mustafa Ameen, Esquire
Personal Injury and Criminal Attorney

TABLE OF CONTENTS

FOREWORD

Since receiving my B.A. from Newcomb College in 1980 and my J.D. from Tulane University School of Law in 1984, I have been passionate about bringing my clients peace of mind by minimizing their legal and business risk exposure in operating their businesses. Having been a business owner myself since 1988, first as the owner of publishing company, and now a law firm, I understand the feeling many business owners experience that, while they are experts in the fields in which they were trained, they were never properly taught how to run a business. This knowledge is invaluable to any professional who runs his own practice.

In *From Lawyer to Law Firm,* Elizabeth Miller and Joryn Jenkins guide law firm owners through the fine points of law firm management. Typically a fairly dry topic, Liz and Joryn will surprise you as they entertain you with personal anecdotes from their experiences working in the trenches as a law firm administrator and a law firm owner, respectively.

But why should you care about my opinion? Well, I'm proud to tell you.

I joined the law firm of Lugenbuhl, Wheaton, Peck, Rankin & Hubbard in January 2016 as a shareholder in the New Orleans office and in 2017, I was elected to the firm's Board of Directors. From 2008 through December 2015, I was a partner with Montgomery Barnett. Prior to that I served as the managing partner of Patrick, Miller, Burnside & Belleau, LLC.

I served as the national president of the Federal Bar Association for the 2011-2012 term. I currently hold a seat on the American Bar Association's House of Delegates as the FBA representative, and I am a vice-chair of the ABA Fidelity and Surety Law General Committee. I am also a contributing editor to the 2017 edition of *Business Torts: A Fifty State Guide* for the Louisiana chapter.

In May, 2016, I was named to the New Orleans City Business 2016 *Leadership in Law* class. In December, 2016, I spoke at the National Business Institute seminar, *LLCs From Start to Finish,* and was a speaker at the ABA's Fidelity and Surety Law Committee's 2017 Midwinter Meeting held in New Orleans in January, 2017. In addition, I was selected to Super Lawyers from 2007 to 2013 and 2015 to 2017 in the area of business litigation.

From 2006 to 2007, I served as a member of a panel of mediators for the Louisiana Department of Insurance Hurricane Mediation Program administered by American Arbitration Association ("AAA"), mediating hurricane wind damage disputes between homeowners and insurance companies. I have also arbitrated and/or mediated for FINRA, f/k/a National Association of Securities Dealers Regulation, Inc.; the New York Stock Exchange; and the AAA Construction and Commercial panels. In 2007, I served as a hearing examiner of property assessment tax appeals for the City of New Orleans.

My current areas of practice include business litigation, business/corporate, estate planning and probate, construction litigation, fidelity, surety and financial institution bonds, insurance, professional malpractice, and alternative dispute resolution. I advise businesses, financial institutions, and individuals concerning bankruptcies, contracts, construction, environmental issues, fidelity, surety and financial institution bonds, insurance, professional malpractice, real estate, corporate, and estate matters. I assist business owners and entrepreneurs with every aspect of the business from inception through growth and development to, when necessary, dissolution. I assist clients in obtaining financing, provide ongoing business advice, advise clients during litigation, and counsel them through the dissolution of the business. I also consult with individuals on how to protect their personal assets through estate and trust vehicles.

My career as a lawyer spans over 30 years. As a lawyer and former business owner, I have been actively involved in law firm management and administration. I know how a business operates from the inside out, as I have been a business owner myself since 1988. I understand the need to be efficient in the management and marketing of the business and how to address the employee and financial aspects of the business.

Through my foregoing described experience, I know that the business of practicing law brings with it challenges that no other profession must overcome. Lawyers sell their time to their clients – their knowledge of the law and the time that they put into representing a client. All the parts of the practice must synchronize in perfect harmony to make it work.

Balancing the profession of practicing law with the business of practicing law can easily become a fulltime career for the attorney who endeavors to take on that role or who has that role thrust upon him. This role can take on a life of its own and easily consume time that, arguably, would be better devoted to serving clients well. Managing the business of practicing law is a role for which law school does not prepare us, yet it is also crucial to the survival of every law firm, regardless of how large or small it may be.

It takes a person with the experience, education, skill, and dedication to manage a law firm so that it is efficient, productive, and profitable, while nevertheless adhering to the ethics and morals that set the legal profession apart from any other. Elizabeth Miller is that person. She began in the trenches as a legal secretary, back when legal secretaries were called "legal secretaries" and not "legal assistants." She climbed up the law firm ladder to become a certified paralegal and, when the opportunity presented itself, segued her career into that of a law firm administrator.

With a legal career that spans more than three decades, Liz currently works as an independent law firm administrator. She works with lawyers who want to start their own law firm, as well as attorneys who are currently in practice, to become more efficient, productive, and profitable, and thus, more successful. Nowadays, as an editorial board advisory member for *Law Office Manager* magazine and newsletter, Liz shares administration techniques learned and developed as a working law firm administrator through articles and blogs that she writes. She is a member of the National Association of Legal Administrators, the Suncoast Chapters of the Association of Legal Administrators, the Society of Human Resource Management, the Hillsborough County Bar Association, and the American Bar Association.

Joryn Jenkins has been practicing law for 37 years. Before relocating to Tampa to, as she imagined, become "a big fish in a little pond," Joryn worked for one of the ten largest firms in the country in Washington, D.C. When she moved, she served as an assistant state attorney and as a specially-appointed assistant U.S. attorney. In fact, before she opened her own firm, Joryn taught trial practice, appellate practice, and bankruptcy practice for Stetson University College of Law. For the last 23 years, Joryn has successfully run her own law practice, through good times and bad, through recessions and growth, with many employees and few, with a heavily weighted trial practice and, more lately, with an emphasis on a courtless family practice.

In *From Lawyer to Law Firm,* law firm administrator Elizabeth Miller and attorney Joryn Jenkins address law office administration issues – *issues that matter.* Buying office furniture, choosing a computer, and leasing a copier are the peripheral fundamentals of running any office. There are specific administrative, non-legal aspects known as the "business of practicing law" fundamentals that can and will make your law practice successful. Do you know the trust account regulations? Do you have billing procedures in place that enable you to collect more than 90% of your monthly billables? Are you really in touch with your clients? Does your law office culture reflect the values and principles that you hold dear and that will attract the clients you want? What is your current office morale? Who is taking care of your clients? We get so tied up in the practice of law that sometimes we don't know anything about our own business. We are so focused only on our clients' needs, and do not take care of our personal business, such as running an efficient law practice or even having a Last Will and Testament to protect our family assets.

You may be the most zealous litigator, the most ardent peacemaker, the most meticulous researcher, the most scrupulous drafter, but if you lack good business knowledge and sense, you will likely flounder, and quite possibly, fail.

Lawyers cannot practice law if no one takes care of the business of practicing law. With the guidance of Liz and Joryn in this book, you do not have to go it alone.

Ashley Belleau, Esquire
Past President – Federal Bar Association
Shareholder – Lugenbuhl, Wheaton, Peck,
Rankin & Hubbard
New Orleans, Louisiana – 2017

WHY WE WROTE THIS BOOK

Joryn has been practicing law for over 37 years and has taught at Stetson Law School. Liz has worked her entire 38-year career in the legal profession, focusing on law office administration for the last 20 years. Through both of our experiences, we are acutely aware that while law school prepares students to practice law, it does not offer any substantive training from professionals who have "been there and done that."

In 2013, California lawyer and associate professor of law at UC Hastings College of Law Morris Ratner stated the dilemma clearly and succinctly when he said:

> In this market, law schools must provide students with a larger tool kit than previous generations of law students were thought to need upon graduating, and that tool kit includes a basic understanding of law practice management . . . . Law students need to learn the business of law.

Not only is this an accurate statement, it is a long overdue sentiment. Law school prepares aspiring lawyers to practice law. They learn statutes, case law, theory, and practical application. They learn in very broad terms what a trust account is and that its purpose is to hold their clients' money. But they do not learn the full extent of managing the clients' funds, managing the account, reconciling the account, or when it is appropriate to disburse the money in terms of when the funds have cleared.

Graduating from law school, passing the bar, and being issued a bar license is not enough anymore to build a successful law business. A law practice is divided into two parts. The first part is the actual practice of law which involves representing the clients. The second part, equally important, is managing the business of practicing law™.

Practicing law keeps a lawyer busy enough. The truth of the matter is that lawyers cannot waste precious billable client hours managing the business of practicing law™. However, a lawyer who is totally and completely unfamiliar with any aspect of management of the law firm is at a complete and total disadvantage. That lawyer will find that she spends valuable billable client hours trying to determine why her marketing strategy isn't working or where she can get the best price on a case of paper.

Although no one expects a lawyer to execute the administrative functions of a firm, the knowledge of what all is involved is a prerequisite, even if it is only for the purpose of hiring the right people to handle those functions and making sure they are being done properly.

Our goal with this book is to teach law students aspiring to open their own practices, as well as lawyers who are already in practice, the nuances of law practice management. Teaching law students about law practice management provides additional challenges because, unlike attorneys who are already practicing, everything is theoretical. Law students generally have not had day-to-day experience to which they can relate, such as dealing with office politics issues, prioritizing management responsibilities, or staffing a law firm.

At the very least, this book gives law students a foundation of the information necessary to manage their businesses. They will learn how to handle the issues they will be facing when they do go into private practice. For law students, it is important to understand law firm accounting, billing, finances, selection of practice areas, client development and marketing, HR, and IT and the important roles they play in the business of running a law firm.

So, why write this book? Because an experienced lawyer and law firm administrator with a combined 75 years' experience in managing law firms can share real-life experiences from which readers can learn. We have both made our share of mistakes. We have learned the right ways to do things (sometimes by doing them the wrong way or the more difficult way first), and along the way, we've discovered the easier ways.

We want to pass on our experiences, both good and bad, and the knowledge that we have acquired over our careers to our readers so they can learn from them. We want to share not only the right way to do things but why it is the right way and why the ways that we tried did not work. Our hope is that this will enable readers to be more efficient, productive, cost-conscious (profitable), and as a result, successful with their law careers.

Introduction

When my friend of more than 28 years, attorney Joryn Jenkins, a published author many times over and a pioneer in both the American Inns of Court and the collaborative divorce movements, suggested that we co-author a book on managing the business of practicing law that will work for today's law firm, I was elated but apprehensive. "Do I really have that much to say?" I asked her.

She laughed. "Well, if your history is any indication, I'd guess that you do!"

So here it goes.

I started my 38-year career in the legal profession right out of high school in January of 1979 as a legal secretary in lower Manhattan. I was anxious to get into the working world. I had worked hard in high school and planned my academic curriculum so that I was able to graduate six months earlier than the rest of my class. Being an overachiever was already an integral part of my persona.

Minimum wage back then was $3.15 an hour and regular secretarial positions started at $135 per week. When I discovered that a legal secretary earned more than a regular secretary, I focused my career goals on being part of the legal profession.

I was a month short of turning 18 when I began my legal career. In New York, the secretaries signed the affidavits of service for pleadings. Because of my age, I was not able to sign the old "blue backs," as they were called back then, until a month after I started the position.

During my first few months at the firm, I was utterly clueless about what it was that I was doing or even why I was doing it. I mechanically went through the motions of typing whatever they assigned to me. This was quite an arduous task some days—typing documents that meant nothing to me. The typewriters of those days were not like the high-tech computers of today. We didn't have 'delete' or 'backspace' buttons. Making just one simple typographical error meant that I had to start the document all over. Using white out was just unacceptable to me. My "Type A" personality was also already well established by then.

One day, after about three months in this position, one of the partner's secretaries sat down beside me. She told me that she was going to give me a crash course in being a legal secretary. I remember vividly how relieved and excited I felt. I don't know what happened, but we were barely ten minutes into her crash course and—as easily as flipping a light switch—I suddenly understood what I was doing and why. Fast-forward to now and that light has yet to go out—and neither has my passion for working in the legal profession. It still burns just as brightly now as it did 38 years ago.

Two years later, I obtained my paralegal degree, and soon after I was offered a hybrid paralegal/office manager position with a plaintiff's firm on Madison Avenue. There I was, barely 21 years old and already a paralegal and an office manager for a law firm in Manhattan.

In 1985, my husband and I decided to move to Tampa, Florida. Within two days of our arrival, I accepted a position with a law firm in downtown Tampa. I worked for the firm a few short months before I took a second job working at night as a paralegal for a general practitioner. Culture shock would be an understatement to describe the salaries in Tampa in the 1980s versus those in New York City.

The attorney I worked for at night offered me a full-time position at twice the salary of the other firm. Unfortunately, three years later, that attorney was disbarred for stealing a client's money from an estate trust account. The firm folded, and, through no fault of my own, I found myself looking for another position.

Naturally, I went to work for another attorney. Coincidentally, not too long after I took that position, my new boss was disbarred, also for stealing money from an estate trust account to buy himself a Corvette.

I did not want to find out if the old saying, "the third time is the charm," would prove to be true, so I decided to be my own boss. For the next 15 years, I owned and operated a paralegal service business performing outsource work for attorneys.

Having gone to work in the legal profession right out of high school, it was always my plan to get a four-year degree and then a graduate degree. So, while working full-time, I attended an accelerated college program that allowed me to earn my bachelor's degree in two-and-a-half years. When I took the LSAT (I thought I might go to law school), I earned a score of 171. Instead, however, I pursued an MBA with a specialty in finance, which I earned in 11 months while working full-time.

Towards the end of my time operating my paralegal service, a client attorney presented me with an offer to segue my career into law firm administration. I didn't exactly jump at the opportunity because I was not sure I wanted to go into office administration. Years later, it seems obvious that that was to be my next step.

I worked in law office administration for several years, including a position with a 500-attorney law firm in Montana. Having had the opportunity to work as an administrator in the solo/small firm environment and with a firm that employed a staff of about 1,400 has given me a very diverse background in law office administration.

When I returned to Tampa from Montana in 2015, I applied for an administrator position that I thought was full-time. After interviewing on the phone and then in-person with both the partner and his staff, it dawned on me that the position was to be part-time. As I was thanking the attorney, and at the same time, apologizing for wasting his time, he let me know that he was not about to let me go so easily. He suggested that I take on other small law firm practices as clients and build a business similar to my paralegal services business, but offering independent law firm administrator services instead. Today, I work as an independent law office administrator and management consultant.

I am very grateful to that attorney for having been so insistent. In fact, he is still a client, and a friend, today.

Although I have taken on more law firms as clients since then, I have also declined some clients along the way. This is because, while attorneys do not have to do things my way, they *do* have to do things the ethical way for me to work with them.

I love what I do, and my track record demonstrates that I am good at it. The firms I have worked for have all been positively impacted by my work.

There are many things that aspiring attorneys learn in law school. However, even if law schools taught courses on law office administration, they would fall far short of the everyday practical application of those skills. It would be difficult to teach someone how to handle every situation that arises on a day-to-day basis.

Thus, in the course of working on this book, I discovered that I do, in fact, have a lot to say about law firm administration. The perceptions I share in this book are the culmination of my education, my expertise, and my experience with the legal profession, not only as an administrator, but also as a working paralegal and intrinsic member of a support staff team. In transitioning from being a paralegal to an administrator, I have gained insights the benefit of which other law firm administrators without my legal background don't have. Without a legal foundation, some administrators don't always make the sane decisions I would make because they lack familiarity with what it's actually like to work in such an environment as a staff member and how clients may feel. There is just no substitute for exposure to legal experience.

My experiences have led me to develop a management style that is built around the unique business environment of a law firm. I'm pleased to see that, in the last few years, the legal profession has come to understand what I have been saying for years: "Law firms are businesses and, while the practice of law is one thing, the 'business' of practicing law is entirely another."

So let's get down to the nitty-gritty and talk about the business of practicing law.

Elizabeth Miller
Tampa, Florida
4/1/2017

I've known Liz for a long time now. When I first suggested to her that she write a book, I was not surprised that she immediately deliberated, taking a breath and pausing, to think about my idea; she always considers my suggestions thoughtfully. What surprised me was that she wondered aloud whether she had enough to share with all of us.

As you will soon see, Liz knows a lot about the business of practicing law. We wrote this book in tandem, but I asked her to write her part first, in part, because I wanted to see if she would really "man up." (And oh, my, did she ever—providing me with a draft of 37,000 written words six weeks after she inquired, "Do I really have that much to say?") As I read what she had written, I discovered that we had a lot more in common than I had originally thought.

Nearly 29 years ago, I developed an interest in the American Inns of Court concept and became deeply involved in supporting its goal of advancing professionalism, civility, excellence, and *ethics* in the practice of law. I began by organizing my first Inn of Court in 1987 (and it's still going strong today). I later had a hand, one way or another, in getting another thirty-plus inns off the ground.

At the same time, I served six years on, and twice chaired, a Florida Bar grievance committee. I began to be recognized by the courts as an expert on questions involving legal ethics. Later, I added legal malpractice, both plaintiff's work and defense, to the repertoire of actions I felt comfortable pursuing on behalf of my clients.

In that context (and as a parent to a wonderful daughter), I have always said, "It's not *whether* you will make a mistake. Everyone makes mistakes. The question is how you will rectify that mistake when it happens." As you will see, most of the problems that one encounters in the business of practicing law can be avoided beforehand or corrected soon after the fact simply by reading this book and acting on our recommendations.

Now, having said that, you probably realize that there are some "mistakes" that simply cannot be fixed. Those are the "mistakes" that lawyers who are simply lacking any sense of ethics will make.

Both Liz and I share a strong ethical standard, which is in part how we met. Liz was working for a lawyer, my husband at the time, who made it through law school despite being a sociopath. (Just as they don't teach the business of practicing law in law school, they also do not apply the Levenson Self-Report Psychopathy Scale Test to applicants to determine whether they have the right personality for the practice of law.) He simply lacked any sense of ethics, and I was, for a very short period of time, married to him. When he came home with that Corvette and explained where he'd "found" the money to buy it, I fixed my mistake by divorcing him. Liz "divorced" him (she quit the job) shortly thereafter.

If you are reading this book, either you want your law practice to excel, or your boss does. You want to avoid the mistakes that lawyers who aren't savvy enough to teach themselves the business of practicing law often make.

There are four elements that can help you succeed in the business of practicing law. In this book, we'll cover management, staffing, client, and financial issues.

Read this book to ensure that you do understand the business of practicing law, and your practice will outshine those who do not.

Joryn Jenkins
Tampa, Florida
4/1/2017

MANAGEMENT

CHAPTER ONE
HOW TO START A LAW FIRM

Liz has always had the entrepreneurial spirit. Back in the 1980's, before the advent of virtual or contract paralegal work, she opened a paralegal business that she managed for 15 years. Had it not been for an attorney client for whom she did paralegal work offering her a position as his office manager, she would probably still own that paralegal business today.

After embarking upon law office administration, she backed into a position as an independent law firm administrator, and she has never been happier. The attorney who pointed her in this direction is still her client and is likely to be her client until one of them retires.

Make no mistake, working on your own in any profession is not as glamorous as it looks from the outside. Liz and Joryn both work harder now than they ever worked when they were employed by someone else. While neither Liz nor Joryn has ever been the type to totally disconnect from work at the end of the day, we certainly did a much better job of that then than we do now. Our clients often find e-mails in their inbox that we sent out at 3 a.m. or 5 a.m. or 11 p.m. and on the weekends. We both giggle when one of us e-mails the other at some ungodly hour and the other responds right away, likewise clinging to her computer in the wee hours of the morning.

There is a lot to do when running your own show. If you do not keep your finger on the pulse, there is always someone who is willing to bump you right out of your place.

With that being said, every single one of you who has ever thought to take the plunge into the deep end of the pool without a life preserver should *just do it.* Joryn, in particular, has given this advice many, many times in her role as mentor to young professionals. In fact, at least three of her associates over the years have done so quite successfully. Liz, too, has encouraged attorneys with bigger firms who were considering going out on their own.

However, do not jump in without a strategic business plan. Do not plan to hang your own shingle and leave the stability of an established firm that will still write you a paycheck if you don't bill your weekly requirement one week and instead choose to bill more hours the next week without a plan. Remember, too, that at that firm, your legal assistant will get paid, the lights will work when you flip the switch, and you will have a place to put your briefcase without you having to worry (at least not the same way) about every hour you bill and collect.

Are you scared right about now? Yeah, you should be. But you should also be excited, thoughtful, and writing that strategic business plan.

Why do we keep emphasizing that business plan? It is a map or a footprint of where you want to go when you go out on your own and how you plan to get there. Now, we can write an entire book about all the things that you must do, consider, buy, and pay for, but we are not going to give you instructions on how to buy a desk, or a chair, or what computer software to purchase. Those are all things that you can figure out on your own once you decide the issues that really *are* important.

We are goal-oriented people. Chances are, if you are reading this book, you are, too. The way to achieve a goal is to write it down, and then to write the plan for how to achieve it. As the scribe once said, "If you don't know your destination, then you'll never get there." The plan can always be altered, but if you don't have a plan in the first place, you are likely not to achieve your objective at all.

If your ambition is to open your own law firm and survive, here are a few important steps that you must take that will help you achieve that goal. Write them down, and you will have a strategic business plan.

- IN WHAT AREA OF LAW WILL YOU SPECIALIZE? This is something you will have to decide before you even think about hourly fees or value billing, flat fee, or contingency. The area or areas of law you choose will impact the fee structure.

- DECIDE WHO YOUR TARGET CLIENT MARKET IS. This will be based on the area of law in which you want to specialize and where you will be practicing. This will be helpful when designing your marketing plan.

- CHOOSE A MENTOR. Take him to lunch and tell him ahead of time why; "I want to find out everything I need to know to open my own law firm." If you choose wisely, you will find someone who will be happy to suggest vendors and service providers they have worked with over time, saving you some headaches along the way.

- DECIDE WHAT KIND OF FEE STRUCTURE YOU WILL USE. You will do this once you have decided the area(s) of law on which you want to concentrate. Researching the competition will help you figure this out. Charge too low an hourly rate and prospective clients will think that you are not as good as the other lawyers because you don't charge enough. Charge too much, and potential clients will think that they cannot afford you because you are charging too much. While fee structures are often closely guarded secrets, there are ways to figure this out in your legal community. One of those would be through the experiences that you have had with attorneys prior to opening your own firm. The other will be through networking with colleagues who are willing to share.

- LOCATION. LOCATION. LOCATION. Where do you want to locate your office? Whether you want to be close to the courthouse, downtown, or in an "up and coming" area, there is likely an abundance of available real estate to rent (and buy). Because of the overflow of available offices, you are likely to be in a good bargaining position when it comes to narrowing down a location. Do remember a few things, though. If you are a trial lawyer, being close to the courthouse might be a plus for many reasons: reduced travel time, less risk of getting stuck in traffic and being late for court, and no need to look for a parking space or rent a space downtown. If you are not a litigator, being downtown might not be as important. If you are a trial attorney, and you want to be close to the courthouse no matter what, consider the parking situation for your clients and how convenient (and affordable) parking will be for them. You might want to factor in the expense of validating parking for clients or others who come to see you at the office.

- PREPARE A BUDGET. It is not a fun thing to do—no one wants to put into the computer (or pad of paper if you prefer) what all of this will cost you. Going into this blind, however, is a huge mistake. While a budget is only good the day that it is written, you need some parameters on expenses and what all of this will cost on a monthly basis. Especially, because it may be as little as 60 or as many as 120 days before you start generating revenues. Check the coffers, and make sure that you are in a position to float the nut on your expenses until you start generating some cash flow.

The good news is that, so far, you haven't spent any money at all. You are still in the strategic planning stage and, by the time it comes to spending money, you will already know what areas of law you want to practice, who your target clients are, where your office will be, and what the parameters are of your budget. Now that the foundation for your practice has been assembled, here is the focus of your practice.

Consider the resources available to generate new clients for your practice. Networking is the least expensive source of new clients. All those years you spent glad-handing, passing out business cards, and talking a good game, you can now call on to send you new business. Think through a marketing plan in which all the moving parts come together to create a masterfully designed source of new business.

Now that these things have been determined, you can focus on your desk and chair, computer system, telephones, software, and staff. Obtaining that chair or computer won't matter if you don't have the important things figured out.

There are many services available to assist with opening a new law practice inexpensively. We have discussed many of those resources or alternatives in this book.

Above all else, remember to manage the firm, *do not let the firm manage you*. If you keep control of the things that matter most—marketing, attracting and retaining new clients, generating revenues, and paying the bills—while it will not be without its peaks and valleys, it will all come together.

Remember that you cannot do everything yourself, and you don't know everything. Steve Jobs once said, "It doesn't make sense to hire smart people and tell them what to do;

we hire smart people so they can tell us what to do." The smartest people we know are smart enough to recognize that they don't know everything, and they hire the people who know how to do what they can't. Luckily for us, we live in an age when creative, out-of-the-box solutions are commonplace. Just because someone else did not think of it first, does not mean it won't work.

Hanging your shingle can be scary and stressful. But once you become a success, it is far more rewarding than working for someone else. There is no better time than the present to begin living your dream!

Lawyers:

1. What areas of law firm administration, or more accurately, "managing the business of practicing law," are your biggest challenges? List these areas. Write down how you might solve each challenge.
2. Does the thought of being responsible for employees, both managing them and compensating them, make you nervous? Why? How can you solve that problem?
3. Do you feel that you lack the technological knowledge to handle all of the technical problems that will surely arise? Make a list of the possible problems you can already envision. Then, make a list of ways that you can prepare for those issues before they arise.
4. Are you terrible with your own finances and feel like you might inadvertently get into trouble managing your firm's finances? How do you solve that problem before it occurs? What procedures can you put into place to ensure your accounting records and budgets are accurate?
5. Are you concerned that you don't have enough connections in your community? List the ways to address your lack of community connections and design a protocol to accomplish those tasks. Also, list the connections that you *do* have. You probably have more than you think!
6. Are you shy? Do you fear that you won't be able to effectively market yourself? Identify a book that speaks to the issue of how personalities impact marketing abilities and read it.
7. Do you fear you don't have the determination and motivation to be successful if you don't have a boss to answer to? Or are you such a workhorse that you're afraid you won't be able to maintain a work/life balance and you'll burn out? Again, identify a book that speaks to this issue and read it.

Law Students:

1. In your life as a student, what tasks do you find especially challenging when managing your educational and personal life? List these tasks and write down how you might solve each challenge.
2. When you have held jobs, have you been given managerial responsibilities? Do you find those responsibilities challenging or do you enjoy them? List the managerial

responsibilities you have been given in the past. List those at which you have excelled, as well as those at which you were less successful. For those responsibilities that you found more challenging, what can you do when faced with similar responsibilities in the future that will help you be more successful?

3. Do you worry because you have never been given management responsibilities and you don't know if you will be successful once you are responsible for those types of tasks? Find a book that speaks to this issue and read it.

4. Are you confident with your computer skills? Or does the thought of the new software you will need to be a successful lawyer intimidate you? Research and make a list of the different software you expect you will need to manage your law firm. Are there courses you can take to become better acquainted with this software?

5. How are you at managing your own finances? If you are not so good at it, how can you correct that so you don't make detrimental financial mistakes when you are running your own firm?

6. Do you have a lot of social connections with members of your community? Write down your connections. How do you plan on maintaining these relationships and developing new ones?

7. Or are you planning on opening a firm in a new community where you don't yet have many connections? If so, how do you plan on making important connections? Write down a list of possible ways in which you can develop new connections.

8. Are you shy and fear that you won't be able to effectively market yourself once you open your own practice? Identify a book that speaks to this issue of how personalities impact marketing abilities. Then read it.

9. Without guidance, are you the type of individual who is motivated and determined enough to be successful? Or do you become lazy and unmotivated when you are not pushed and managed? If so, how do you plan on changing that part of your personality? Again, identify a book that speaks to this issue and then read it.

10. Do you understand the importance of maintaining a good work/life balance so you don't burn out? Write down what is important to you in your life other than your work. Do you have hobbies? If so, how can you maintain them? If not, find something that interests you, and join a related club.

11. Are you confident that you have done well in law school, but fear that you won't be a good attorney? Did you struggle in law school, and are you nervous that you won't be successful? If so, talk with lawyers whom you admire, and ask them if they struggled in law school. When you find one who did, discuss how he overcame the lack of confidence this may have created.

12. Are you concerned that you don't know anything about running a business? List your concerns, and begin to brainstorm ways to overcome them.

Chapter Two
How to Go Solo or Begin Your Own Small Firm

Some people think of a solo practitioner as the lawyer who could not make it in the big firms, the renegade lawyer who refuses to conform, or the lawyer who is not serious about practicing law so he went out on his own. After all, don't solo practitioners do the simple-minded legal work that big firm lawyers don't do? And they couldn't possibly be making any money because no one is going to pay a solo practitioner $300 or $400 an hour when they can hire a big-time lawyer with a firm that employs 200 or 300 lawyers or more, right?

The reality of these misconceptions is that solo or small firm lawyers handle "big law" matters such as commercial litigation, tax matters, construction litigation, complex litigation, and corporate work as well as matters usually associated with smaller firms, such as personal injury, family law, and bankruptcy. Solo and small firm lawyers provide the same high-quality legal services that the big firm lawyers do. While it takes a little while to get a solo or small firm up and running and to become established, the reality is that, because of their increased efficiency, productivity, access to top-notch staffing and administrative help through outsourcing, and their lower overhead, solo and smaller firms actually realize larger profits on the revenues that they generate.

Solo and small firm lawyers are not losers who couldn't cut it in the "big law" sandbox. They are independent, entrepreneurial lawyers who are finding ways to build a better—and more cost efficient—mousetrap.

For some lawyers, "going solo" or small firm is an aspiration. The concept of running one's own show and answering to no one is very attractive. Some lawyers, through happenstance or otherwise, find themselves practicing as solo practitioners through downsizing or right-sizing. Law schools are turning out more lawyers every year. The competition for jobs is tough, and the supply and demand ratio of lawyers and jobs has driven salaries way down. Liz has even had three-year associates tell her that they are making less than paralegals working for someone else.

The competitive legal market, the demand for alternative fee arrangements by clients, and the need for firms to be more efficient and productive have contributed to the creation of more solo and small firm practitioners. Over the years, the percentage of lawyers who are running their own solo or small firms has reached and now surpassed the number of lawyers working in large firms.

According to the American Bar Foundation's 2005 *Lawyer Statistical Report,* updated in 2012:

- 75% of American lawyers are in private practice. Of these:
    - 62% work as solo practitioners or in offices of five or fewer lawyers;
    - 18% work in offices of between six and 50 lawyers; and
    - 20% work in firms of more than 50 lawyers.

- The other 25% are lawyers who work for government agencies, private industries, or legal aid; public defenders; in legal education; members of the judiciary; or are retired.

Clients of larger firms have access to lawyers with a variety of areas of specialization within the same firm. Thus, the large firm lawyer's experience tends to be limited to one area of proficiency. Clients who have more than one legal issue or conflict will find themselves represented by more than one lawyer in the same firm.

Solo practitioners must handle a variety of legal matters alone and often practice in more than one area, although their practice areas are not as diverse as the larger firms. As a result, solo practitioners either establish a network with other solo practitioners in whom they can refer clients to lawyers with other specialties, or they hire contract lawyers when the need arises. Contract lawyers allow solo practitioners to keep clients in-house without having to refer them to other attorneys and to risk losing the client. If you build a network of lawyers whose areas of specialty are diverse from your own, you will find that you can build a source of referrals from other lawyers for cases within your realm of specialty. As a solo practitioner, referrals of new business that cost nothing are important and cost-effective.

Undertaking the opening of a solo or small firm without a strategic business plan is like flying a plane in the dark. To decide that you are opening a law firm without any strategic planning is actually a plan . . . *for failure.* We recommend preparing a strategic business plan either on your own or with the assistance of someone who has experience with managing the business of practicing law because that person has all the business experience of running an efficient, productive, and profitable law firm.

Aside from preparing that very important strategic business plan, there are three important items to consider if you want to go out on your own or to open a small firm with other like-minded attorneys:

1. TECHNOLOGY. There are software programs available specifically geared for law firms from case management and e-mail to accounting and billing. Blindly going into a search for software that will work for your firm is akin to looking for a needle in a haystack. Contacting software companies and speaking with salespeople is not likely to offer any real solutions in selecting software; it will, in fact, convolute the issue even more. Each salesperson will tell you that their software is premiere, that it is the best on the market, that it can do the best for increased efficiency, and that it is user friendly. Unfortunately, that is

what salespeople do. It is always important to be a well-informed consumer when buying any product and to know what you want the software to accomplish for you.

Determine what your software must do: e-mail, telephone, facsimile, legal research, access the internet, document management, docketing/calendaring, and/or billing and accounting.

There are many considerations when selecting your software. One of the important ones, as a solo or small firm, is cost. Some software companies try to soft-sell how expensive their product is by telling you that it will only cost you $100 per month to buy the software. Your question should be, for how long? Some companies will charge a monthly fee to use their software, almost like a leasing program. If you plan to use the software for a long time, ask how much the software will actually cost. Is it less expensive to just buy the software that you are researching?

What is the extent of the technical support available for the program? Is it 90 days, one year, or, as in the case of a billing program with which Liz worked in the past, is support available until the new version comes out and then your version is no longer supported? In this situation, after two years, a billing program was no longer supported because the new version came out. Liz could still get technical support, but the cost was $180 for 15 minutes.

Are updates included in the price of the software, or is there an additional fee for updates? It always makes sense to have the most updated version of a program, and updates should be included in the price, especially if updates have to do with solving bugs with the original programs.

Going out on your own as a solo practitioner, you have probably had no experience being involved in evaluating and choosing software programs for the firm. Rather than listening to one endless sales pitch after another in which it seems that each program does something better than the one before, reach out to colleagues for recommendations. They will be just as pleased to tell you about what works well with their software as well as what doesn't. Colleagues could include not only other attorneys but also law firm administrators and paralegals. These individuals have all had an opportunity to work with different programs on the market, and their input can be invaluable for narrowing down the best options for your firm.

Software programs are not cheap. The last thing you need while trying to be efficient or productive is a program that does not serve your needs, one that is quickly outdated, or one that requires technical support that isn't available when you need it. Downtime in a solo or small firm environment can be devastating.

And changing software is often a huge chore; try to choose right the first time.

2. STAFFING. The mantra "keep it small and keep it all" is the initial advice Liz gives to lawyers who go out on their own as a solo practitioner. Unless you are leaving a larger firm and taking clients with you, building up a client base will likely be a slow process. Virtual offices, outsourcing help, and cell phones enable solos to get started with little to no support staff overhead.

Be sure that keeping the overhead low does not interfere with your ability to provide outstanding service to clients. You do not want clients to associate the fact that you are a solo practitioner with providing inferior or inadequate legal work. Remember, money can buy everything but a reputation. When you are just starting out on your own, you cannot afford to provide less than stellar service to your clients.

3. LOCATION. LOCATION. LOCATION. There are many considerations when deciding where to locate your office and what kind of office to get. Liz and Joryn have both known solo practitioners who have gone out on their own and rented space that barely qualified as an office and certainly not as a law office. With creative office space options these days, you don't have to rent a dive just to have an office because it's cheap and you don't think anything better is affordable. Space sharing, virtual offices, and space for services are all viable options that can get you an office space where you can be proud to have clients visit you.

Solo and small firm practitioners can reduce their rent overhead by leasing professional offices together. In this way, each lawyer gets a professional office and can share common areas with other attorneys and split the rent. In terms of client referrals, if possible, it would be a good idea to rent space with other lawyers who practice in different areas. First, no one has to worry about someone stealing his client. Obviously, when you are starting out, this is a concern. Second, you can start building a network with your co-tenants that is something you can continue even when you all move to other offices. Always be thinking about establishing and maintaining referral networks that will bring in more business.

Virtual offices are more common today than ever. With remote capabilities, fax, Skype, FaceTime, and e-mail, lawyers can effectively work from home. And while it is certainly understandable that you might not want clients coming to your home—especially if you have small children—you can always rent an executive room or conference room space on a per hour or per half-day basis where you can meet clients when necessary. Of course, as you become busier and meet with clients more frequently, you may find that an office sharing arrangement is cheaper than renting conference room space several times per month. Joryn splits the baby, renting the use of her conference room on a first come, first serve monthly basis for a fairly low fee to what she fondly calls her "ghost tenants." These are lawyers who work from home but occasionally need a conference room in which to meet clients.

Space for services is a concept Liz remembers from 20 or 30 years ago with a law firm for which she worked. A firm provides office space (usually a small office, desk, chair, and phone access) in exchange for a certain number of hours per month on their cases. In this way, you are investing time in exchange for office space as opposed to laying out money. This is especially useful when you have a slow month. Sometimes investing time is better than investing money, especially when cash flow is tight. Joryn currently has a tenant with whom she has made that arrangement, to their mutual satisfaction.

We cannot stress enough the importance of a strategic business plan. And not only to map out the opening of a solo or small firm but also to manage it over the course of your practice. It is a good idea to re-evaluate and update your business plan as your practice grows and your goals change. Putting something in writing helps many people to visualize their accomplishments and often highlights obstacles or problems that may not have been evident while they were formulating their goals.

When you go out on your own, you don't work for your firm—you *are* the firm! You are the firm whether you are at the office, at home in the evenings, spending time with your family, or on vacation. Work/life balance is important for everyone. As a solo practitioner, it can be a little tricky to achieve that balance because you don't want to miss a telephone call or wait too long to respond to an e-mail that may be a potential new client. The best advice we can give you is that you will have to muddle through and figure out what you need to do to achieve work/life balance. For both of us, it means taking the opportunity whenever we can to have downtime. We still answer e-mails on the weekends, and someone still monitors phone calls. We are accessible while on a vacation, or, alternatively, have made arrangements for coverage so that we can have a little peace of mind. It may mean taking more frequent three or four-day weekend vacations instead of taking a month off to travel through Europe. There is no question that you make concessions, but you don't have to work 24/7 to be a successful solo or small firm practitioner.

If you broach the subject of going out on your own with people who have done it, you will get mixed reviews. Some will tell you that they love it and would never consider going back to work for someone else. Some will tell you that they hate it. We suspect that the ones who hate it are struggling more with managing the business than with the practice of law. You cannot fly by the seat of your pants. You need a business plan, and you need to be organized.

Successful solo and small firm practitioners have one thing in common—the desire to start their own firms and practice law their own way. They enjoy the entrepreneurial spirit and mentality. With this drive, they can face the challenges of being a solo practitioner. Ask the ones who are successful whether they would go back to work for someone else. The answer is generally a resounding "*no!*"

CHAPTER THREE
HOW TO DEVELOP YOUR BUSINESS PLAN

Opening a start-up law firm is not a simple undertaking. There are so many items to consider and for which you must plan. All law firms start with great ideas and good intentions, yet not all new law firms succeed. Thomas Edison once said, "A good intention with a bad approach often leads to a poor result." Starting a law firm without a business plan is a plan for failure. A business plan is a roadmap of where you want to go and the route you are going to take to get there.

Right now, you are probably thinking, "How do I develop a business plan to start a law firm when I have never owned my own firm?" If you are asking yourself that question, then you have just realized the importance of a business plan.

In its simplest terms, a business plan describes the goals that you want to accomplish, gives structure to your ideas, and helps you plan out the financial aspects of achieving your goals.

So why do you want to start your own law firm? Here are some questions you should ask yourself that will help you decide if you are doing this for the right reasons:

1) Am I motivated to own my own law firm?
2) Do I have good organizational and time management skills (or am I willing to hire someone who does)?
3) Am I aware of my strengths and weaknesses?
4) Do I have a vision for the future of my new law firm?
5) Do I have attainable personal and professional goals?
6) Have I weighed the risks and benefits of starting my own practice?
7) Am I committed to being successful?

If you answered "yes" to these questions and have decided to take the leap of faith and start your own law firm, let's go through the important items to address in your business plan:

- EXECUTIVE SUMMARY. Although this is the first part of your business plan, it should be written last as it will summarize everything in your business plan.

- BUSINESS DESCRIPTION. This is a generalized but brief statement that generally includes the name of your firm, the areas in which you will specialize, and who your target client base is, at least initially.

- VISION STATEMENT. The vision statement for your firm should be to attract and retain new clients through a marketing strategy focused on the firm's area of specialty, to establish the firm's presence in the legal community, and to establish a referral system within the legal community.

- MISSION STATEMENT. Your mission statement should be to provide exceptional legal services to all clients so they will be repeat clients when necessary and refer others who require your services to the firm.

- INITIATIVES/OBJECTIVES/GOALS. Everyone wants to be successful. No one in his right mind would start a law firm without the goal of being successful. Like your marketing strategy, your business strategy will evolve. In this section, identify your long-term goals (usually your five-year goals), as well as your shorter-term goals (such as your three-year goals, one-year goals, and six-month goals).

- CLIENT DEVELOPMENT/MARKETING OPPORTUNITIES. Before developing this business plan, perform market research to determine the competition in your community. If there is a particular target market, such as an ethnic group (for example, if you speak Spanish and want to target that market) or an age group (for example, if you practice elder law), you might consider preparing a client development strategy for that particular segment of the public. Research and examine the marketing that other law firms are doing. Really think about the message you want to convey to potential new clients, and consider what your budget is to get that message out there to achieve your goal. It is important to plan a marketing strategy separate from this business plan. Your marketing strategy should include your marketing budget and potential marketing strategies that will not cost you anything. Several forms of social media, for example, are available at no cost except your time.

- COMPETITIVE ADVANTAGES/STRENGTHS. What will you offer your target market that will attract clients to your firm? Do you have some special experience in a particular area? If, for example, you want to do personal injury work and you have a medical license, this might be an advantage over your competition.

- COMPETITIVE DISADVANTAGES/WEAKNESSES. You may be wondering why we are even addressing disadvantages and weaknesses. Starting a law firm requires a significant emotional investment—for the rest of your career. You cannot go into this with blinders on. The reality is that you should acknowledge your weaknesses, not so they will stop you from opening your firm, but so that you can plan to overcome them. A disadvantage or weakness for all start-up firms is the already-strong presence that other law firms have within the community. But this is something that you can't change, so don't let it hold you back from reaching for your dreams. You can overcome weaknesses such as lack of presence in the community and less experience than other lawyers. Meet the challenges head on, eyes open. Acknowledge the weaknesses in your business plan, and it will help you overcome them.

• OPPORTUNITIES. Identify the opportunities for success. Did you come from a larger, well-known firm in which you were able to network with business people in the community? This is an opportunity. Were you born and raised in the same town in which you are now opening your practice? This is an opportunity, as well. Are you well known within a particular practice area? Identifying these opportunities can also help you determine how best to market your firm's services.

• THREATS. Identify anything that would be a threat to the success of your firm, with the intention of planning to overcome it. Are you lacking in financial management skills? Is there a similar type of firm just down the block from your intended office location? You cannot stick your head in the sand about obstacles that are present. The plan here is not to acknowledge them and walk away from your goal of starting a firm. The intent is to identify threats or obstacles and plan to overcome them.

• INDUSTRY ANALYSIS. This does not have to be lengthy or comprehensive. You should conduct a market analysis to identify new opportunities.

• FINANCIAL PROJECTIONS. Every business is driven by money—income and expenses. While you cannot plan how many new clients will retain the firm in the first six months of business, you can project with some accuracy your business expenses, such as rent, utilities, marketing, etc.

• ACTION PLAN. This is the point in your business plan at which you itemize what you are going to do to accomplish the goals laid out in the plan.

A business plan is necessary when planning a new business venture. Like your budget, it is a plan for where you are going and how you will get there. A business plan will:

1) Define the purpose of your business;
2) Identify the operational needs to make the business a success;
3) Provide structure to your business ideas; and
4) Help you plan your business execution.

Joryn first decided to open her own firm nearly 25 years ago. She had worked at large firms, small firms, and medium-sized firms; she had worked in the government; she had worked for a university as a law professor. But nothing she had done had prepared her for the business of owning and operating her own law firm. It wasn't until she realized that she would require a line of credit for her firm and asked for one from the local bank that she was informed she would need to create a business plan. The bank would not consider making her a loan without one.

Years later, she appreciates the value of that prerequisite. So, if no one has made that suggestion to you yet, we make it now because we both know how very important it is that you create a business plan and revisit it regularly over the years to revise it in order to achieve the goals you have set for yourself. Consider it a living document that can—and should—be altered as your goals change.

You would never take a road trip to a new destination without Google Maps, or at least a roadmap. Think of this as taking a road trip to your new firm—you shouldn't do that without a roadmap either!

CHAPTER FOUR
HOW TO BALANCE YOUR WORK WITH YOUR LIFE

People find it hard to believe that Liz has worked in the legal profession for 38 years. The expression on their faces says, "I've never met anyone who has been in this field for so long." Liz is quick to reply, "I know! By the time most people have been doing this for 15 or 20 years, they are so burned out, they prefer to weave baskets at the flea market."

The legal profession can be a tough career path for anyone—lawyer, paralegal, or administrator. It is stressful in general and even more stressful when there is a final hearing, trial, appeal, or some other kind of deadline that must be met. You deal with clients who often have never been involved in a legal proceeding or litigation asking you the same questions over and over. They take a long time to provide necessary documents or information. They want assurances on how things will turn out and they want you to predict what will happen next. Of course, no one can prophesize how a case will turn out, and when you tell them that, there is yet more anxiety and more questions.

It does not matter whether you are an attorney or a paralegal or even the firm administrator. This is an intense and highly stressful profession. There is so much work involved in some cases. And if it isn't the legal cases, it's HR, or billing, or payroll, or some kind of problem that must be addressed. For anyone who takes her profession in the legal field seriously, it never turns off—and, if a firm specializes in litigation, the pressure is even worse.

Fortunately, in the last few years, many professions are recognizing the importance of work/life balance to give staff an opportunity to decompress and recharge.

It used to be that, if you went downtown in the early evening when it was just getting dark, you could look up at the skyscrapers and tell by the lights in the windows which offices had the three- to five-year associates burning the midnight oil trying to make partner. With the new attitude about work/life balance, even associates striving to make partner are taking some time off to clear their heads and feed their need for a life outside the office.

There are a few signs that will tell you if you are suffering from a lack of work/life balance. The need to excel, bill hours, and be successful still exists. People are just trying to balance it more with life because, as the saying goes, "all work and no play…"

Here are some questions to ask yourself to assess your physical and mental health and the need to bring some work/life balance into your life:

1. Do you feel overwhelmed before you even get to the office and wonder how late you will have to stay tonight to get a day's work done?

2. When you are working on projects, do you find yourself not only trying to work on the current project but also thinking about the other five things you must do before you leave the office at 9 PM?
3. Do you feel exhausted all the time?
4. Do you feel like the only thing that you do is work and that there is no "me" time or no downtime?
5. Can you remember when you last took a vacation?
6. Do you have a vacation planned, or have you even thought about taking a vacation?
7. Are you so exhausted that you cannot sleep at night thinking about all the things you didn't accomplish today that you have to do tomorrow before you will be able to get to the things that you have to do tomorrow?
8. Do you sleep with your cell phone or some other device by your bedside?

There is a lot to be said for the cliché "work smarter, not harder." Remember, a client is not impressed by the number of billable hours that you work on her case, she is impressed by the result. Time management and organizational skills are very important in both maintaining a work/life balance and also completing work in an orderly manner without burning out before the day is over.

Many years ago, Liz was the workaholic who showed up at the office between 30 to 45 minutes early to get a "jump" on the day. She ate lunch at her desk while she continued to work because she could pump out another hour if she didn't take a break. She didn't go home until the last piece of mail went out, the last pleading was filed, and the last e-mail answered. Sometimes that meant another 30 to 45 minutes at the end of the day. The result was that her eight-hour day was now nearly a ten-hour day. She returned home frustrated and exhausted. Despite all she'd accomplished in those ten hours, she was already thinking about what she had on her plate for the next day. Not to mention worrying about what she had not achieved that day.

When Liz shared this story with Joryn, Joryn laughed. Ever competitive, for years, she made sure to be the first in her office every morning, which meant that she was there by 6:30. Burning the candle at both ends, she always skipped lunch and also insisted on being the last to leave, which regularly meant that she was there until 9 PM at night, still wearing her high heels. She did the same thing on Saturdays. Sunday was the easy day; she only worked six or seven hours and could do that in jeans and sneakers.

Clearly, times have changed. Here's what you can do to ensure that you, and your staff, have a work/life balance and to avoid burnout:

1. TAKE YOUR LUNCH BREAK. While it might seem more productive to work through lunch and to eat at your desk, it really isn't. Everyone should enjoy a full lunch hour. Even if you think you can only drag yourself away from your desk for 30 minutes, it's a start. Taking a lunch break away from your desk, even if you stay in the office, may be what you need to

sharpen your mind and to restart your work with a clear head. When you get back to your desk, you will be re-energized and able to focus on what takes priority.

2. DRINK WATER. Hydrating helps boost your energy.

3. EAT HEALTHY. In the mid-afternoon when your energy starts to wane, eat some protein. It will give you a boost, and you will feel rejuvenated.

4. GET ENOUGH SLEEP. This may be hard to do at first because, when your head hits the pillow, your brain will still turn on and you'll have a hard time falling to sleep. You may lie in bed thinking about everything that happened that day, what should have happened, and how you could have handled a situation differently. Additionally, you'll think about everything you have to do the next day and what you have to do before anything else so you don't have to stay too late again. Some folks turn on the television when they first lie down to sleep and find it helps them fall asleep because it stops them from thinking so much. Eventually, when you are able to achieve a work/life balance and do not think about work all the time, sleep will come more easily, too.

5. PRIORITIZE. Really prioritize—not with an "everything has to get done now" attitude, but, rather by being realistic about deadlines. Does it really matter if you get things done ahead of schedule by one day instead of two? Or is what really matters that you get it done on time?

6. HIRE COMPETENT PEOPLE. Sometimes it is a little costlier monetarily to hire people who are more experienced. The trade-off is that they will get their work accomplished more efficiently and more productively, which will not only contribute to the bottom line but will also afford you more peace of mind in the work/balance scheme.

7. DELEGATE. Do not try to do everything yourself. You alone cannot be the secretary, the paralegal, the attorney, and the administrator. First, hire competent help to assist with non-billable functions in the office so that you can spend more time on the work that you do best, billable work for clients. Then go ahead and delegate that other work to the staff you hired.

8. TAKE A MENTAL DAY OFF. If you notice that certain staff members never take a day off or never go on vacation, urge them, and even force them, if you must, to take some time off for themselves. And hold yourself to the same rule. They (and you) will return to the office rejuvenated and they will appreciate you more for realizing that they needed a break. Even an afternoon off can make a big difference. Joryn always closes her office the afternoon after her annual holiday lunch so that employees have time to get their holiday shopping finished. During such a busy time of year, that kind of thoughtfulness is appreciated, and the time off from the office revitalizing.

Work/life balance is important for everyone. When achieved, work will be finished more efficiently and with fewer errors, and clients will receive exceptional service because your staff is not burnt out from putting in long unproductive hours just for the sake of putting in hours. Everyone needs downtime—even you!

CHAPTER FIVE
HOW TO BE A HAPPY LAWYER

We can hear the snickering now—somehow the words "happy" and "lawyer" seem like they don't belong in the same sentence. Or do they? Everyone's definition of happiness is different. The first thing you need to do is figure what out what makes YOU happy.

When people ask Joryn or Liz for career advice, we tell them to do what makes them happy and what they have a passion for. Unless you are independently wealthy or have some inside information that you will win the lottery, most of us will spend at least the next 40 or 50 years doing whatever it is that we have chosen to do to make a living. If you choose a career because you think it will make you wealthy, you will soon realize how much truth there is to the saying that money doesn't buy happiness. What money does buy is the perception of happiness to others looking in. However, it really doesn't matter what someone else's perception is of your happiness—what matters is whether you are happy.

Can you be a happy lawyer? That depends on whether you plan to control your career or let your career control you.

1.   DO WHAT YOU LOVE. Some lawyers are meant to be litigators, others prefer to avoid the stress of trial. Whether you would rather be in court every day or sit at your desk preparing wills, do what you love. Everyone is not cut out to be Perry Mason. Make sure the area of practice you choose is something you envision yourself doing for the rest of your career. If you love what you do, you will be happy.

2.   NETWORK. Not just to get referrals. Network to spend time with people like you who face the same challenges you do every day. Sometimes you feel better just venting to someone who understands, and it helps to know that you are not alone.

3.   WORK/LIFE BALANCE. You can get just as much work done in 40 hours as you can in 50 hours if you are not all stressed out. Does it make you happy spending 50 hours to get 40 hours of work done—or do you just feel better because you think you should be putting in long hours? Look around you and you will see proof that there is a great deal of truth to the benefits of work/life balance.

4.   GET INVOLVED IN YOUR BAR ASSOCIATION. All work and no play make Jack or Jill dull and unhappy. You will still be involved in the profession but can get involved in charitable

endeavors through the bar association. The camaraderie will be a good diversion and everyone feels good when he is giving something back.

5. UNHAPPY WORK ENVIRONMENT—CHANGE IT! That could mean getting a new job or just moving your desk to another position in the office so it looks out the window—hopefully, you have a great view. Bring in some personal items. If it means getting a new job, maybe you need to explore your options. Before you do, make a list of what it is that is making you unhappy. You might find that you need to not just change your job but your profession or your area of practice, as well. There are plenty of jobs other than being a lawyer for someone with a law degree and bar license.

You have the ability to be in control of your happiness. The first thing you have to do is figure out what it is that is making you an unhappy lawyer. The wonderful thing is that we all have the free will to change our lives and be happy by changing whatever it is about our careers that is making us unhappy.

Albert Schweitzer once said, *"Success is not the key to happiness. Happiness is the key to success. If you love what you are doing, you will be successful."* Make sure you love what you are doing—happiness and success will follow.

Review Questions Two

Lawyers:

1. What have you learned through your experiences in private practice?
2. Are there certain mistakes you continue to make over and over again? What are they? List them.
3. How can you develop better skills or patterns so you don't continue to make those mistakes? List the actions you could take to prevent future mistakes.
4. Do you sometimes feel that the more you learn, the less you know? Why is this? List the reasons.
5. What is your reaction when you make a mistake? Does it make you work harder so you don't make a similar mistake again? Or, instead, does it crush your self-esteem? If so, what can you do so you experience a more positive, beneficial reaction when, inevitably, mistakes are made? Make a list of the actions you can take so you are already prepared when the time comes.
6. What do you do so that you and your practice continue to evolve? List the actions you've already taken to ensure evolution in your practice. What effect did each of them have?

Law Students:

1. In your life, do you feel like you make the same mistakes over and over again? What are they? List them.
7. How can you develop better skills or patterns so you don't continue to make those mistakes? List the actions you can take to prevent future mistakes.
2. Do you sometimes feel that the more you learn, the less you know? Why is this? List the reasons.
3. What is your reaction when you make a mistake? Does it make you work harder so you don't make a similar mistake again? Or instead, does it crush your self-esteem? If so, what can you do so you experience a more positive, beneficial reaction when, inevitably, mistakes are made? Make a list of these actions you can take so you are already prepared when the time comes.
4. What do you do so that you as a person and as a soon-to-be professional continue to evolve? List the actions you've already taken to ensure evolution in yourself. What effect did each of them have?

CHAPTER SIX
HOW TO REMAIN ETHICAL AS YOU MANAGE THE BUSINESS OF PRACTICING LAW

Everyone recognizes the famous quote from Shakespeare's *Henry VI*, "First thing we do, let's kill all the lawyers." This phrase is actually a tribute to lawyers, recognizing their critical role as the ones who maintain the Rule of Law. Thus, the line was spoken by a conspirator who planned to overthrow the English government and establish a dictatorship.

Over 400 years ago, lawyers were recognized as the professionals who kept the peace and ensured that everyone abided by the laws that were meant to protect the public. That remains the role of the lawyer today: To ensure peace and to ensure that the rights of one party are not improperly infringed on by another.

Lawyers are held to a higher standard of conduct while protecting and enforcing the rights of their clients. The American Bar Association Canon of Professional Ethics was adopted as a general guide to the duties and responsibilities of lawyers to conduct themselves in a professional manner. As the preamble states, it is "peculiarly essential that the system for establishing and dispensing Justice be developed to a high point of efficiency and so maintained that the public shall have absolute confidence in the integrity and impartiality of its administration." In short—do the right thing.

That may sound a bit oversimplified, but ethical behavior, in a nutshell, is all about doing the right thing. It is about having integrity and employing civility and professionalism in dealing with opposing counsel, the courts, experts, and, of course, your clients. That means being a professional at all times, even if opposing counsel is not. Ethics involves being committed to honesty, integrity, and appropriate behavior even when moral dilemmas present themselves and ethical behavior is not the easy choice. It will always be the *right choice*.

In the practice of law, there are ethical considerations both in the actual practice of law and also in the management of the business of law that will affect the best interests of your client.

1. CONFLICTS OF INTEREST. Before meeting with a prospective client for the first time, perform a thorough conflict check. Most case management software programs are designed to allow a computer conflict check. If there is a clear-cut conflict, such as prior representation of a party associated with the matter, refer the client elsewhere. Disclose any possible conflicts (as opposed to direct conflicts) to a potential client and any interest or connections to any of the parties involved in a case. Identify potential conflicts, notify clients and other appropriate parties, and take the necessary steps to avoid future issues. If the client wants

to retain you to represent him after full disclosure of any possible conflict, obtain written consent from the client, and be sure to include the conflict in the written consent.

This may not always be as easy as it sounds. Joryn was once referred a client who refused to disclose the name of the person who had referred him. This is not unusual so Joryn thought nothing of it; she is often referred business by the opposing spouses in her divorce matters, with the caveat that the prospective clients not reveal their names. (They are more impressed with Joryn than they are with their own lawyers!)

But, in this case, it became an issue. First, Joryn discovered that the woman who had referred the client was his girlfriend. This was not an issue by itself—until he and his girlfriend's ex-husband got into an altercation with each other. It turns out the ex-husband was Joryn's prior client and he was dating Joryn's current client's wife. All of this became so messy that, without pinpointing a specific reason for why it felt like a conflict, Joryn withdrew from the representation. "Better safe than sorry."

2. CONFIDENTIALITY. Protect your client at all costs. If complicated circumstances present themselves and you cannot maintain client confidentiality, withdraw from the representation. Never compromise the best interests of the client for the sake of collecting fees.

3. PROFESSIONAL CONDUCT. Lawyers must be respectful and professional in their interactions with the court, opposing counsel, and others. Refrain from endeavoring to undertake *ex parte* communications with judges except in rare circumstances when it is appropriate. If you are about to hit "send" and there is any question in your mind as to the professionalism of a correspondence, wait 24 hours before you send it. Ask a trusted advisor to review it for you first.

4. CLIENT ADVOCACY. A huge part of what a lawyer does for his client is to advocate for him. Even when a lawyer represents a criminal client who he believes is guilty, he cannot encourage the client to perjure himself to the court but must zealously represent his client and afford him the best defense possible.

5. FIDUCIARY RESPONSIBILITY. Lawyers are entrusted with client's funds through their IOLTA or trust accounts. They accept monies from, for, or on behalf of clients and deposit those funds into their firm trust accounts. To avoid the appearance of impropriety or the possibility that the client may be harmed through misappropriation of client funds, the fiduciary responsibility set forth by the bar association regulations and guidelines state that these funds must be held separately from law firm funds and cannot be commingled. There are specific regulations for identifying the actual owner or beneficiary of those funds.

Lawyers are required to reconcile trust funds on a monthly basis to ensure that the funds are used for their intended purposes. Although bookkeepers or administrators are usually responsible for maintenance of the trust account and reconciliation, the ultimate responsibility for the trust funds rests with the lawyer.

6. PROFESSIONAL RESPONSIBILITY. Bar associations establish professional responsibility rules for their member-lawyers. As mentioned earlier, the American Bar Association, as well as your local state bar association, maintains a canon of ethics that sets out guidelines for lawyers. Adhering to these regulations of professional responsibility is of prime importance, even before generating revenues and advocating for your clients. Codes of professional responsibility govern effective communication with other lawyers. Attorneys must avoid behavior that is dishonest or criminal, manage their personal and professional financial obligations, and refrain from defrauding anyone, including clients or other persons. Failure to adhere to these rules subjects the lawyer and the firm to being sued. In addition, sanctions by the state bar association, private or public reprimands, suspension, and in some cases, disbarment do occur.

In the chapter on trust accounting, we discuss real-life experiences when attorneys' behaviors and failures to adhere to the local canons of ethics resulted in disbarment and criminal charges. Bar associations take seriously their duty to protect the public from the actions of lawyers who are placed in a position of trust by their clients every day.

Firm protocols and software can protect the client and the firm. Case management software allows a lawyer to perform conflict checks by inputting information regarding a potential new case. Using this software *each and every time* the lawyer conducts a new client consult will avoid problems later in the representation of unknown conflicts that could have been discovered during the consultation.

When used properly, accounting software will track deposits of client funds, disbursements, and balances. It generates a reconciliation report on a monthly basis as part of the reconciliation process that should accurately reflect each client's balance at the close of the month. The billing program used in conjunction with the accounting software should generate accurate client balances on each client bill and should show the disbursements made that month for each client.

Client confidentiality, professional conduct, client advocacy, and professional responsibility all involve the moral compass of the lawyer and staff. The lawyer sets the example of appropriate behavior. The need for confidentiality is a topic that must be included in your policy and procedure manual.

While the canons of ethics of both the American Bar Association and the state bar associations are directed to attorneys, it is incumbent on the lawyer to hold each and every staff member to the same high standard of ethical and moral behavior in the best interests of his clients. Any breach of ethical behavior in the firm *by any employee*, be it lawyer, paralegal, legal assistant, receptionist, or firm administrator, must be grounds for termination. There is no margin for error, and there is no gray area. Unethical or questionable behavior absolutely cannot be tolerated. It is detrimental to the client's best interests. It could jeopardize a client's case, and it will affect the firm's reputation within the legal community. While money can buy a lot of things, it cannot buy you or your firm a good reputation once it has been tarnished.

CHAPTER SEVEN
HOW TO PUT TOGETHER A MONTHLY "TO DO" LIST

Whether you have been running your own practice for years or have just hung your shingle, you are likely very familiar with the feeling that there is something pressing that must be completed. While even important due dates like tax deadlines or employee annual reviews can often be extended, if you do so continuously, you will feel as though you can never catch up. Rather than completing tasks in an orderly fashion without stress, you will find yourself running around like a chicken with your head cut off and wasting time worrying. Tax time can be especially stressful when you feel as though your accountant is tap dancing on your forehead and demanding to know where your tax documents are and your employees send you emails on January 31 asking when to expect their W-2s.

Sound familiar?

Joryn and Liz believe in time management and organization. With combined experience of over 70 years, they understand that the best way to get things accomplished timely and to truly maximize efficiency is by being organized. In fact, organization is a good way to get many things completed in a law firm, including managing your caseload.

If you've ever read the bestseller *The Checklist Manifesto*, you already know that Atul Gawande has demonstrated in a very readable style what the simple idea of the checklist reveals about the complexity of our lives and how we can deal with it.

We have amazing know-how in the modern age. Yet the news is replete with stories about preventable failures plaguing us in health care, government, the law, the financial industry—in almost every realm of organized activity. And the reason is simple: the volume and complexity of knowledge today have exceeded our ability as individuals to properly deliver it to people consistently, correctly, and safely. We train longer, specialize more, use ever-advancing technologies, and still, we fail. Gawande makes a compelling argument that we can do better using the simplest of methods: the checklist. In riveting stories, he reveals what checklists can do, what they can't, and how they can bring about striking improvements in a variety of fields, from medicine and disaster recovery to professions and businesses of all kinds. And the insights are making a difference. Already, a simple surgical checklist from the World Health Organization designed by following the ideas described here has been adopted in more than twenty countries as a standard for care and has been heralded as "the biggest clinical invention in thirty years." (*The Independent*.)

So, to help you manage your year and get monthly tasks accomplished efficiently and on time, here is a list of monthly "to dos" that will get you through the year and help ensure that everything is done in a timely fashion:

January

1. HELP STAFF SET AND ACHIEVE GOALS. Review last year's profit and loss statement if you have not done so already. Review timekeeper quotas and income. Meet with your staff, and discuss their goals and how they align with your firm goals. Consider asking questions like, "What is on your agenda for the coming year?"; "What areas of work do you need to improve?"; and "What areas can the firm improve to make things more efficient and enable you to be more productive?"

2. CUT COSTS (WITHOUT CUTTING CORNERS). The beginning of the year is a good time to look back at the prior year to analyze how much the firm was spending on what and where money can be saved without making sacrifices. If you provide refreshments and are using a beverage service that charges $18 for a case of soda, consider purchasing beverages from a retail warehouse store that only charges $9 to $12. In your legal cases, take a look at the life cycle of a file, and ensure that processes are in place to cut back on waste. Consider legal project management services or process improvement. If your lawyers are performing secretarial or clerical work instead of exclusively billable services, ensure that such tasks are being completed by more appropriate staff members.

3. REVIEW, AND POSSIBLY, RAISE YOUR FEES. Raising fees is best accomplished at the beginning of the year. While clients generally won't thank you for raising your fees, it is expected more at the beginning of the year than mid-year. Be sure to give your clients 30 day's written notice that you are increasing your fees, and be reasonable. If you double your hourly rate, you will lose clients.

4. KEEP TIMEKEEPERS INFORMED OF THEIR BILLABLE HOURS AND WHETHER THEY ARE MEETING THEIR QUOTAS. Review annual timekeeper reports. Talk to timekeepers whose hourly quotas were not met in the previous year. Discuss obstacles that prevented them from meeting their quotas. Then, keep an eye on your billables. Around the 15th of the month, check to determine where timekeepers are in terms of meeting their goals. Immediately discuss how to address the issue with timekeepers who are falling short of their goals. The end of the month will be too late.

5. SCHEDULE EVERYTHING FOR THE COMING YEAR NOW. We aren't talking about hearings or depositions. Ensure that the expiration of your office lease, copier lease, and any other service with whom you have a contract is scheduled 30 and 60 days in advance of expiration so you have plenty of notice to take appropriate action. Now is the time to renegotiate or to shop around for a better copier, for more (or less) office space, or for lower rent. Being prepared puts you in a position of power to negotiate a better deal for the firm. And a better deal for the firm is a better deal for the bottom line.

6. PERFORM COMPUTER MAINTENANCE. Have your computer or IT guy perform maintenance work on your computer, server, scanner, etc. Make sure all updates have been performed, that everything is working at maximum efficiency, and that you have plenty of memory and computer storage. Take care of this now, and you will be good to go for the rest of the year.

7. ENSURE THAT YOU HAVE YOUR W-2'S AND 1099'S READY FOR DISTRIBUTION TO YOUR EMPLOYEES AND CONTRACTORS.

8. FINALIZE YOUR BUDGET FOR THE CURRENT YEAR. Remember, *the budget is only accurate on the date when it is prepared.* Be sure to review the budget on a regular basis, and make adjustments as necessary.

FEBRUARY

1. REVIEW DEPARTMENT REVENUES. If your firm has more than one area of specialty, compare the annual revenues from each department. If litigation showed enormous profits, and real estate barely covered its overhead expenses, consider re-assigning personnel to the litigation department to spread out the workload. Also, review marketing for the real estate department, and determine if it is appropriate to step up your marketing strategy to bring in more real estate work. Or consider discontinuing offering legal services in a practice area that is not generating sufficient revenue.

2. REVIEW STAFFING NEEDS. Review origination and realization reports and profit and loss reports. If new business taken on last year has been sustainable for six to nine months, plan to review this again in another three months. If the growth continues, consider re-assigning a staff member or taking on a new staff member for this new business. Don't move too fast and hire a half dozen new people because you do not want to have to let them go in three months if the growth doesn't continue.

3. PREPARE FOR TAX TIME. Start accumulating tax documents in anticipation of tax time. Most of this should be fairly easy as reports can be generated by your accounting software, provided the information entered is accurate and current. You don't want to scramble at the last minute or file for an extension if it isn't absolutely necessary. Your accountant will thank you.

4. UPDATE YOUR WEBSITE. Ensure that bios and photos are current. Potential clients connect with you through your website. We have heard clients say time and again that they felt a connection with a photo or that someone looked like they would care about them, etc. If you have discontinued an area of practice or if you have added a new area of specialty, be sure to include that on your website. Existing and current clients must have the most up-to-date information to make an informed decision.

5. BOOST MORALE. The holidays are over, and by February, people are feeling a little bit blah. Shake things up a little bit with a staff luncheon. Order pizzas and sodas or get barbecue and arrange for everyone to contribute a side dish or a dessert. Take an hour and lunch with your staff. Everyone will feel rejuvenated.

MARCH

1. CLEAN UP THE RECEPTION AREA. Get rid of old magazines. No one wants Christmas cookie recipes or Christmas gifts under $10 in March. Repot or replace plants, if necessary. Get some silk flowers. Have upholstered chairs cleaned, and spruce up the reception area. Burn some candles for ambiance.

2. HELP STAFF MEET THEIR GOALS. It's almost three months into the new year. Start conducting quarterly reviews with employees, not to discuss raises, but to evaluate where

employees are and discuss any areas of concern. Be sure these conversations are constructive and not destructive. It is counter-productive to wait to discuss issues only annually. When an issue arises, but you wait a year to discuss it with an employee, it's only natural that they file it under "old news."

3. CONSIDER HIRING SUMMER ASSOCIATES. Does your firm hire summer associates? If so, start looking now, and consider your recruiting methods. Are you going to attend recruiting events or have a luncheon? Prepare an on-boarding package including welcome letters, job descriptions, and training letters. Make sure that you have sufficient support staff for the additional associates.

4. REVIEW YOUR ROI FOR THE PAST YEAR, AND CONSIDER RE-STRATEGIZING YOUR MARKETING PLAN. Remember to do some market analysis and size up your competition. See what they are offering new clients, and consider re-working your own marketing strategy. Remember, for the client, it is always about, "What can you do for me?"

APRIL

1. ENSURE THAT 941 RETURNS ARE FILED. Do you have a payroll company that does your payroll? Confirm that they have filed your 941 returns. Ask for a copy for your records. If you file your own 941 returns, prepare and file them. Be sure to pay any taxes you owe. Interest and penalties add up quickly.

2. PAY REAL ESTATE TAXES, IF APPROPRIATE. If you pay real estate taxes in one installment, they are usually due by April 30. Check where you live/work to ensure that you are timely.

3. REVIEW FIRST QUARTER BILLABLE HOUR REPORTS TO VERIFY HOW YOUR TIMEKEEPERS ARE PERFORMING. Assess where timekeepers are in terms of reaching their annual goals, and discuss any changes that must be made, such as adjustments in procedures for capturing time or time management techniques.

4. REVIEW YOUR FIRST QUARTER EXPENSES. Compare them to the budget that you prepared for the current year. Did you have unexpected expenditures in the first three months of the year? If so, adjust your budget. Do you anticipate any expenditures for the rest of the year that were not expected when you prepared the budget? If so, make the adjustment to the budget. Try to keep the budget as accurate as possible.

5. PLAN MARKETING EVENTS FOR THE FIRM. If you are considering a client event in the coming months, start planning (and budgeting) for it now.

6. UPDATE YOUR FIRM BROCHURE. If you have added (or lost) attorneys, or if partners have joined the firm, ensure the information in your firm brochure is current.

7. PREPARE FOR ADMINISTRATIVE PROFESSIONALS WEEK (DAY). This is usually during the last week of April. Any gesture of appreciation goes a long way to thank the staff that helps the firm succeed throughout the year. Don't overlook them.

MAY

1. START PLANNING COVERAGE FOR VACATIONS. Few firms use temporary staffing to cover for legal assistants or secretaries. With great strides in office efficiencies, legal assistants and

secretaries (or even law firm administrators, if they have legal experience) can cover for support staff while they are on vacation. Look at the schedules for the coming months now, and ensure that you will have sufficient coverage. If outside help is really necessary, start searching in advance and pre-screen applicants. Get a temp who will actually be productive. We both have stories to tell about temporary help who were actually more trouble (and expense) than they were worth.

2.   START PLANNING YOUR SUMMER EVENT. If your firm schedules a summer event for the firm, start planning it now. Clear dates with attorneys and staff, being mindful that people take vacations during the summer when their kids are out of school. To be effective, you really want as many of the staff to attend as possible. Plan fun family activities in which everyone can participate.

3.   ASSESS PROFITABILITY OF THE FIRM. No law firm can afford to support staff who are not profitable and generating revenues for the firm. Keep in mind that this is purely about business. Attorneys and staff with great educations or skills are not enough to justify employment with the firm if they are not contributing to the bottom line. Be sure to track the monthly profitability of the firm, and verify who is and who is not performing.

JUNE

1.   REVIEW THE BUDGET. Did we say that already? Yes, we sure did! That's because you cannot check the budget too often to keep expenses under control.

2.   REVIEW THE CURRENT PROFIT AND LOSS STATEMENT, AND COMPARE IT TO THE BUDGET. This will tell you if the firm is on track. If there are adjustments that should be made to the budget or to work, productivity, or billing, now is the time to make them. If despite having a budget, spending is somehow getting out of hand, it's time to investigate what is causing the bleeding and why.

3.   REVIEW THE FIRM'S BENEFIT PLANS. Shop insurance and other benefits for better rates and better coverages. This includes legal malpractice insurance. Shopping around gets you the best rates. Remember to negotiate.

4.   MEET WITH THE STAFF. Conduct mid-year performance reviews or "stay" interviews with your staff. Remember to maintain a "no retaliation/no retribution" policy. Staff will be open and honest with you if they know that their jobs are not on the line. Ask about efficiency in the office, and seek any input they might have on how things can be improved. This is often your best source of information.

JULY

1.   REVIEW YOUR MARKETING PLAN. You have just passed the halfway point of the year, and this is a good time to look at the tracking and conversion on your return on investment. Review your spending and returns. If you advertise in more than one area, determine which area is getting a better return on the money. Consider redistributing the marketing budget if one area is performing better than another. Or examine the marketing strategy for the under-performing marketing, and make the necessary changes.

2.   ASSIGN WORK TO SUMMER ASSOCIATES. You have the extra help so put it to good use! The summers are slower, and the court docket slows down. But come the fall, your workload will pick up fast. You likely have trials and depositions that are already scheduled for later in the year. Witnesses must be subpoenaed and prepped. Documents should be subpoenaed, reviewed, and summarized. Make good use of the extra help, and put those summer associates to work. If your summer associates don't earn their keep, you don't really need them.

3.   CLEAN UP YOUR CASE FILES. If you still have some closed paper files hanging around, follow your closing file procedure, and move them out of the office. Even if you cannot go through the proper closing procedure now, move them to the closed list, and make room by moving them out.

4.   SCHEDULE A STAFF UPDATE MEETING. Call it a "this is where we are, and this is where we are (or need to be) going" meeting. Everyone wants to know that the firm at which they work is stable and financially secure. The professional staff understands the concept of how their work contributes to the bottom line of the firm. If anyone on your staff does *not* get that or doesn't want to be part of that, you may need to employ new staff.

Don't discuss specific dollars and cents with your employees. They don't need to know the gross revenues of the firm or the firm's expenses. This is primarily because of human nature; all they will hear are the gross revenues of the firm. Somehow, no one ever hears what the expenses are. Your staff will be more inclined to take ownership of their positions and how their work affects the firm if they feel that they are really part of a team. Inclusion in a meeting like this will reinforce these feelings.

AUGUST

1.   START REVIEWING OUTSTANDING CLIENT ACCOUNTS IN TERMS OF COLLECTIONS. If clients have old past-due balances that might not be collectible, before turning them over to collections, offer the clients a 20% discount but only if paid in full within seven or ten days. This is preferable to sending it to collections or to suit because that will cost the firm even more money. This comes under the heading of "cut your losses" and helps avoid a total write-off.

2.   REVIEW YOUR BUDGET AGAIN! With almost three-quarters of the year behind you, review your budget to determine where the firm is in terms of staying on track. Reign in your year-end spending, especially if you have gone over-budget. Make necessary adjustments in order to stay on track.

3.   REVIEW BILLABLE HOURS. With the last quarter of the year just ahead, you can already project the firm's income thus far. In all likelihood, barring the loss of any client or influx of new business, most timekeepers remain steady in their billable hours. Discuss with timekeepers who are falling short how they can step up their game for the rest of the year.

SEPTEMBER

1.   REVIEW YOUR INCOME AND EXPENSES FOR THE YEAR THUS FAR. Does the business that the firm is generating warrant hiring a new legal assistant, paralegal, or associate? Is the

sustainability of new business sufficient to justify the new hire? Or has there been a slowdown in business that is affecting the profits of the firm based upon the cost of employee overhead versus fees generated? If so, consider "right-sizing" the firm or reassigning job descriptions so that everyone has enough work to do and is productive.

If there must be a "right-sizing," plan its timing carefully; don't wait until the holidays to do it.

2. REMEMBER YOUR SUMMER STAFF. Consider summer staff for a full-time position if the firm is in a position to add staff. The benefit is that they are already familiar with the other staff, clients, and office procedures, which reduces their learning curve.

3. PREPARE YOUR DRAFT BUDGET FOR THE FOLLOWING YEAR. By now you have a pretty good idea of your current year budget. The expenses for the rest of the year should be routine, except for year-end or performance bonuses. Now is a good time to prepare a draft budget for the following year and to add or delete items from the current budget as needed.

4. SCRUTINIZE THE MARKETING BUDGET FOR THE PAST YEAR AND THE CONVERSION OF PROSPECTS TO CLIENTS. Calculate whether the new business generated justified the expense of marketing dollars. Always be flexible enough with your marketing dollars to move them around if something isn't working.

5. CONTACT CLIENTS AFTER THE SUMMER. Reach out to clients with an email asking if they had a good summer and enjoyed their time off. You might mention what the firm did over the summer to get ready for another year, and remind them that the firm is ready to help them with their legal needs. Be sure to list the firm's services, especially if you have added new practice areas. Perhaps even more importantly, say "thank you" for their faith in you. Let them know that you value their business.

6. CONTACT REFERRING ATTORNEYS. Everyone is back from summer vacation, including referring attorneys. Reach out to them. Send a thank you letter or email for referrals that they have made in the past. (An actual thank you note is really unusual these days and you'll be surprised by how much they will appreciate it. There is still something to be said for the personal touch.) Outline the areas in which your firm specializes, and mention that you are available to assist any referrals.

Be sure to mention any referral fees that you pay, and ask them in which areas they currently practice so that you can refer business to them, as well. Offer to take them to lunch or a coffee. Networking often results in the referral of new business.

7. DEVELOP A BUSINESS CONTINUITY PLAN. Do you have a plan to keep operations running in a power outage or crisis? Be sure to have a business continuity plan in place that includes computer back up and contact information for everyone including employees, clients, opposing counsel, and the courts.

OCTOBER

1. RUN THE PROFIT AND LOSS STATEMENTS THROUGH THE THIRD QUARTER. You will know where you are for the year and can make revisions to the budget you are working on for next year. Start evaluating the budget for year-end or performance bonuses based on the firm's revenues through the third quarter.

2. REVIEW TIMEKEEPER BILLABLES THROUGH THE THIRD QUARTER, AND COMPARE QUOTAS TO THE REALITY. Are timekeepers meeting their requirements? If not, discuss the shortfall. Sometimes it's something as simple as forgetting to bill for travel time.

3. TIME TO THINK ABOUT SOME FUN! The Christmas or year-end party is just around the corner. Now is the time to look at the budget (did you budget for a party?), and start making calls to check prices and availability. Be creative, and decide early so you can get the place you really want.

NOVEMBER

1. ORDER YOUR HOLIDAY CARDS. If your firm traditionally sends out holiday cards, start putting your list together, and choose a firm card now. Surprisingly, even with emails replacing snail mail, many firms still send holiday cards, and clients and other professionals still expect them. Again, there is something to be said for the personal touch.

2. PLAN YOUR GIFT GIVING. Does your firm give gifts to other professionals who refer business to the firm? If so, start putting together your list, and, using your budget, figure out the gift budget. Everyone sends chocolates, cookies, or some kind of gift basket. Try to be a bit more creative, and choose (or make) a gift that is person specific. The extra thought goes a long way.

3. DOUBLE-CHECK THE BUDGET FOR THE YEAR-END BONUSES. Now is a good time to determine the overall annual picture of how well the firm did, what your timekeepers contributed, and what it cost to run the firm. Apportion any money that might be available to fund year-end bonuses. Some firms give a week's salary across the board, for example. Others distribute bonuses according to billable time and revenues generated for the firm.

4. CHECK YOUR RECEIVABLES. See what monies you might be able to collect before year end. Remember that, usually by December 15, you have collected all the money your firm will get for the year. Most clients are in holiday mode with their own families by December 15 and you will not see any receivables until sometime after the first of the new year.

5. PLAN FOR A PRODUCTIVE NEW YEAR. Schedule a year-end meeting with your staff, and determine what the firm's needs are for the coming year in terms of a new scanner, phone system, or software update. Be sure to include those items in your upcoming annual budget.

DECEMBER

1. PLAN FOR YOUR OFFICE COVERAGE OVER THE HOLIDAYS. By the 22nd or 23rd of December, at the latest, business slows down tremendously. The phones stop ringing because clients are busy with their families. Many law firms either close the office completely from December 23rd through January 2 (making sure that someone checks emails and messages), or they arrange for a rotating skeleton crew. If this is feasible, it is certainly a good opportunity for everyone to enjoy some downtime, recharge, and get ready for the coming year of success.

2. START THINKING ABOUT THE FIRM'S TAXES. Are there any bills that you can pay by December 31 that can offset any expected income or reduce tax liabilities for the firm?

Consider paying them before December 31st, as they have to be paid anyway.

3. EVALUATE YOUR ADVERTISING BUDGET. Review the income that your marketing strategy has generated through the year. Include ads in magazines, newspapers, television, Google, Twitter, etc. If you are unable to calculate the ROI from each of the sources on which you spent money, you may need to consider implementing a better way to track conversion.

4. ANALYZE BILLABLE HOURS FOR THE YEAR. Who is underperforming and why? If there isn't enough work to justify the overhead, consider right-sizing or reassigning workloads. Be sure to re-evaluate this in 90 days. The best way to determine whether something is working is to review it regularly until you are sure of the answer.

5. REVIEW FIRM'S FEES INCLUDING FEE STRUCTURES. Ensure that your firm is competitive in the hourly rates that you charge, as well as in the fee structures that you offer clients. Many firms have worked out alternative fee arrangements with clients because of the client's demand for value. Ensure that you remain competitive within your legal community.

6. ACCOMMODATE WORK/LIFE BALANCE. Review your PTO policy, and ensure that your employees have enough downtime to keep them happy and productive. Studies have shown that employees who work more hours don't necessarily get more work finished; they simply accomplish the same amount of work over a longer period of time.

7. REDUCE THE STRESS OF GIFT GIVING IN THE OFFICE. If your staff observes Christmas, consider a secret Santa, a white elephant, or some other limited gift exchange. The economy being what it is, everyone is struggling (no matter how well-paid you might think some of your staff are), and no one wants to feel as though they aren't participating. A secret Santa eliminates much of the financial burden of multiple gift giving in the office because everyone buys for just one person. This practice ensures no one will feel left out. No one feels obligated to buy gifts they cannot afford or is embarrassed when they receive gifts and don't, or can't, reciprocate. Be sure to set a limit; $25 is reasonable.

8. SCHEDULE PERFORMANCE REVIEWS. If you met with everyone at the beginning of the year to discuss expectations, now is a good time to schedule a meeting to discuss performance. At the meeting, present a summary in bullet form of goals that have been met, as well as an overview of achievements. Be sure to include the financial impact of meeting these goals because everyone can relate to numbers (i.e. to money).

9. PLAN A LIST OF ACCOMPLISHMENTS THAT YOU WANT THE FIRM TO ACHIEVE FOR THE UPCOMING YEAR. There is no better way to accomplish a goal than to create one—or more. Celebrate the firm's accomplishments, and plant the seed for your successes in the coming year. The power of suggestion does work, and you will find that everyone will work towards a goal—if they know what it is.

10. CLEAN HOUSE FOR THE NEW YEAR, LITERALLY. Now is the time to clean out your desk, file cabinets, inboxes, contacts, the refrigerator, etc. You will come back in the new year ready to perform with a clean desk and a clear head.

Henry Ford once said, "Before everything else, getting ready is the secret to success." Follow this outline of monthly "to dos," and you will be ready to achieve success!

REVIEW QUESTIONS THREE

Lawyers:

1. How do you keep track of tasks that must be performed throughout the year without having deadlines creep up on you? Whether it's monthly responsibilities like billing and reconciling bank accounts or annual tasks like preparing your taxes or planning the annual holiday party, do you have a system in place so you don't wake up one morning to realize that a deadline is looming and you have not prepared appropriately to be able to meet it? What is your system?
2. Do you have checks and balances in place to ensure deadlines are not missed? If so, what are they?
3. Have you ever missed a deadline? How did that may you feel? List the important deadlines you have missed in the past five years. Write down how you felt and what resulted from the missed deadline.
4. What can you do differently to improve your system to ensure you never miss a deadline again? Brainstorm ideas. Now implement them!

Law Students:

1. In your life, have you had responsibilities that needed to be performed throughout the year? List examples of those responsibilities. Don't forget important school deadlines. How have you kept track of those tasks without having deadlines creep up on you?
2. Do you have a system in place so you don't wake up one morning to realize that a deadline is looming and you have not prepared appropriately to be able to meet it? What is your system? Is it effective? Write down ways in which you could improve your systems.
3. Do you have checks and balances in place so deadlines are not missed? If so, what are they? List them. How can you improve them as your deadlines become more important?
4. Have you ever missed a deadline? List the important deadlines you have missed in the past five years. Write down how you felt and what resulted from the missed deadline.
5. What can you do differently to improve your system to ensure you never miss a deadline again? Brainstorm ideas. Now implement them!

CHAPTER EIGHT
HOW TO PRIORITIZE MANAGEMENT PRIORITIES

Ever think to yourself, "How much more could I accomplish if there were just one more hour in a day?" We would all make each day longer to fit just one more thing into the work day—and one more thing, and one more thing, and one more... Impeccable time management and organizational skills are an absolute necessity, no matter what business you are in. An organized law firm admin can always find time to accomplish "one more thing."

Management priorities differ in law firms from day to day and from moment to moment. There are often competing priorities. Unless there is an existing crisis, it is not always easy to determine which priority is more important.

Priority should always be given to anything that involves the clients. But really, everything in the office is about the clients, isn't it? Serving clients is why the law firm exists, and without clients, there is no law firm. If you are struggling with an HR issue, that involves the clients because if work is not accomplished, that affects them. At the same time, when there are information technology ("IT") problems, it involves the clients because "no computers" means "no work," which results in unsatisfied clients when you are unable to meet their deadlines.

Law firm administrators handle most day-to-day functions of the practice. The list of those functions in a job description for a law firm administrator would be quite short— *everything.*

There are six overarching administrative functions of a law firm:

1. Human Resources;
2. Accounting/finance (including billing);
3. IT;
4. Client development/marketing;
5. Office services; and
6. Facilities management.

It is not an accident that we have listed these primary areas of firm administration in order of everyday significance in terms of deciding what is most important when there are competing priorities.

We consider two areas—human resources and accounting—to be top priorities in trying to manage administrative duties. Human resources encompass all staffing issues, benefits, payroll, conflict resolution, performance evaluation, bonuses, paid time off, vacation, and the like. Human resource issues affect personnel. Personnel is the means to the end of performing work for clients so that they are satisfied with the services they receive from your firm. Happy clients are paying clients, and every firm needs paying clients to generate revenues because revenues sustain the practice. Happy clients also refer new clients. So, clients are the number one priority. *Always.*

Accounting includes managing bank accounts, billing, collections, client trust funds, the firm's revenues, and anything having to do with the law firm's finances. The bottom line is *money matters.* The fact that your legal staff completes the work and provides quality legal services to the client is not enough. Once the work is completed, timekeepers must make time entries so that clients can be billed.

Time must be captured efficiently. To ensure that *all* time is captured, it is necessary that timekeepers enter their time contemporaneously with completing a client project or assignment. The amount of firm revenues lost when a timekeeper enters time later is significant. Trying to remember a week or even a day later everything that was accomplished on a client file leads to errors and forgotten time. Unless of course, the timekeeper records all of his time, in which case he could have made the time entry in a billing program and be done with it. We have both had an associate tell us that, even though he does not contemporaneously enter his time or write it down, he captures all his time by reviewing his e-mails to see what he did. We know for certain that all time cannot be captured this way.

Sometimes it is difficult to enable staff to understand the consequences to the firm of losing even .2 billable hours a few times a day. After all, it is just .2 hours, right? Well, at the end of the month, and at the end of the year, those .2 hours add up to several hours of lost time. Several hours every month at $250 or $350 an hour is not inconsequential.

If you are a sole proprietor, you probably are the human resources and IT departments. It may seem like you don't have enough hours in your day to make sure that all time is captured and that technical issues are addressed immediately. After all, you are working on cases so that you can bill clients for your time and make money for the firm. But HR and IT matters must be addressed as soon as possible before they evolve into bigger problems that will cause the rest of your staff to lose valuable time.

It goes without saying that a crisis that interferes with the efficiency and productivity of the legal staff takes priority when it impedes work. If the printer is down, take one minute and call for service. If there is an IT problem, troubleshoot the problem yourself if you can or call IT. Some things can't wait. While it is a judgment call, the priority should be obvious.

In these days of firms endeavoring to do more with less, it is important for management to recognize the need to address everyday priorities so that the reduced staff can operate efficiently and cost-effectively. Good for the client equals good for the bottom line.

What is good for the bottom line is definitely good for the firm!

CHAPTER NINE
HOW TO DO MORE WITH LESS
(PROBLEM SOLVING AND PROCESS IMPROVEMENT)

"Doing more with less." The goal for every law firm today. Providing maximum efficiency is an endless challenge for today's law firms, especially for smaller and medium-sized firms as there is often less staff to perform the work. Law firms must stay competitive in today's legal market. That means providing outstanding service and giving every client value for his legal dollar. But often, reduced staffing resources due to reduced revenues cause an unsustainable work model for law firms.

The one thing that no law firm can afford to sacrifice or compromise on is meeting a client's expectations. Not in terms of outcome, because no one can guarantee what will happen, but in terms of quality of service. Undertaking the problem solving, process improvement, and doing-more-with-less philosophy, you can increase client development, growth, and retention opportunities for your firm.

Twenty or thirty years ago, before computers replaced electric typewriters (anyone remember those?), preparation of documents was an arduous task in which every pleading required that the wheel be reinvented over and over. Bookkeeping and trust accounting were done with a calculator, checkbooks, and ledgers and accounting tasks required painstaking attention to detail. There were no computerized calendars—everyone used the big red lawyer diary. We communicated by snail mail, telephone, and telefax.

All of those tools are now obsolete, and those of us who remember those days remember how difficult it was to be productive. Those who don't remember find it unimaginable. Case management software, accounting and financial software, e-mail, text, and cell phones all enable us to prepare documents, communicate, schedule, and manage finances much more easily, quickly and more accurately.

There are more attorneys per capita today than there were 20 years ago. Competition for clients is tough, and law firms sometimes spend a significant amount of their revenues executing marketing plans to attract new clients. Some clients are very tech savvy, and they expect improved services for their money. As a result of reduced staffing necessitated by the competitive legal market, firm staff is often overloaded with work and often feels a little overwhelmed.

No firm can afford to sacrifice what clients expect in terms of quality of service. When a client needs legal services, the business value of the service and the firm's profitability can be reduced as a result of failing to meet client demands. This can significantly affect a firm's revenues.

Could your firm benefit from problem solving and process improvement? Ask yourself:

- Is your case management software being used to its fullest potential?
- Are your forms up-to-date and actually used as forms with templates and merge codes, or is your staff reinventing the wheel every time a letter or pleading must be generated?
- Are you utilizing accounting software for office bookkeeping, trust accounting, and maintaining client ledgers, thereby reducing the errors made by numerous entries in different places of the same information?
- Can you easily access information for a client?

It's easy to fall into the trap of believing that your firm is too busy to undertake process improvement. A review of the current systems that are in place will help you determine what changes you can and must make.

What are the steps involved in problem solving and process improvement? Here's what you must do:

- Define the problem;
- Measure the current performance of the process currently being used; and
- After identifying the problem, control it by implementing solutions designed to eliminate the problem and improve the process.

Measure the benefits of problem solving and process improvement for your firm:

- Better client services (and therefore improved client satisfaction);
- Improved efficiency and higher levels of production;
- Reduced errors in work product; and
- Lower costs (and therefore increased profitability).

So, for example, when using form templates, be sure to always keep them up-to-date. Be leery of any form that is more than a few years old. Always stay apprised of statutory amendments that necessitate a revision to your forms.

Also, many software programs offer free tutorials so that you and your staff are able to learn how to more effectively utilize all that the program has to offer. Watch these tutorials or talk to your salesperson to learn how to most efficiently use these programs. Once you do, you will be amazed at what many of these programs can do and how this will save you time and help you to offer an improved service.

If you believe you are too busy to undertake process improvement but know that your firm would benefit from it, there is only one way to break that cycle—just do it!

CHAPTER TEN
HOW TO USE SUMMER "DOWNTIME" EFFICIENTLY

Summertime brings with it the inevitable slowdown of both office practice and court dockets as kids come home for the summer and everyone, including judges, judicial assistants, and legal assistants, take vacations. There are many ways to make productive use of the summer slowdown that will benefit the firm and get you ready to wind down the year on a successful and profitable note. Here are some suggestions for making efficient and cost-effective use of that time.

- ENCOURAGE YOUR SUPPORT STAFF TO TAKE TIME OFF. During summer downtime, your firm may not be in need of as many hands as the rest of the year. Allowing staff to take time off during summer slowdown may be especially beneficial for those who have children on break from school. Try to rotate schedules so that there is sufficient coverage in the office without creating the need to incur the added expense of employing a temporary staff person. There's no benefit to hiring temporary help for the sake of having someone in the office. Doing so is counter cost productive. With a less hectic schedule in the court dockets, and consequently the office, staff members should be able to cover for those taking time off without much inconvenience.

- REJUVENATE, REFRESH, AND RESTART. Don't forget that the summer is also an opportunity for you to take some time for yourself so you can begin the fall rejuvenated. Plan your own family vacation. Leave work early to watch your kids play sports or to attend dance recitals. While it is important to work hard throughout the year, it is also important to recognize when to take some downtime. Remember to always work towards a good work/life balance so that you can be successful long term.

- CREATE OPPORTUNITIES FOR BONDING. If your firm likes to hold summer outing or office bonding events, April or May are good months to start planning. Attorneys' schedules are lighter and a bit more relaxed during those months. Check with everyone well in advance to avoid conflict with staff's personal family vacation time. This is also a nice way to show your staff that you appreciate their work. Plan appropriate activities that will keep both the adults and the children entertained. Interactive activities will be good for boosting morale as they will encourage interaction without imposition on the office hierarchy.

- ASSESS FINANCIAL PROGRESS. June 30 marks the halfway point of the firm's profits for the year. By this time, you will have a good indication of the profits and losses thus far. Sit down with the firm's decision-makers to take a detailed look at the firm's income and expenses. This should be a close item-by-item examination. Liz always tells her clients, she may not have a way to save $1,000, but she can find 1,000 ways to save $1. In the end, it's the same thing.

- TACKLE QUOTAS FOR BILLABLE HOURS. Take the summer slowdown to examine your firm's billable hours. Determine if staff is meeting their quotas and how to improve areas of shortcomings. This process should include all of the attorneys and paralegals of the firm. It is best to address any pressing issues during the time when office operation is slow, rather than letting it fester for another six months until the end of the year when the principals assess the firm's annual goals achievements. Be sure that when you provide clients with their monthly bills, you also provide your timekeepers with reports reflecting the billable hours they've generated in each bill. It's important for staff to know whether they are meeting their quotas. Everyone wants a healthy bottom line during evaluations as it impacts their pay increases, bonuses, or other forms of compensation.

- PRIOR PLANNING PREVENTS POOR PERFORMANCE. Summer slowdown also allows for time to prepare for any trials or evidentiary hearings in the fall. Put summer associates and extra help available during the summer to work. Complete key research, organize files and exhibits, gather and prep key witnesses—get as much legwork as possible finished while you have the support in the office. Doing so will save chaos as the days before the hearing or trial approach.

- INCREASE YOUR KNOWLEDGE BASE. Fill low caseload and slow days in the office by taking the time to attend seminars, workshops, and trainings or to complete CLE credits. This would be a wise use of time if you are considering shifting the direction of the firm by perhaps adding another area to your practice that calls for additional training.

- EVALUATE MARKETING STRATEGIES. Use the summer as a time to hone the marketing *fortes* discussed in the marketing chapter. For example, summer is a great time to write your book, to blog more often, or to prepare your Power Points for autumn, when you can offer to present. Along those same lines, get any special projects, like article writing, out of the way as well.

Time management and organizational skills are essential to any firm's success. The summer slowdown gives your firm a few months in which to accomplish many things—as long you have an agenda and stay focused and organized on what you wish to achieve. By summer's end, you can have accomplished far more than you thought possible and still have a very productive summer!

CHAPTER ELEVEN
HOW TO EFFECTIVELY COMMUNICATE BY E-MAIL

Over the last 20 or 30 years, technology has paved the way for efficiency and productivity in the law office of today. Communications—with clients, opposing counsels, the courts, and others—is an everyday necessity. The evolution of e-mail technology and all forms of electronic communications have expedited how we do business in a law firm.

Snail mail has really slowed to a crawl. With few exceptions, most law firms send little to no mail anymore. Court filings in state and federal courts are now accomplished via e-portals to speed up the process and to make it more convenient. Discovery is also effectuated through the use of electronic communications (e-discovery).

Correspondence is still used, but these days, any letters one writes are attached in PDF format to an e-mail that is then transmitted electronically to recipients. Many law firm bills are also paid on online.

But of course, when there is progress in technology, there are concerns that must be addressed and precautions that should be taken to preserve client confidentiality and the security of legal documents and other information. Rule 1.1 of the American Bar Association's Model Rules of Professional Conduct states that attorneys must be aware of, familiar with, and guided by "the benefits and risks associated with relevant technology."

E-mail communications can prove to be a double-edged sword. While it has improved the expediency of client and other communications, there are many ways in which e-mail can be a source of concern in a law firm. This is true not only of confidentiality issues but because of errors that may be made, as well. If you follow these guidelines for e-mail etiquette and procedure, you will find that e-mail communications can be efficient and productive in your law firm.

1.   Every e-mail that is sent from a law office *to anyone* should be written with the expectation that someday that e-mail will find its way into some form of litigation or discovery. Be sure that even the most informal e-mail sent to a client or opposing counsel is accurate, free of errors, and addresses only the matters to which the e-mail actually pertains, clearly and without the possibility of its being misconstrued.

If you must e-mail the same opposing counsel on more than one matter, send separate e-mails for each. You do not want to disclose confidential client information on another case to unrelated persons if that e-mail must be disclosed later.

2.   Be sure e-mails contain a subject that accurately describes the purpose of the e-

mail. Simply writing "John Smith case" is not an appropriate subject. "John Smith—motion to compel" is an appropriate subject that tells the recipient what the e-mail is about. Although e-mails should be monitored and responses prepared in a timely fashion (see below), an appropriate subject signals the recipient that she may have just received an e-mail for which she has been waiting.

3. With regard to e-mails inadvertently sent to the wrong parties, unfortunately, this comes under the heading of *you can't un-ring the bell*. Microsoft Outlook provides instructions to recall e-mails if they have not been opened by the recipient. The American Bar Association Rule 4.4(a) provides that if a lawyer inadvertently receives a document that he knows is not related to the representation of a client, he has a duty to notify the sender. Additional procedures may vary according to your state's bar rules, however, professional courtesy dictates that the recipient should delete the e-mail without reading more of it than is necessary to determine that it was sent in error.

Also note that you have a professional duty to notify your client that this error occurred if the error is in any way damaging to your client.

4. Be careful using e-mail addresses that automatically populate when you start typing a name. It is easy to send an e-mail intended to one person named "John" to the wrong "John," especially if their last names start with the same letter. While it is easy to turn off this function in Microsoft Outlook, the auto-complete does facilitate e-mail addresses and dispenses with having to look them up and re-type them. Just take the extra necessary precautions to ensure your e-mails are properly addressed to the correct recipients.

5. Because many law firms utilize e-mail as their primary form of communication, be sure everyone in the firm regularly monitors their e-mail messages. While lawyers and staff should not be expected to monitor their e-mails 24/7, when unread e-mails pile up, deadlines or necessary client contacts can be easily overlooked.

Ensure that everyone in your firm is diligent about reviewing *and* responding to their e-mails. This is especially true with clients. If a client sends you an update on his case or pertinent information that does not appear to require a response, *send a response anyway*. This lets the client know you are reading his e-mails and are aware of his concerns and information. Remember: most bar grievances are filed by clients who complain that their lawyers did not communicate with them in a timely manner.

6. When retained by a new client, discuss with him that the firm communicates via e-mail. Many clients use telephones, laptops, iPads, or tablets to send and retrieve e-mail communications. Discuss with your client the parameters of and the need for confidentiality concerning communications regarding his representation. Some clients allow family members to use their e-mail addresses. Some clients retrieve their personal e-mails from an employer's computer during work hours. Clients should consider an employer's policies regarding e-mail communications of a personal nature on the employer's equipment during working hours. If an employer reviews an employee's use of company computers, there is

likely no expectation of privacy for the client, even though he is communicating with his lawyer.

Similarly, clients should be aware of security concerns with any mobile device. To ensure that your law firm is protected from a breach of confidentiality claim by a client who reads or writes law firm communications on devices that have questionable security, cover communication in your retainer agreement or engagement letter. It will save you headaches in the event that there is a breakdown of the attorney-client relationship.

In addition to the foregoing, there are three overwhelmingly important aspects of e-mail communications that should be observed.

1. MAINTAINING ATTORNEY-CLIENT PRIVILEGE. There are ethical and risk management considerations that should be observed with regard to client and non-client e-mails. The expectation of client confidentiality with e-mail communication is the same as it would be with any other form of communication: letter, fax, or telephone call. Confidentiality of e-mail communications (whether it is to the client, opposing counsel, the court, or experts) must be maintained. Lawyers must exercise due diligence and reasonable care to avoid inadvertently disclosing confidential client information.

2. KEEPING A CLIENT INFORMED. E-mail is an easy way to keep the information highway open to a client so that he remains informed on the status of his case. It would be simple enough to include the client as a "cc" or "bcc" on communications with opposing counsel, the court, or experts. The problem arises if a client decides that he wants to respond to something in the e-mail, provide information, or render an opinion about what is transpiring. If a client inadvertently hits "reply all" and sends his e-mail to all recipients, rather than just "reply" to respond to your e-mail, the client can inadvertently breach confidentiality and provide information to other parties that should not be shared.

How does one avoid this problem? Again, e-mail is a very easy way to keep a client informed. So first send the e-mail to your opposing counsel or expert, and then go into your sent folder and forward the e-mail to your client. Do not include in the forwarded e-mail anyone other than those in your office working on the client's file. This involves two or three extra but quick steps. The upside is that it will prevent inadvertent disclosure by your client of confidential information that could hurt his case.

3. E-MAIL RETENTION. Just as it is important to retain correspondence, pleadings, and other important documents in client files, retention of e-mails is equally critical. E-mails can be printed and placed in the paper file (if you are not yet paperless). Almost all case management programs interface with e-mail software such as Outlook. Retention of e-mails is as important as retention of all other client documents, especially because, for many firms, it is our primary form of communication in a case.

As we have discussed in other chapters, high on the list of client complaints to the bar association is the lack of information or status updates on a client's case. E-mail has made it much easier to keep clients informed about the status of their cases. Following these guidelines will reduce the number of clients who complain that they don't know what is going on in their cases and will actually enhance attorney-client relationships. And happy clients refer new cases.

Chapter Twelve
How to Go Paperless in Three Easy Steps

The concept of going paperless seems overwhelming for law firms. This is one of those things where you conjure up in your mind all the added work that it is going to take, then decide that it is more time efficient and less work to just keep things the way they are. The next time you are looking for a file as you are rushing out the door, already late to court, might be a good time to reconsider whether going paperless will really be that much of an inconvenience. In the long run, the ends will justify the means.

For decades, lawyers have surrounded themselves with paperwork. The thought of not being tethered to every file, to be able to reach out and touch it, or to see the product of all your work in a thick red file is incomprehensible to some lawyers. When meeting with a client, that thick red file and all that paper are tangible evidence of all the hard work you did on that client's case.

In a paperless law firm, when you meet with a client, you sit with a desktop or laptop computer and click around looking at documents while talking to a client. Somehow that does not seem as impressive as having a lot of paperwork scattered around a desk or a conference room table.

Going paperless, however, is very cost-effective and time-efficient. Courts require paperless filing via the e-portal. Service of pleadings is also done via email. Rarely does a law firm mail a letter to anyone unless a client does not have access to email. If communication is in letter form, it is attached as a PDF to an email and sent electronically. Most communications between attorneys, experts, clients, and the court are done via email. No need to buy as much paper or pay for shredding (if you have not yet negotiated to get your shredding done for free).

Many firms have already been paperless for years and have reaped the many benefits of a paperless office:

- Even if you print your own letterhead, the reduction of the cost of paper to print letterhead, make copies, send emails instead of letters, e-file court documents, and respond to discovery with pdfs or even a CD will substantially reduce the cost of paper for your office. Not to mention all the time spent by someone in your office to stand at the copier and make copies.

- No more file cabinets for storing current files or closed files. No more space to store the file cabinets. Imagine the cost savings of not having to rent office space to store six or 12 file cabinets.

- File folders never get lost.

- No more costs for off-site storage or the time and expense it takes to retrieve a file when it is needed.

- You have the ability to access a file without having to be in the office.

Liz recently had a consultation with a law firm that wanted to go paperless. The office manager met with Liz to discuss implementing a paperless protocol but was very clear that when it comes to being paperless in the office with client files, she was resistant to that kind of change. She conjured up in her mind the difficulty of not being able to "put her hands" on something that she needed. Liz explained to her that paperless computer files are set up exactly the way paper files are set up—same folders, same names, same procedures for filing documents. So, it should not be any more difficult to know which folder to look in for a document than it would be in a paper file. If someone is going to misfile something in a paperless file, that is likely the same person who would have misfiled it in a paper file. The document is not being misfiled because the file is paperless, it is being misfiled because the person doing the filing does not know where to put it or he inadvertently put it in the wrong folder. At least with a computer file, if the document was named correctly, it can be found with a simple computer search.

The single most important aspect of transitioning your law firm to a paperless office, before any procedures are put in place, is *consistency*. Consistency is *key* for a paperless practice to be successful. The firm must set up protocols for storing documents and entering consistent data in whichever case management software is used for storing files and documents or this will not work. No one will ever be able to find anything and more time will be wasted looking for documents. This would be counter-productive in every aspect. Everyone in the firm needs to know what the specific procedures are for opening files, setting them up, and naming documents or no one will ever be able to find anything. There will be no cost or time-saving benefit. In fact, people will likely get more frustrated. Going paperless requires buy-in from everyone in the firm.

Here are three steps that will get your firm started:

- Choose an appropriate and user-friendly document management system that will work for your firm. There are many companies selling different document management systems specifically geared for the practice of law. Shop some demos that these companies offer, and if all else fails, get information on available programs from another lawyer whose firm has instituted a paperless protocol.

Start your paperless procedures with the next file that you open. Phase out your paper files. Many firms that have gone paperless have spent time and money having someone scan current files into the new system. The ends do not justify the means. Each new matter that comes into the office should be opened as a paperless file.

- Set up your paperless files the same way you would set up your paper file. You can have correspondence, memos, pleadings, discovery, billing, etc. Do not break down file folders to 10 sub-folders. This is going to make things way too confusing for people and when someone is in a hurry—and in a law office it happens—someone is going to save something to a wrong subfolder and it will be hard for the next person to find it. Make sure documents are stored in chronological order by using dates as part of the naming process.

Going paperless is a time-saving and cost-saving protocol. If you take the time to implement the procedure and get everyone on board, you will see the benefits rather quickly and wonder why you didn't do it sooner.

REVIEW QUESTIONS FOUR

Lawyers:

1. Do you appreciate the importance of going paperless, not only to save time and money but also to remain competitive in the legal community? Identify the advantages and disadvantages of going paperless.
2. Are you so accustomed to the old way of doing things that you are uncomfortable making necessary changes? Are you old school and fear that you don't completely understand or trust technology? If so, find a book you can read on the subject. Better yet, consult with an expert.
3. Has your firm gone paperless? If not, why not? What are your challenges? List them.

Law Students:

1. Do you appreciate the importance of running a paperless practice, not only to save time and money but also to remain competitive in the legal community? Identify the advantages and disadvantages of going paperless.
2. When you graduate and open your own firm, do you plan to be a paperless firm? If so, why? If not, why not? List your reasons.

CHAPTER THIRTEEN
HOW TO USE SOCIAL MEDIA EFFECTIVELY

Not every marketing tool, including social media, will work for every area of law. Each area of law requires a different marketing strategy, as does your target client market.

Technology and social media have forever changed the way that we communicate—whether it is in our businesses or our personal lives. Some people would sooner send five texts than pick up the telephone and actually talk with whomever they are texting. In many ways, social media and texting have taken the "person" out of "personal" communications.

It is a huge mistake for any firm to fail to enter into the social media arena. Even if it is not for a direct marketing strategy *per se*, there is much to say for having a presence and marketing your brand, if not your work. Many consider social media to be the new gateway into client development and marketing that has not yet been saturated in the same way that television ads and billboards have.

The time to get active and to pave the way for your firm to be recognized in the social media arena is now. To stay in the game, you need to keep pace with the competition. To rely on outdated marketing ploys, such as yellow page ads, will only ensure that you are left in the dust. All generations are participating in social media.

These are some of the realities about social media—whether we want to face them or not:

1. Social media is a longer-term commitment than any other advertising. It requires a great deal of maintenance and builds up momentum over time. As you continue to use social media, new clients will find you and prior clients will return to your firm for additional services, so tracking the return on your investment of time expended on your social media "advertising" will be difficult. Social media is more about having a presence in that world so that you are not left behind.

2. Your social media strategy will depend on the area of law you practice, as well as on your personality and your brand.

3. Determine what part of your overall marketing budget you want to use on social media, if any. Much of social media is free and so are the corresponding analytics. If you plan to use free social media, be cautious about what social media you choose to use. Do not sign up with every new social media product

or service that pops up out there before it's proven. As with everything, you are judged by the company you keep. There are unpalatable social media service providers out there, so ensure that whatever form you use, it is professional and will attract the type of client you want.

4. Even though it is difficult to track the ROI on social media (especially when it's free), be sure to track *all* avenues of client referrals, including social media. There are analytics available for Facebook, LinkedIn, AVVO, and most other social media. They allow you to track the number of views and your standing as compared to others and also provide you access to what other professionals are doing to advertise their services.

5. Do not give up if it seems that, initially, it is taking a long time to see any active traffic from social media. Unlike direct marketing or advertising, the process with social media will likely take longer. You are in the social media game, and your firm is getting "face time" in the social media arena, which is critical.

6. If you advertise on paid sites that cater to lawyer advertisers *en masse*, ensure that you are prepared to work that from your end, as well. You should not spend thousands of dollars a month for referral sources that e-mail inquiries to you if you then fail to respond to those inquiries. If you participate in this kind of a marketing strategy, the key is to be the first to respond to the potential client's inquiries—even if they arrive during non-traditional office hours. When a prospect has what he considers to be an emergency, he wants someone who will address that inquiry immediately. In her replies, Liz specifically reiterates the inquirers' questions. This lets the client know that she actually read his inquiry and that he is not receiving a cookie cutter "thanks for writing, here's our bio, here's our intake form" answer. When lawyers and paralegals defer their response to *later* or *tomorrow*, they guarantee that that potential client already has another attorney.

Even if you do not practice the type of law the client requires, reply that this is the case, offer him a referral, thank him, and then inform him of the services your law firm does offer. You never know where your next million-dollar case will come from.

Use social media as a means to inform people about your firm's structures, the services it offers, and the level of qualifications your staff possesses. Post pictures of firm activities, articles written by members of the firm, and newsworthy information that is of a professional, but also a personal nature. Many potential tech savvy clients will want to verify that your firm has a web page. Whether you have one will be a factor in their decision to retain your services.

Liz worked for a firm that paid their IT person to manage social media. The "management" that the IT person provided consisted of posting and reposting the same information over and over again, and updating the firm's new information. He also ensured that the information on the website was consistent with the firm's Facebook and Twitter accounts. The content consisted of practical videos in which the attorneys answered clients' frequently asked questions in the context of *How Do I...?* The most useful or popular topics were recycled every six months, or when the firm was unable to post new videos due to other high demands of the practice. Through their analytics, the firm discovered that the content on the website had a higher rate of being viewed by clients than did the firm's newsletters sent by e-mail.

Viewers and potential clients want to see new postings. If your social media marketing campaign simply regurgitates the same information over and over again, and it looks like "news" is being recycled endlessly because no one is actively managing your social media marketing, people will lose interest. It is crucial that the content of the page is always fresh.

Let us make two important points regarding the use of "How To" videos as a means to connect with viewers and prospective clients. First, it is important that the firm only produces videos that will actually be used. Recording videos requires the firm's time, money, and other resources. Thus, it is important to plan strategically to ensure that each production will ultimately be useful and worth the expense.

Second, be mindful that most viewers seeking your firm's services will not be knowledgeable of the legal process and many legal terms. Clients want to know that your firm can relate to their problems. Using lay terms in the contents of the videos is key not only for conveying assurance to viewers that your firm is familiar with the type of problem they are bringing to you but it also prevents the videos from coming across as boring.

Another creative tactic is to incorporate videos into related blog topics. Consider writing a bi-weekly blog. Typically, blogs are under 500 words, so they are not difficult to write. To get ideas, look at what is happening in the media and in your personal life. Incorporate some of the videos into the blog ideas to add variety and to offer a more personal appeal.

As with any form of social media, always respond to anyone who comments on your posts or blogs. This is how you will develop your fan base and how you will get new clients.

First impressions always matter. This is even truer in social media than in normal space and time. Someone surfing the Internet, "attorney shopping" through some of the popular sites in which attorneys advertise, will make the decision as to whether they will continue exploring a particular site within the first 30 seconds. Make sure that whatever people first see when visiting your site is something that will capture their attention and make them want to see more.

Statistics show that recruiters spend less than ten seconds looking at a resume to decide whether they are interested in a candidate. Similarly, potential clients spend that same amount of time or even less looking at your website.

Finally, it's important to know what prospective clients see when visiting your firm's website. From time to time, look at what people are seeing through their eyes. Google yourself. Do a search, not only of your firm, but also of yourself, your associates, and of your area of practice. Search as if you were looking for an attorney to do what you do. You will see an interesting difference between what your firm's IT person shows you during the process of approving your page's content and what ultimately becomes your website. You do not want to be surprised by inconsistencies or poor representation of your firm *after* you've paid for it—or even worse, *after* it has been published and seen by 'might have been' clients.

So, the question then becomes, "Is the company or person you hired who has no law firm experience really the right choice to do your blogging, write your newsletters, and manage your social media?" Conversely, must the person you hire to write your blog and newsletters and to manage your social media have law firm experience?

Can he relate to your law firm's desired clientele? Can he write about topics that will interest both current *and* potential clients, not only encouraging them to return to read your newsletters, but to go further and look at your Facebook, LinkedIn, and Twitter page? More importantly, do the themes you blog about or which you explore in your newsletters stand out enough in the mind of the reader that when a friend or family member needs a referral, she will remember your firm? Do you update your website regularly?

Social media changes rapidly, so make sure that you, or the person responsible for it in your office, stay apprised of this quickly evolving form of advertisement. Always offer fresh, current information. And, most of all, have fun with it. The biggest reason that social media has been such an overwhelming success is because it is so much fun!

REVIEW QUESTIONS FIVE

Lawyers:

1. Do you understand the importance of the business of practicing law? List the reasons.
2. Have you always understood the importance? If not, when did you realize it? Did something bad happen that made you understand the importance? How did that realization change the way that you run your business? Write down what happened and how it changed the way you do things.
3. Did you retain new non-attorney employees to help you more effectively manage your practice? List the advantages and disadvantages of doing so.

Law Students:

1. Do you understand the importance of the business of practicing law? List the reasons.
2. What do you find intimidating about it? List those items.
3. What do you find exciting about it? List those items.
4. Do you plan to open your own practice right out of law school? Why or why not? List the advantages and disadvantages.
5. Do you plan to work for a few years at another firm and then open your own practice? Why or why not? List the advantages and disadvantages.
6. Do you feel that you never want the responsibility of running your own practice? Why or why not? List the advantages and disadvantages.

STAFFING

CHAPTER FOURTEEN
HOW TO ATTRACT AND RETAIN EXCEPTIONAL STAFF

Richard Branson is quoted as saying, "Clients do not come first; employees come first. If you take care of your employees, they will take care of the clients." Truer words have never been spoken.

It is truly a misconception for anyone in any industry, including the legal profession, to believe that salary is what keeps an employee from moving to another position. The truth of the matter is salary is *one* of the things that will *attract* an employee to a position. Employees who tell you that they are motivated only by the amount of their paycheck will soon realize that the size of their paycheck alone is not enough to keep them satisfied in their position.

Aside from salary, what else attracts competent staff, and how do you retain them? Now, we do not mean the job hoppers who have had six positions in the last 18 months and who would jump ship if someone else paid them another $25 a week. That is not the staff person you want to attract or retain. Those types of employees have a knack for claiming it is always the employer's fault that a job situation did not work out. The truth of the matter is that after the second or third position, it is time for that employee to take a good hard look in the mirror. It is also important for your firm to decline hiring future employees with this kind of employment history. Unless, of course, you do not mind the revolving door stigma.

If you want to attract top-notch professional staff for your legal team, a fair salary that compensates for talent and experience will attract an applicant's attention to apply for the position. After that, it is the benefits package and the work environment that can keep your staff engaged, including paid time off because every professional knows that, at some point, everyone needs to recharge their batteries, a stable and friendly work environment, and a firm with a good reputation.

If you find that you are having difficulty retaining quality staff, it is important to investigate. Employers can stick their heads in the sand and pretend they are ignorant as to why people leave their employ. Few administrators are really clueless, although the lawyers may well be. To learn more about your turnover, conduct exit interviews with employees who are leaving and ask, with genuine interest and employing active listening skills, why they have chosen to move on.

Constant turnover affects a practice. Clients like to have continuity in your staff. They want to call one week and speak to Mary and call in a month and still speak to Mary because Mary knows all about their case. In addition, turnover can be costly as it necessitates hiring and retraining. It can disrupt your processes and affect employee morale.

So, what are the reasons that employees leave a firm? Here are a few:

- THE POSITION DOES NOT TURN OUT TO BE WHAT WAS POSTED OR WHAT WAS DESCRIBED DURING THE INTERVIEW. If you hire a paralegal who ends up working as a receptionist, a file clerk, or someone's flunky, she will leave the firm. If she wanted to be a receptionist, she would have taken a job as a receptionist. She also would not have gone to school to earn (and pay for) a paralegal degree.

- THE POSITION AND THE PERSON ARE NOT A GOOD FIT. It is difficult to tell from just an interview, a resume, and a reference check everything you must know about someone's personality to make sure that she will mesh well with the firm. For this reason, we recommend utilizing personality testing as part of the hiring process. That, at least, will give you one more indicator of qualification for the position you have in mind.

- THE EMPLOYEE DOES NOT RECEIVE ENOUGH FEEDBACK OR SUPPORT. No one can or wants to operate in a vacuum. Feedback is important. Make sure it is constructive criticism prefaced with something positive. Destructive feedback is worse than no feedback at all. For example, "Mary, I really appreciate how hard you've been working to get the electronic files better organized. Can we ensure that all documents are scanned in a timely fashion so files will be complete when someone has a deposition or court appearance?" Starting with a positive statement works better than the alternative, "Mary, lawyers are going to court and depositions with incomplete files. When are you going to get the documents scanned in on time?"

- THE POSITION OFFERS NO OPPORTUNITY TO ADVANCE. If you hire a receptionist, that individual may have her sights set on receiving training and moving into a legal assistant position, or a legal assistant to a paralegal position. For some positions in a firm, there are no opportunities for advancement. If you hire a paralegal, unless the paralegal goes to law school, the paralegal may always remain a paralegal. In a larger firm, there may be an opportunity for the paralegal to become a paralegal manager.

In this situation, it is helpful to ask someone at the interview where they see themselves in five or ten years. You can gauge whether or not an employee will be happy being a paralegal at your firm for the length of their employment. If you know there is no room for advancement, be sure to mention that at the interview.

- EMPLOYEES FEEL UNDERAPPRECIATED AND UNRECOGNIZED. *Everyone* wants to be appreciated and recognized for his or her accomplishments. We all know that employees get their paychecks and their benefits. And we all know that people are far more likely to complain when they are unhappy than they are to compliment when they are satisfied. Taking the time to encourage staff can boost morale and help staff feel appreciated. A "thank you" or an "atta boy" (or girl) does not cost anything more than the few seconds it takes to say it, but the goodwill that it shows is immeasurable.

In the chapter on office morale, there is a list of things that a firm can do to show its employees appreciation for a job well done that cost little or nothing in terms of dollars and cents but that will add considerably to the firm's revenues with cheerful and productive employees.

- THE EMPLOYEE IS UNABLE TO BALANCE WORK AND LIFE STRESS. All industries are recognizing the need for work/life balance, including law firms. Monthly billable requirements will never go away in hourly firms. On the other hand, there is something to be said for happy employees being productive employees.

The focus is now on working "smarter, not harder," productivity, and efficiency. Studies have shown that people who work ten hours do not necessarily accomplish more work than people who work eight hours—they just take longer to do it. Sitting at a desk and toiling away but being unproductive because employees are tired or stressed accomplishes nothing. Instead, what it *will* do is cause an otherwise valuable employee to look for another job.

What attracts an employee to a position will not be the same concerns that keep him there. That is why there is so much truth to the fact that compensation is not what keeps an employee at a firm in the long run, it is what attracts him to a firm in the beginning.

Here are some of the things that will keep an employee at a firm—besides office morale:

- ENSURE THAT EMPLOYEES KNOW WHAT IS EXPECTED OF THEM. Clarity of their job and the description of their duties will ensure that they are doing their job because they know exactly what their job is. Ambiguity creates stress. A clear set of expectations creates a framework for employees to work within.

- PROVIDE SUFFICIENT SUPERVISION, BUT DON'T MICROMANAGE. What if I am one of those employees who does not respond well to being micromanaged? Like many others in the profession, I know what my responsibilities are and what your expectations are. We believe in accountability, as do many of us who do our jobs.

Nevertheless, require accountability of your staff to ensure that the work is being completed timely and that no deadlines are missed. You don't need them to report to you every five minutes, but make it known that they are being supervised, and that, if they need help, someone can provide the supervision or answer questions. Once you start checking accountability, you may find that one of them is having difficulty accomplishing his work correctly or in a timely fashion. You can then implement different processes to help ensure that this person is able to live up to the expectations of his position. Do not treat everyone the same way when it comes to supervision.

- MAINTAIN A "NO RETRIBUTION/NO RETALIATION" POLICY. "No retribution/No retaliation" is Liz's mantra, and it is a part of her open-door management style. Liz instructs all members of her teams that, when a problem arises—be it a client issue, meeting a deadline, or anything else—they are encouraged to talk to her about it, without concern of retribution or retaliation. Provided, of course, that the problem does not harm the client or the firm. If you maintain this policy, your staff will feel comfortable talking to management, and you will always know what is happening inside your firm.

- ALLOW EMPLOYEES TO GROW THEIR SKILLS AND TO THRIVE AT WHAT THEY DO. We do not believe in smothering someone's desire to improve his skills, to think/work outside-the-box, or to try something new. The more skills that your employees can exercise, and the more they are able to perform in their positions, the better it is for everyone inside the firm, as well as for its clients.

- PROVIDE TRAINING. No one knows everything. We have both worked for firms at which we did not have as much experience with certain software or computer programs as we would have liked. There is so much software out there that it is impossible for everyone to be familiar with every program, but we are always willing to learn, and so is your staff. If your staff is using the case management software as a word processing program and little else, then you should get them some training. Let employees know that their willingness to learn new programs and to work efficiently with the tools in the office is viewed positively. Do not ever make an employee who is lacking a skill but willing to learn it feel like he is coming up short.

- ENCOURAGE CONTINUING EDUCATION. Paralegals and attorneys must attend continuing legal education ("CLE") courses to keep up with changing rules, law, regulations, and procedures. They will need the CLE courses to maintain their bar licenses or their paralegal certifications. They also need them to stay current in specific areas of law.

Encourage attendance at educational courses, and offer to pay for them, too. Do not dock salaries or scrutinize billable hours more closely because they attended a CLE. This benefits the firm and the clients. More importantly, attendance at CLE courses makes your staff feel that what they do is valued within the firm and that they have the firm's respect.

- CONDUCT STAY INTERVIEWS. In order to prevent a situation rising to the level at which an employee feels she has no choice but to leave, consider conducting "stay" interviews with your employees once or twice a year. A stay interview is a casual, non-threatening (off-the-record, if you will) discussion of the employee's position, how the employee perceives her job performance, how she fits into the staff structure, how she likes (or dislikes) the firm culture, and anything else the employee wants to bring to your attention.

During her stay interview, ask how things are going. Inquire if she needs assistance of any kind or if she feels that additional training is necessary or would be helpful. Discuss the possible workshops or trainings that might be available to her. It is important to ask the employee if there is anything she would change to improve the office philosophy or the working conditions of the firm.

Again, active listening here is a prerequisite; do not conduct a stay interview if you don't have the time to ask pointed questions and to hear what you might be told. If you have made it clear that there is a "no retaliation/no retribution" policy, employees will provide you with valuable information about your own firm that you might not otherwise know.

- ENSURE THAT THERE IS SOMEONE IN MANAGEMENT TO DEAL WITH EMPLOYEE ISSUES. Many employees feel that lawyers are somehow a little disconnected from the reality of the day-to-day operations of their firms. When an administrator, someone who knows the day-to-day goings on and who has experience as a secretary or paralegal, is out there in the trenches with them, she can identify with the staff more than you do. Empower your firm administrator to be a liaison and an ally to the staff.

Attracting and keeping qualified staff can help your firm be more productive and keep your clients satisfied. Keeping your staff happy requires more than a good paycheck and health benefits—it requires a commitment to an open, constructive work environment and positive employee relations. A good salary will attract a good employee, but it is everything else that will keep them hard working for you.

REVIEW QUESTIONS SIX

Lawyers:

1. Do you have a problem with staff turnover? List the employees who have left your firm in the past three years.
2. To what do you attribute this turnover? List the reasons why these staff members left.
3. Do you know what you can do to attract and retain exceptional staff? Brainstorm ideas.
4. Do you nurture your employees' professional and educational growth so they remain challenged? Identify how you do so. List new ways you can nurture their growth.
5. When a good employee tells you she is leaving, what attempts do you make, if any, to try to keep her? List them.
6. How do you share with clients that a beloved employee is leaving your firm? Have you ever lost clients when an employee has left? What did you do to try to retain those clients? Were you successful? List strategies you have implemented and that you can implement in the future to help you keep clients when a beloved employee leaves.

Law Students:

1. When you notice a high staff turnover rate at an establishment where you frequent, what does it make you think of that establishment? Do you feel that the employees are not treated well there? Conversely, does it make you consider that if the employees are not treated well, the customers may not be treated well either?
2. Have you ever stopped going to a business because it lost one of your favorite employees? Write down your experience.
3. What do you think a business owner should do to ensure that she attracts and retains exceptional staff? List those actions.
4. Have you ever left a job? Why did you leave? Could your employer have done anything differently to keep you as an employee? Write down your experience.

CHAPTER FIFTEEN
HOW TO KNOW WHEN TO HIRE STAFF AND WHAT STAFF IS NECESSARY

There are many reasons why an attorney who opens his own solo firm after departing from another firm prefers to remain solo, at least for a time. After working under the direction (well, perhaps a better word might be "control") of other lawyers, he likely enjoys his newfound autonomy and the ability to finally do things his own way. Additionally, a solo practitioner enjoys a certain flexibility that is not possible once he hires staff he must guide, manage, and mentor.

Liz has dubbed solo practitioners as "the ones who give the orders in the morning and carry them out in the afternoon." Solo practitioners often wear many hats in the office. They do not generally employ a great many support staff. And those few employees who are able to bill (whether a paralegal or an associate), should spend their time doing so. But there are so many other tasks that must be completed in a law office. Sometimes lawyers focus their attention elsewhere, thus falling behind on the actual client work, the work that pays the bills.

Once you open your own firm, you will soon face the dilemma of if and when to hire staff. When considering whether it is time to do so, answer the following questions:

1. How much of your time is actually billed to your clients, and how much is spent instead on administrative and non-billable tasks?

2. Are the processes, procedures, and legal project management systems in your office up to date so that you are not reinventing the wheel every time you generate a document, pleading, or letter?

3. Do you waste valuable time going back to documents that you have already created in other files and editing them for use in other cases, rather than working with ready-to-use forms and templates?

4. Do you have good organizational and time management skills?

5. Are you utilizing your available technology the way that it was intended to be used, or are you using your very expensive case management software as a word processing program, thereby wasting firm revenues and valuable time?

6. Are you wasting time strategizing your own marketing and client development plan when your billable time would be better spent elsewhere?

7. Are you using the appropriate fee structure to benefit your clients and to maximize the generation of revenues for your firm?

If some of the items mentioned above require reorganization of the administration of your firm, hire someone, even on a part-time basis, to assist with the non-billable administrative tasks for the firm. If you are a solo practitioner, you do not need a full-time employee. But hiring a part-time employee will help your bottom line as you are freed to spend more billable time working on your clients' files.

This is a good formula to use when trying to decide whether to seek administrative help:

1. Calculate the approximate number of hours that you devote to your firm's administrative tasks. Multiply that by the typical hourly rate of a contract law firm administrator, which is approximately $50 per hour. Let's estimate that you spend 10 hours per week on administrative tasks. By multiplying that number by $50, you see that hiring an administrator will cost you a maximum of $500 per week. (It may well be less if the experienced admin can accomplish the same tasks more time-effectively, which is highly likely.) This is significantly less than it would cost to employ a full-time law firm administrator with the same experience.

2. Now, take those same ten hours for which you could be paying a professional administrator at $50 per hour and multiply them by your hourly rate, let's say $250. If you had been able to bill clients for those ten hours instead of wasting your time on administrative work, you would have earned $2,500 extra each week. In other words, for just the cost of two hours of *your* time, an administrator can handle all of your firm's affairs for the week. If you deduct the $500 that you should be paying to a part-time or contract administrator from the $2,500 in additional fees that you would be able to earn, the firm sees a return on its investment of $2,000 per week. Over the course of the year, your firm will realize an additional $104,000 in revenue!

Initially, it may be that you should not hire an associate because what you really need is an administrator. But hopefully, at some point, your marketing strategy will really begin to pay off. You will be getting referrals from clients and other firms. Eventually, you will have more work than you can handle.

This is not something that happens overnight; the momentum builds over time. You will realize that you are opening the same number of files in a week that, a year ago, you were opening in a month. You will stop going to lunch, and you will find yourself working additional hours. Your work/life balance will become almost non-existent.

If you have been analyzing your profit and loss statements every month, preparing and keeping up with an annual budget, and watching your collection reports, you should have a good sense of whether the finances will support adding an associate. Before you decide that you are ready to hire an associate, however, determine whether you need an actual body in the office. You may just need to increase efficiency by improving your processes and legal project management. Or, you may just need a paralegal or legal assistant who can bill clients, but whom you can pay at a lower rate than an associate attorney.

If you are not sure what you need, consider outsourcing work to a contract or part-time attorney for a test period of time. If after 60, 90, or 120 days you realize that the additional business and income are sustained, then it may well be time to hire an associate.

If, after crunching and re-crunching the numbers, you can financially justify hiring an associate rather than outsourcing work, there are some important things that you must consider.

1.   Consider hiring someone for a trial period of six months to see if the person will work hard enough to justify her salary. This means meeting the firm's billable hour quota or measuring up to whatever metric the firm is using for profitability.

2.   Avoid hiring someone just to do the work that you don't like doing or you don't know how to do. If you do, you will be opening yourself up to a legal malpractice complaint.

3.   Find a good fit for your firm. This does not necessarily mean hiring someone who is the mirror image of yourself. Everyone has their shortcomings. If you are in touch with who you really are, you know what your shortcomings are. If you, by your own admission, tend to be a little emotionally removed from your clients and don't have that nurturing instinct, consider hiring someone who has those qualities. It will be a good balance for the firm. Not every client is the same. Some are all business. But some want someone to ask how they are holding up, to wish them a happy birthday, or to be a little more personal. There is no right or wrong when it comes to your own personality. But if you have the opportunity to hire someone, take advantage of it to hire someone who complements what you bring to your table.

4.   While at the time of hiring, you may need someone who has experience in the same area that the firm currently practices, consider looking for someone with some experience in another area as well. This will enable you to grow the firm and spread out into different areas, thereby offering your clients additional services. The more services that you can provide to a client, the more you can keep them in-house without the need to refer them elsewhere.

5.   If you have a legal assistant, paralegal, or receptionist working for the firm, allow them to meet with any potential candidates, not so much to interview them, but more as an opportunity to see if they will be able to work together. First impressions are usually accurate. We find that we know very quickly whether we will click with someone. Your staff and your lawyers will have to work together. The more you do to make sure the relationship works well before the hire, the smoother the transition will be.

6.   Decide how much experience you need for the associate position. Do you need someone who has court experience and can take depositions? Or do you need someone who can work behind the scenes and draft pleadings, answer discovery, and perform research while you attend depositions, motion hearings, and trials?

7.   Consider whether hiring someone right out of law school who has an interest in the firm's specialties will work for you. While there may be a learning curve upfront, sometimes it is worthwhile to hire someone with little to no experience for two very good reasons.

- First, the starting salary will be less than it is for a more experienced attorney. Thus, the attorney (and his salary) can grow with the firm as the firm's business grows.

- Second, lawyers (and staff generally) with less experience have fewer preconceived notions on procedures and how things should be done. Liz and Joryn can both tell you that it is almost inevitable when you hire someone with experience, be it a lawyer or a paralegal, that you will frequently hear the phrases, "This is how we did it at my other firm," or "That isn't how *we* used to do it." (Just as an aside, we tell new hires who say this to first try it our way for a while, and then if they have suggestions to make things better, we'd certainly be willing to listen and consider them.)

The skills and level of experience that you need for the associate position will help you to determine the compensation package for the position, including benefits and bonuses. Many compensation packages now have a pay-for-performance component as an incentive, with a lower starting salary. Given that clients are seeking alternative fee schedules and value billing, these demands can be passed on to the associates, incentivizing them to perform well and to produce results that will give clients the value and service they seek.

If you are at the point that it is time to hire staff, congratulations! It means that your firm is succeeding. Hire the right staff for the right positions, and your firm will continue to thrive.

CHAPTER SIXTEEN
HOW TO STAFF YOUR LAW FIRM

It is important that you not only hire employees who are good at their jobs but who also positively contribute to your work atmosphere. You will likely find yourself spending the vast majority of the day with your employees, and even if someone is the best lawyer in town, if you don't like him, you will have a hard time working with him.

Depending on the size of your firm, you'll likely need at least the following employees: a receptionist, a paralegal, and an associate attorney. You may also need an office manager, an IT manager, and an HR manager. Only hire the employees who you really need. Consider outsourcing as much as possible because it should save you money as you will only be paying hourly for specific assignments, and you will not need to pay benefits. You may find outsource staff by word of mouth, temp agencies, or by placing ads in relevant magazines.

Make the extra effort to be as thorough as you can be in posting a position and in the interview process.

Additionally, hire employees who complement one another. Rather than hiring employees who are simply mirror images of yourself, consider that you need different personalities to have a well-rounded firm.

Before Joryn hires a new employee, she has them take the Myers-Briggs Type Indicator. This not only gives her good insight as to who the person really is, but also whether she is a good fit for Joryn's firm. The Myers-Briggs Type Indicator differentiates personalities based on a person's degree of extraversion versus introversion, sensing versus intuition, thinking versus feeling, and judging versus perceiving.

In the office, each employee has their Myer-Briggs personality types on display on their desks so that the other employees and lawyers are always reminded how best to approach a particular colleague. Every couple of years, we have a psychologist friend give a brief seminar during lunch to discuss the personality types and how best to deal with each type. Each personality type learns differently, communicates differently, handles stress differently, and excels at different skills, etc., so it is important to understand your employees.

What should you consider when staffing your law firm? Think about this:

1. Does the candidate have the relevant experience to do the job for which he applied? If you are a litigation firm, you need someone with litigation experience. *Period.* Unless you are willing to make the investment to train someone with no experience in your

area of specialization, this will not be a smooth transition—for the firm or for the employee.

The only training you should have to do is for the office procedures in your firm. Do not waste your time or your money with a "make do" or "we'll make it work" situation if your firm cannot afford a huge learning curve. It rarely works, and everyone just ends up frustrated. Make no mistake, the employee will figure out he is not achieving the level of work that is required of him, which can actually make the whole situation worse.

2. How current are his technology skills? There is software for everything—e-mail, contacts, accounting, word processing, case management, marketing, etc. If the candidate in front of you does not have the tech skills to keep up, you will be investing time and money in training and a learning curve. If you need someone to hit the ground running, make sure he has the technological skills and experience that the job requires and that he will use the systems that you have in place.

3. How professional is the candidate? If he shows up in flip-flops and jeans to the interview, chances are his attire will not improve. Although business casual is becoming an acceptable trend, casual and worse-than-casual, otherwise known as sloppy, still belongs at the beach, even if in Florida. Clients do gauge whether they think you and your firm will do a good job by the appearance of your staff. First impressions will always matter. Professionalism has not gone out of style.

4. When you hire a new employee, be sure to look for qualities that show you that the person you are hiring is not someone who will take advantage of your looking the other way if he is a few minutes late arriving or if he needs to leave a few minutes early for whatever reason. Hire professionals who will act like professionals and commit to treating them that way.

A little bit of goodwill with the right employee will certainly go a long way when you need someone to stay five, ten, or 30 minutes late to get a project which is due out the door or if a client is in your office waiting for something. As Liz has told employees in the past, "Show me that I can depend on you and that you will act like a professional, and I will treat you like one."

5. If you plan to hire someone that you know from the interview has limited experience or skill in a certain area, provide the employee with all the training and resources that she needs to be efficient and productive in carrying out her job description. Training is very important. Some law firms spend thousands of dollars on case management software systems only to have employees haphazardly use certain parts of the program. This usually occurs because they do not know how to efficiently work the program and are afraid to ask for help. It does not make sense to spend money on programs to make the office more efficient, especially these days when clients are looking for value billing and flat fee work, and to then have employees who cannot use the software because they don't know how.

Do not ever make an employee feel that she cannot ask for training to improve the job she does for your law firm.

6. Check references. This has become a touchy subject for former employers who are afraid of being sued for being honest about the work of a former employee. We live in a society that is more litigious than ever. As a result, employers are unwilling to provide any kind of reference other than name, rank, serial number, salary, and dates of employment. We have tried to check references with some law firms who actually require a written release before they would even confirm employment.

Rather than ask specifics about the employee's performance, simply ask if the employee would be considered for rehire. Former employers will respond better to that question, and a "yes" or "no" answer really provides a great deal of information.

Reference letters do not usually impress us either. Sometimes you really have to read between the lines to see that these forms usually say a whole lot about nothing.

Follow these tips, and you'll find yourself doing less hiring as you hire well-suited, professional employees who remain at your firm for many years.

CHAPTER SEVENTEEN
HOW TO NEGOTIATE ASSOCIATE COMPENSATION

As much as we might like them to, employees will not work for free. We have already discussed the decision-making process regarding whether to hire an associate. Based on the needs of your firm, you must decide whether you should hire a seasoned attorney or a recent law school graduate. Obviously, you can hire a recent graduate at a much lower salary than an experienced attorney.

Lawyer compensation, like alternative client fee arrangements, has evolved in recent years and has become quite creative. Hard-working attorneys with ambition and initiative are not afraid to accept positions in which pay-for-performance is part of the compensation package. Joryn and Liz are both drawn to hiring lawyers who are willing to accept a pay-for-performance component as part of their compensation. Most people are well-aware of their own ambition and drive to succeed. A potential candidate who agrees to base his pay on his performance as part of his compensation is willing to work hard, knows he will strive to perform, and recognizes the financial rewards of his efforts. Someone who is reluctant to agree to a creative compensation package is likely to be an underperformer and someone who will probably not contribute sufficiently to the firm's bottom-line to justify his employment.

There are many considerations on which candidates for a lawyer position will reflect when they negotiate their salaries. Understand what those considerations are from the candidate's perspective because that knowledge will enable you to negotiate his salary more effectively.

1. HOW MUCH MUST THE LAWYER MAKE TO PAY HER BILLS? Even if the hire is someone with a few years' experience, barring unusual circumstances, it is likely that she is carrying some student loan debt. Additionally, factor in the cost of professional clothing, dry cleaning, and maintenance of a professional appearance. While suits are not bought every month (unless the attorney is a clothes horse), the cost of purchasing a new suit, tie, shoes, etc. can be expensive. Impressions do matter. Both female and male lawyers know that, even if they prefer to dress business casual, they still have to invest money in their appearances. Add to that rent or mortgage payments, car payments, and the bills that we all pay every day. These are the expenses that a potential candidate is considering when she is seeking a position and negotiating her compensation.

2. EGO IS USUALLY A COMPONENT. While most will not admit it, a candidate's ego should be factored into salary negotiations. She is, after all, a lawyer. Most lawyers believe that they should be paid a lot of money. It simply comes with the territory. Part of the justification is that friends, family, and the general public expect lawyers to earn a large salary. Many lawyers feel that they must live up to that expectation. Period. It's that simple. Just as the expectation that someone who flips hamburgers for a living does *not* make a lot of money, lawyers are supposed to make a lot of money. So if they don't, there must be something wrong with them.

By the same token, consider what the prosecutors and the public defenders are paid in your jurisdiction. While Joryn recommends that all beginning attorneys try to spend a couple of years getting the experience that one of those jobs will gift them, those positions (despite the low level of pay) are pretty difficult to come by. If you are offering your candidates the same in-the-trenches experience, that has value. So consider the salaries that those jobs pay before settling on a high wage.

As the employer, there are a number of considerations that the firm should take into account when developing a job posting and determining the salary and other compensation that the firm can afford to pay for the position you seek to fill.

1. KNOW THE MARKET IN YOUR LEGAL COMMUNITY FOR AN ASSOCIATE WITH THE EXPERIENCE YOUR FIRM NEEDS. Law firm salaries depend first on geographic location. Law firms in large metropolitan areas such as New York, Chicago, and Dallas pay higher salaries than smaller cities or more rural areas. Part of the reason for this is the cost of living. Salaries always have to take into consideration the cost of living where the firm is located. Perform some market research in your city or town to determine the average salary for the position you want to fill. Among other things, you can check job postings to see what firms are offering in terms of salary and benefits. Talk to attorneys at other firms and gather information from them on what firms similar to yours are paying.

Avoid depending on salary websites because there are many variables that go into those calculations, and they tend to be wildly inaccurate.

2. CONSIDER WHAT TYPE OF FIRM YOU RUN. Is it plaintiff or defense-oriented? What is the size of your firm? How big is the staff you have to support? Considering this information is critical because it, too, will likely impact the salary you are willing to pay. Insurance defense firms usually pay less because insurance companies generally pay lower hourly rates. In addition, insurance companies scrutinize law firm bills closely, frequently slashing billable time, and insisting that the lowest paid hourly timekeeper do the most amount of work on a file. They will not pay attorney rates for any work that a paralegal can do at a lower hourly rate. Therefore, there are less attorney billable hours and insurance defense firms pay less as a general rule, out of necessity.

3. CONSIDER YOUR FEE ARRANGEMENTS WITH YOUR CLIENTS.

- CONTINGENCY FIRMS: There is often an ebb and flow of income. Generally, the income varies on a monthly basis—although your lawyers' salaries do not. Keep in mind that, while you are waiting for cases to settle, your associates must still be paid. In addition, a lawyer handling this type of case for your firm must work efficiently. If an associate devotes 100 hours on a personal injury case with a $10,000 BI policy, and the firm's fee after settlement is $3,300, this means that the associate only billed $33 per hour for the work done on that file. You cannot afford to pay an associate attorney $60,000 a year for a return of $33 per hour on a contingency case.

- BILLABLE HOURS: If your firm is an hourly billable firm, consider the monthly billable requirement for an associate when determining the appropriate salary. You cannot have an associate billing 20 or 30 hours a month and pay them $60,000 a year. Not only will the associate not cover her own overhead, but the firm will lose money by the time the costs for benefits, bonuses, and other perks are added to her annual salary.

- FLAT FEE: For straightforward legal matters (and rarely can we say that anything is ever a truly "straightforward" legal matter), clients want flat fee billing. Clients believe this encourages lawyers to work efficiently on their cases, and if the lawyer is not efficient and productive, the cost of the lawyer's time does not matter much to the client. If your firm does offer flat fee legal services to clients, associates must really understand the concept and have the ability to be efficient and productive.

When preparing a job posting, it is best not to post a salary or even a salary range. Instead, include the years of experience for which you are looking, the type of practice, the responsibilities of the position, and the geographic location. As to actual compensation, the posting should simply state, "Salary is commensurate with experience. Compensation includes benefits and pay for performance."

Most firms today still do offer benefits in addition to salary. Some of these include:

- Health including medical/dental/vision or some combination for the employee with the option of paying for spouse or family coverage;
- Short/long-term disability;
- Paid time off;
- Retirement plan;
- Reimbursement or payment for bar dues and CLE courses;
- Parking;
- Profit sharing;
- Reimbursement for meals when working late;

- Reimbursement for expenses of entertaining clients; and
- Mileage reimbursement.

A new trend with some firms is payment of monthly student loan obligations or contribution thereto in exchange for an associate's agreement to stay with the firm for a pre-agreed upon period of time, usually three to five years. If the associate leaves before the pre-agreed time, the associate must repay the firm. If the agreed time expires, there is no repayment requirement.

In the actual salary negotiation, always ask the candidate what her salary expectations are. It is typically a good idea to ascertain whether the candidate's salary demand is grounded in reality and whether she, too, has done her homework on what the market is paying for someone with her experience. If the salary that you are considering is lower than that which the candidate requested, this is a good time to discuss in general terms that the firm provides additional benefits. The cost of the benefits is part of the actual compensation plan.

Liz recently had an opportunity to interview and hire an associate for a client. With many years of experience in the Tampa area, Liz is always aware of salary trends for associates with varying degrees of experience. The compensation package included a pay-for-performance component that Liz and the firm's owner designed to not only encourage the associate to exceed the monthly billable hour requirement, but also to supplement the salary offer that was made. The associate accepted, and after a few months, she is already regularly exceeding the firm's monthly billing expectations, earning several hundred dollars in additional income based on the percentage of the pay-for-performance bonus structure that the firm offered her. Because of this, the associate appreciates the bonus more than if it were part of her annual salary since the accomplishment of exceeding the billable requirement and receiving a bonus highlights the additional income she is earning by working hard for the firm.

Negotiating fair compensation, keeping in mind not only the revenues of the firm to pay the lawyer but also how the firm generates the revenues, will ensure that you make a good hire for the firm. It is important that the associate you hire is paid a fair salary and that the compensation package motivates her to do a good job, with that pot of gold at the end of the rainbow. The return on your investment will show up in your bottom line.

REVIEW QUESTIONS SEVEN

Lawyers:

1. What do you think is more important than salary to your employees, and why? List those items. Put a check next to the items you provide. For those you don't, brainstorm ideas so you can offer those items to employees.
2. When you were employed by someone else, what was important to you? List those benefits.
3. Do you recognize that some employees are financially driven, while others are more driven by motives such as feeling appreciated and feeling that they are doing a good job? Explain why, in writing.
4. Do you modify compensation and benefits structures for your employees based on what motivates them? List the advantages of doing so.
5. How do you determine what motivates a specific employee? List the strategies that you use. Do you ask them during the interview process?
6. Have you ever lost a good employee because you were wrong about what motivates them?

Law Students:

1. What motivates you and why? Write down your motivations and reasons.
2. Are you financially driven? Why? Write down your reasons.
3. Are you driven by the idea that if you work hard, you'll get more time off? Why? Write down your reasons.
4. Are you driven when you know you are appreciated? Why? Write down your reasons.
5. Are you driven when you are rewarded for doing a good job? Why? Write down your reasons.
6. Are you driven when you get good results from the hard work that you have performed? Why? Write down your reasons.
7. Is it easy for you to ascertain what motivates those around you? Or do you struggle with that and assume that everyone must be driven by the same things that drive you? If so, identify a book on the subject, and read it.
8. What happens when you are not rewarded in the way that drives you? Does it cause you to work harder? Or to give up? Think of a time when you were not appropriately rewarded for your work, and write down how it made you feel.

CHAPTER EIGHTEEN
HOW TO HIRE A LAW FIRM ADMINISTRATOR

Every business, including a law firm, requires someone to manage the business itself. The manager is the person who keeps everything running smoothly so the business can thrive, often working behind the scenes. A law firm is no exception; it requires a person whose specific responsibility is to manage the business of the law practice.

The best advice that we can give to any law practitioner—including a solo practitioner who thinks he cannot afford a law firm administrator—is to hire a law firm administrator. You cannot afford *not* to do so.

We have heard the position of the law firm administrator described as "the glue that holds a firm together and makes the engine go." With the right law firm administrator, that is a very accurate description. The very short list of what a law firm administrator does is *everything.* The longer list includes: managing all finances for the firm; updating office procedures; handling client billing, collections, accounting, budgeting, and financial matters; human resources; IT; client development/marketing; facilities management; and the list goes on.

It includes everything that makes up "the business of practicing law."

The success of a law firm revolves around its financials. Without the revenues generated by and managed for the firm, the firm will cease to exist. A qualified law firm administrator will have a strong financial background, with the ability to handle the overall financial planning, budgeting, and management of the firm. The short list of experience that a law firm administrator requires to successfully manage your practice includes:

1. PERSONNEL AND HUMAN RESOURCE MANAGEMENT. The competent law firm administrator will have a knowledgeable background in personnel and human resource management as she is responsible for all overall non-attorney personnel management, including:

- Determining the non-attorney staff needs based upon the caseload and workflow of the firm.
- Interviewing and screening applications for non-attorney positions. On occasion, an experienced law firm administrator may also pre-screen and conduct preliminary interviews for associate positions. Prior experience in a support staff capacity is invaluable when

interviewing potential candidates for positions with the firm.
- Training and/or supervising new personnel.
- Conducting performance evaluations of non-attorney personnel.
- Conducting performance evaluations of timekeepers, including associate attorneys, and reporting findings to partner attorneys and/or discussing findings and responsibilities with timekeepers.
- Overseeing compliance with law firm policies and procedures, *and* taking appropriate action in the absence of compliance.
- Conducting staff meetings, including accountability updates.
- Maintaining all attorney and non-attorney personnel files.
- Terminating employment of non-attorney personnel after making reasonable efforts to resolve employee performance issues.
- Reviewing work performances and recommendations concerning pay increases and/or bonus compensation.
- Managing the benefits package for the firm, including recommending changes as appropriate for cost.
- Conducting stay and exit interviews.

2. MANAGEMENT OF FIRM FINANCES AND ACCOUNTING/BILLING. A law firm administrator should also handle the following responsibilities:

- Preparing the firm's annual budget;
- Periodically (at minimum monthly) reviewing the annual budget and updating it as needed for changes in expenses;
- Performing billing and collections responsibilities;
- Performing accounting responsibilities like general ledger and trust accounting, including reconciliation of the trust account in accordance with state bar rules;
- Handling tasks related to payroll and benefits (bonus) pay;
- Managing cash flow;
- Preparing financial reports, including collections, trust fund reports, profit and loss reports (monthly and annual), expense reports, and client fee reports; and
- Managing banking relationships, including the establishment of banking and other financial relationships to benefit the firm.

3. MANAGEMENT OF COMPUTER AND INFORMATION TECHNOLOGY SERVICES. There is generally no expectation that a law firm administrator is an "IT guy." In fact, hiring an IT guy to be your law firm administrator would be a mistake. However, the firm administrator should be experienced enough with software programs, such as email, accounting, and case management software, to steer the firm in the right direction and to recommend appropriate software that will enable the firm to operate efficiently and productively.

Broad knowledge concerning hardware and the needs of the firm in terms of equipment, memory, servers, printers, and the like is also a necessity. In addition, general experience should include the ability to:

- Evaluate the firm's computer system, including all hardware and software.
- Periodically discuss the system and programs that are available to the firm with employees, especially the support staff.
- Recommend changes based upon both productivity and efficiency, as well as cost effectiveness. If employees do not use computer programs for the purposes intended, the firm is wasting money, and the employees are wasting time and reducing efficiency and productivity. For example, if employees use expensive case management software as a word processing program, then just purchase a word processing program and save money on the cost of the case management program, updates, and staff training.
- Secure a maintenance contract with a reliable and effective IT guy or firm. Many IT support companies can service computers and handle problems remotely. However, ensure that if there is a problem that requires on-site service, your IT guy will respond within a reasonable time to your office. The computer system is at the core of a law firm's operations and its ability to accomplish work. A computer issue, especially a server problem, will bring all work to a screeching halt because there is no alternative method for performing services. In fact, some firms now use VoIP phone systems so when the computers go down, so do the phones, your lifeline to both clients and prospects. Specifically address this matter when you retain your IT company, and if you find that after one or two service calls, you are not getting the response that you need, find another IT guy.
- Develop and manage records retention protocols. We used to retain paper files for seven years before destroying them. Now, many law firms scan files to computer folders or external drives and destroy the actual paper files when they close them. Of course, if you have already "gone paperless," you simply move the now closed files to an external drive, and you are done. This is especially efficient because, if a client calls a few years from now needing a document, it is easily retrievable from a drive, as opposed to ordering a file from closed storage.
- Manage the library, including legal research memberships and other resources.
- Manage the telephone system. Ensure that the firm's phone system is up-to-date and that all features are always in working order.

4. FACILITIES MANAGEMENT. This includes management of the firm's office space and related functions, such as:

- Office space planning;
- Redesigning and renovating the office space to accommodate growth or a reduced need for space;
- Negotiating with the rental agent or landlord of the space, including lease renewal;
- Purchasing and/or leasing office furniture and equipment, including copy, scan, and fax machines, shredders, postage machines, and the like; and
- Purchasing office and break room supplies, including appliances and refreshments.

5. MARKETING AND BUSINESS DEVELOPMENT. The firm administrator, armed with knowledge about the services that the firm provides and the needs of its clients, will assist attorneys with marketing and client development activities, such as:

- Maintaining the firm website, including updating firm and attorney information, bios, photographs, and recent successes, as well as addressing the question that clients ask when searching for legal representation, i.e. "What can your firm do for me?";
- Preparing a firm brochure to include highlights of the firm's services, attorney bios, years of experience, and the like; and
- Preparing firm announcements and law firm advertising.

6. OTHER ACTIVITIES/OFFICE SERVICES. This is the catchall responsibility of the law firm administrator position. Any other activity not specifically assigned to someone else in the firm, especially when it is related to improving the quality and practice of law for the firm and the clients, comes under this heading and falls under the responsibilities of a law firm administrator. An experienced and savvy law firm administrator will, on her own, determine what additional duties are necessary for her to further the interests of the firm and to benefit the bottom line.

This is not an exhaustive list by any means. Anything that involves administrative functions for the firm is part of the responsibilities of a true law firm administrator.

You might wonder why we refer to it as a "true" law firm administrator.

Perhaps your law firm has an office manager, and, as you read this chapter, you think, "I have a law firm administrator. It's the same thing, right?" No, actually it is not. A law firm administrator is a non-attorney law office employee who is responsible for the law firm's overall day-to-day operations. The person in this position should always have an undergraduate business-related degree and will often also have a master's degree.

Law firm administrators are responsible both for ensuring the delivery of legal services by supervising staff and for identifying and developing additional business opportunities.

The ideal law firm administrator is one who has come up through the ranks in a law firm with previous experience as a legal secretary/assistant or paralegal. Law firms are unique from other corporations because law firms sell time. As a result, law firms develop on-going relationships with their clients for the duration of their representation and, hopefully, beyond. Maintaining this on-going relationship and, in fact, nurturing it, is vital to the success of a law firm. It is important for a law firm administrator to experience interacting with clients through her work inside the legal process and with their files. This firsthand "in the trenches" experience is invaluable for a law firm administrator.

A law office manager, on the other hand, is more involved with the day-to-day operations of the firm under the direct supervision of an attorney or an administrator. The position of office manager often has no involvement in the business aspects of the firm, such as finances or marketing. The office manager also has limited decision-making authority.

Some law firms will hire a law firm administrator totally outside of and unconnected to the practice of law. We have seen firms hire CEOs from auto manufacturers and soft drink companies. Hiring a CFO or a COO from one of these industries seems like a good idea to some as they are impressed with the title and the capacity of the work that person did with the company.

We are not so impressed. Someone with this kind of background does not have the legal foundation or even the law firm administrator foundation to effectively run a law firm. Even HR people from diverse backgrounds are not qualified for this position. These potential employees are limited in the scope of their experience. The CFO or COO will focus on the firm's finances. The HR person will focus on the firm's HR needs. This is all fine and good, but what about the other areas that make up the business of practicing law?

Does it make good financial sense to hire a former CFO or an HR person who will handle only one part of the firm's administration and then to pay additional salaries to others who will handle the other administrative functions of the firm? Do the math. The result is several employees who must coordinate with one another because no one person has all of the actual experience to be a law firm administrator and to take care of the business of practicing law, all of which is more time-consuming and less cost-effective.

In the past ten or so years, the position of law firm administrator has been recognized as invaluable in building and maintaining the law firm foundation. Administrators and attorneys can together determine the firm's mission, set goals, and formulate a strategic plan to achieve the goals of the firm.

Finally, there is the cost consideration. Even if you hire a law firm administrator to handle all the administrative functions of the firm, it is still another salary for the firm to pay. Although a firm administrator is not a timekeeper and does not generate billables for the firm, an effective law firm administrator pays for herself in the efficacy of the work that she performs. Bringing all the areas of managing the business of practicing law together to effectuate efficiency and productivity pays for itself.

If you own a small(er) firm, it may not be necessary for your law firm administrator to hold a full-time position. But it is still not cost-effective for any of the attorneys to handle billing or HR. A lawyer should not spend his time shopping for the best price on a case of paper or figuring out how to get shredding done for free; performing such tasks does not generate firm revenue.

Today, independent contractors effectively fill many roles in a law firm: paralegal, legal assistant, attorney—and also law firm administrator. As we discuss in *How to Outsource (and Why)*, hiring an independent contractor as a law firm administrator enables the firm to obtain competent and experienced services without spending the salary or offering the benefits usually associated with such a position. An independent law firm administrator can provide the services that your firm needs as often as you need them.

A smaller firm does not need a bookkeeper every day. Most firms only bill once a month. HR issues do not arise every day. Payroll is done twice a month or every two weeks for most firms. You can see where efficiency and cost-effectiveness can be achieved, even in a law firm administrator role.

There is nothing worse than oversight, uninformed decisions, or mistakes that expose firms to costly claims and lawsuits. Most often, these are due to unqualified administrators (or, worse yet, no administrator) in positions that result in poor judgment, lack of internal/ethical controls, failure to establish policies, outdated employee manuals, and/or unfamiliarity with labor law requirements.

If your vision includes growing your practice, you need an experienced law firm administrator. A good law firm administrator is the management support system with outside knowledge and resources that will keep your firm updated and competitive in your legal community.

REVIEW QUESTIONS EIGHT

Lawyers:

1. What can a law firm administrator do for your firm that would allow you to generate more revenues? List those tasks.
2. What tasks do you feel you are unable to perform adequately because you lack the knowledge to perform them? List those tasks.
3. What tasks is an administrator more suitable to perform, based on her unique skill set? List those tasks.
4. Have you considered the amount of money you could save if you were able to bill clients for all of the time you spend performing administrative tasks? Calculate your savings.

Law Students:

1. When you think of eventually graduating and opening your own firm, what tasks do you feel you will be unable to perform adequately because you lack the knowledge to perform them? List those tasks. Are they administrative tasks? Financial tasks? Technology-related tasks? Financial tasks? Marketing tasks?
2. Are you open to the idea of hiring an administrator to perform these tasks? Why or why not? List the advantages and disadvantages.
3. Do you understand the money that you will save in doing so because you will be able to bill clients for the time you would be spending performing administrative tasks? Calculate your savings if you bill at $200 an hour and pay an administrator $50 an hour for 20 hours of administrative work.
4. Does the idea of being financially and managerially responsible for another person when you are just starting out concern you? If so, list the reasons why. Find a book on the subject, and read it.
5. At what point do you feel you could be comfortable hiring an administrator? Once you've been in practice for a period of time? Once you have a certain number of clients? Once you've consistently earned a certain amount of money? List the things that would need to happen for you to be comfortable hiring an administrator.

CHAPTER NINETEEN
HOW TO DECIDE WHETHER YOU NEED A POLICY AND PROCEDURE MANUAL

Every law firm, regardless of its size, should have a written manual setting forth a description of its processes, procedures, and policies relating, in part, to employment with the firm. The firm should provide that handbook to all lawyers and staff employees to ensure that they are aware of the law firm's operations and how it functions.

It is important to include a disclaimer in the manual that the handbook itself does not constitute a contract of employment, but, rather, serves as a guide to both the employer (the firm) and its employees throughout the duration of the employment relationship. The policies set out in the manual are designed to protect both the firm and its employees.

There are four primary areas that should be included in a law firm procedure manual. These include the rules of the firm, employee conduct, firm procedures, and firm management. Firm procedures and firm management are usually firm-specific and will vary from firm to firm. Rules of the firm and employee conduct are typically boilerplate information about hours, paid time off, employment benefits, etc.

Although some of the information contained in your firm's policy and procedure manual will be firm-specific, in order to protect the firm, you should always include the following areas. While yours may differ, we've included some sample language to assist you.

1. FIRM OBJECTIVES: Examples of firm objectives include:
   - To be a well-organized, well-managed, efficient, and productive law firm that advances the best interests of our clients and the legal system;
   - To provide a work product that is timely, professional, and of value to our clients;
   - To be fair, honest, and ethical in representing our clients and in dealing with court personnel, vendors, and opposing counsels; and
   - To build a law firm culture which makes this firm a quality workplace with a reputation in the legal community for providing ethical, excellent, and reasonably priced legal services.

2. FIRM HOURS: The firm's hours are 8:30 a.m. to 5:00 p.m., Monday through Friday, with one hour for lunch taken between noon and 1:00 p.m. All employees must return from lunch no later than 1:00 p.m., except in special circumstances. The work week is 37.5 hours.

3. PROBATIONARY PERIOD: There will be a ninety-day probationary period for all employees (including lawyers) after the date of hire. During that period, the law firm may terminate the employee for any reason whatsoever.

4. PAID TIME OFF (PTO): The firm provides every employee with PTO. Rather than designate "vacation" time, "sick" time, and "personal" time, the firm provides all employees 112.5 hours of PTO during the first year of employment. Every four months during the first year, an employee accrues 37.5 hours PTO for a first-year annual total of 112.5 hours. This time may be used for vacation, sick, or personal time and may be taken in increments as small as a half day or as large as a full week at a time. Unless specifically authorized in advance, no employee may take more than 37.5 hours consecutively. Employees must coordinate all extended leave with the firm as management needs to be mindful of coverage in the office. After the first year, each employee will accrue another 7.5 hours PTO per year for every year of employment to be added to the original 112.5 hours. In the event that the employee leaves the firm, any unused PTO shall not be paid to the employee.

5. OVERTIME: There will be no overtime except in special circumstances. The responsible partner, managing attorney, or law firm administrator must authorize, in advance, any special circumstance requiring overtime work. Any employee working over 37.5 hours shall be paid straight time hourly up to 40 hours. Any hours authorized and worked over 40 hours will be paid time and a half. Only legal assistants, paralegals, or other hourly employees will be paid overtime if they work overtime hours. Employees who are paid salary are not eligible for overtime compensation.

6. COMPENSATION: Each employee will be compensated pursuant to the salary or wage agreement made at the time of hire. Employees understand that there is to be no discussion with other employees of the firm concerning compensation paid by the firm to individual employees. Such behavior is detrimental to the morale of the firm. Legal assistants and paralegals will be paid an hourly wage. Lawyers, law firm administrators, and any other overtime-exempt employees will be paid salary.

7. PAYROLL: All employees are paid twice a month, on the 15th and the 30th. Payroll is paid via direct deposit, except the first pay period.

8. DRESS CODE: All employees shall wear appropriate office attire. No one in the firm is permitted to wear flip-flops, jeans, t-shirts, shorts, sneakers, or any attire that does not conform with professional attire. "Business casual" attire is acceptable for employees in the office. Lawyers or paralegals appearing in court will wear court-appropriate attire.

9. BENEFITS: The firm provides the following benefits to full-time employees:

- Health insurance: The firm will provide health insurance to cover the employee only. There are two options for health insurance coverage from which employees may choose. The firm will provide either coverage for which the firm will pay 100% of the premium or a second option with lower co-pays and lower deductibles. If the employee chooses the second option, the employee will contribute to its increased cost. The employer's contribution to the second option will be the equivalent of the premium for the first option. The difference will be paid by the employee and will be deducted from the employee's paycheck. Any employee who wishes to cover a spouse or family on his health insurance will pay 100% of the premium for the additional spouse or family coverage.

- Short-term disability: The firm allows the employee the option of purchasing short-term disability coverage. If the employee wants this coverage, the employee will pay 100% of the premium, which will be deducted from the employee's paycheck.

- Long-term disability: The firm will provide long-term disability coverage for the employee only, and the firm will pay 100% of the premium.

- Workers' compensation: The firm is required to carry workers' compensation insurance for work-related accidents. This is provided through the state compensation fund and paid by the firm. Any employee who sustains an accident or injury during the course and scope of his employment with this firm should follow the procedures outlined in the notice posted in the breakroom (or the law firm administrator's office or other conspicuous place to which all employees have access). Written notice must include the date, time, place, and manner of the injury.

- Sam's Club membership: The firm provides a Sam's Club membership for all full-time employees. This is optional, and you can obtain information through the firm administrator.

- Aflac: This is discretionary coverage available through the firm. Employees can select whatever coverages they want. Any coverage selected will be paid 100% by the employee and will be deducted from the employee's paycheck.

- Bonuses: Bonuses are discretionary, whether they are year-end bonuses, pay-for-performance bonuses or some other type of bonus. The firm will provide for any employee who has negotiated a pay-for-performance bonus as part of his compensation package separately from this procedure manual.

10. FAMILY AND MEDICAL LEAVE: This firm observes the FMLA Act of 1993, which is a federal law requiring that employers provide up to 12 weeks of unpaid, job-protected family medical leave to eligible employees for certain family and medical reasons. Anyone wanting additional information concerning the eligibility for FMLA or the guidelines should see the firm administrator or managing partner.

11. ATTITUDE AND COOPERATION: All employees need to work together in the best interests of the firm and for the benefit of our clients. Everyone is, from time-to-time, required to pitch in and help others when workloads or time constraints demand this. There is no room for egos in this firm. This will quickly destroy the team spirit that we work hard to establish in this firm. There is no place for gossip or office politics, and engaging in such destructive behavior will result in a written warning and may possibly lead to termination if the toxic behavior continues.

12. CONFIDENTIALITY: The ethical codes of both the local state bar association and also the American Bar Association applies to all employees of this firm, not only to the lawyers. All communications to, by, or through this office are strictly confidential and are not to be discussed with anyone outside the firm. It is unethical to confirm representation of any client to anyone outside the firm without the client's permission or consent. Violation of client confidentiality under any circumstances will be grounds for termination.

13. SMOKING AND DRUG USE: Smoking is not permitted in the workplace or within 25 feet of the workplace. All employees must dispose of all cigarette material before entering the workplace. In the event that an employee consistently smells of smoke, the firm may require the employee to change clothes prior to beginning work. Smoking breaks are not permitted. Use of illegal drugs or the illegal use of legal drugs, including alcohol, is forbidden in the workplace or during employment-related activities. The use, possession, distribution, or sale of controlled substances, such as drugs or alcohol, or being under the influence of such controlled substances is strictly prohibited while on duty and while on the firm's premises or worksites. Violation of this policy will result in disciplinary action up to and including termination.

14. EMPLOYMENT AT WILL: Employment with this law firm is voluntary, and both the employee and employer are free to terminate employment at any time. This manual does not constitute a contract of employment between the firm and any of its employees. The provisions contained in this manual may be withdrawn, amended, or rewritten at any time by the firm at the firm's sole discretion.

15. DISCIPLINARY ACTION: If a problem arises with an employee, the firm agrees to counsel the employee verbally with follow up in the immediate future. If the problem continues, the firm will issue a written warning that will be presented to the employee. The

employee will be asked to sign acceptance of the warning. A copy of the written warning will be placed in the employee's personnel file. If the problem continues beyond the written warning, further disciplinary action will be taken, up to and including termination.

16. EQUAL EMPLOYMENT OPPORTUNITY: This firm is an equal opportunity employer and provides equal employment and advancement opportunities to all individuals. Employment or hiring decisions at the firm will be based on merit, qualifications, and abilities. The firm does not discriminate against an applicant for employment because of race, color, creed, religion, national origin, sex, handicap, physical or mental disability, perceived disability, age, marital status, sexual orientation, citizenship status, military status, status of public assistance, or any other characteristic protected by federal, state, or local law.

As we mentioned, every practice is different, and therefore, procedural and law office management information will vary from firm to firm. The section on law office procedures and management may include topics on accepting payments, bookkeeping, docket control, answering the telephone, maintaining client files, firm software, use of computers, and the like.

It is important that your procedure manual be clear, accurate, and concise. It does not have to be unnecessarily long, but including basic office practices will avoid problems in the future when employees do not adhere to accepted practices in the office.

CHAPTER TWENTY
HOW TO DETERMINE YOUR FIRM'S PTO POLICY

Paid Time Off ("PTO") is important for everyone in the firm. In the chapter on *How to Have Work/Life Balance*, we discussed the importance of time off for everyone in the firm, including the partners. PTO encourages employees to take time off when they are sick, have a commitment out of the office, or just need a vacation without worrying about a loss of income.

Although staff and lawyers alike will get paid under a PTO policy for time away from the office, there will be employees who have unused PTO at the end of the year. Firms develop different policies on how to address any leftover PTO at the end of the year. How your firm addresses PTO in its policy and procedure manual will likely depend on one or more aspects of the make-up of your firm, including the financial posture of your firm. Keeping this in mind, here are a few ways that firms can deal with unused PTO at year-end:

1. USE IT OR LOSE IT. Employees who do not use all of their PTO by the end of the year lose that time. This encourages employees to have work/life balance by using their PTO during the year. If this is your firm's policy, be sure to track PTO throughout the year so that come December, you are not faced with an empty office as the majority of your staff takes time off at the same time to avoid forfeiting their PTO.

2. USE IT OR ROLL IT OVER. Employees who do not use all of their PTO by the end of the year are permitted to roll over a specific number of unused hours. In this scenario, one week or less is usually the standard amount of time to be rolled over to the following calendar year. Employees forfeit any additional time.

3. USE IT OR CASH IT IN. Employees are paid any unused PTO. Typically, in this scenario, the amount is due by January 31st of the following year. This option encourages some employees to use as little PTO as is necessary because they want to get paid for the time. Some employees are very financially motivated and will see a payout of their PTO as a way to get some additional income. It would be beneficial to set a maximum amount of time that will be paid out so that employees use some of their time and have some down time. Be sure that if your PTO policy allows employees to cash out some of their unused PTO, your firm is in a financial position in to pay employees when they are due.

PTO is an important way to encourage your employees to maintain a healthy work/life balance, as well as a way for some employees to earn additional funds by working hard throughout the year.

CHAPTER TWENTY-ONE
HOW TO MANAGE THE PERFORMANCE OF YOUR STAFF

Like so many things, trends in human resources have changed over the years. Arguably, HR has changed for the better because we are putting the "human" back into "human resources."

Unfortunately, sometimes, life happens. Traffic runs amok, the car breaks down, or the alarm doesn't go off. There is just no getting around it. We have all been there. Of course, there are always employees who take advantage of a situation, whatever that might be. That is an entirely different situation. A few people taking advantage of an employer's flexibility can ruin it for everyone.

Liz read an HR professional's suggestion that law firms have "feel-good pow-wows" with their staff. This involved having an office meeting at which everyone is given a piece of paper to write his name at the top. Then, the paper gets passed to the person to the left. That person writes something positive about the person who handed her the paper. The papers keep getting passed around until everyone has written something positive about each person at the table. The HR manager or administrator then puts those papers into each employee's personnel files. When an employee feels bad about herself, she can go to the HR person or administrator and ask to read all the good things that were written about her so she might feel better.

What? Yes, that one still has us scratching our heads and wondering if the person who wrote it had any law firm experience at all. If you have ever met a true legal staff professional, he would tell you that there is no time to participate in these HR games. Everyone is too focused on client service and billable hours to participate in these types of HR exercises. What works in huge corporations absolutely does not work for a law firm. Anyone who thinks so is really disconnected from the legal profession.

Handling human resource issues in a law firm is different than any other type of company, regardless of what HR professionals would have you believe. One size does not fit all. Flexibility and a little creativity go a long way when valuable employees have issues.

Liz had an interesting experience a few years ago with an exceptional legal secretary. This lady had to be the fastest and most accurate typist Liz had ever seen. But she was habitually late 15 minutes every single day. You could set your watch by her. She could not be on time to save her life. There was never an issue with her getting her work done and she never missed a deadline. She always worked 37.5 hours every week just like everyone else. She stayed late 15 minutes every day, and she always made sure that her boss, a partner, was always prepared and had everything he needed.

In an effort to alleviate this problem with an otherwise model employee, Liz worked with her and changed her hours to accommodate the 15 minutes that she couldn't be on time. Her regular hours were supposed to be from 8:30 to 5:00. When Liz changed her hours to 8:45 to 5:15, she came in at 9:00 and left at 5:30. When Liz changed her hours to 9:00 to 5:30, she came in at 9:15 and left at 5:45. At one point, Liz even bought her an alarm clock thinking that would help. It did not.

As she worked with her on this problem, Liz came to realize that it was not about the 15 minutes; it was actually that *she just could not be on time.* When Liz finally realized that it really was not about the hours, she discussed the situation with her attorney. What they agreed to do was to unofficially change her hours, from 8:45 to 5:15. However, they never told the secretary that they had changed her hours. They never informed human resources that they had changed the secretary's hours, and for all intents and purposes, her hours were from 8:30 to 5:00, just like everyone else's.

After that, she was on time every single day. Without reservation, she is one of the best legal secretaries with whom Liz has ever had the pleasure of working.

Going to these lengths may seem a little extraordinary. (We can hear HR people muttering under their breaths that she should have been fired.) But in our many years, we have both learned that sometimes you go the extra mile for an outstanding employee. Occasionally, this may mean being a little creative in dealing with employees who are worth keeping. A smaller law firm may have more flexibility in this than larger corporations with more rigid HR procedures.

Performance evaluations are a critical component, both to human resources and informing your employees of how they are meeting your expectations. In the past, both employers and employees dreaded evaluations, mostly because they were not effectively handled. The true purpose of the evaluation was lost with the employer pointing out the employee's shortcomings and the employee trying to get through the evaluation with her job still intact.

Performance evaluations should be utilized as a positive tool to work with the employee on improving skills, highlighting the positive contributions the employee has made, and pointing out areas where the employee could make improvements that would benefit everyone.

During a performance evaluation, there are three critical questions you should ask every employee. Use your active listening skills as you discuss them with the employee and you will discover un-mined gold that you can excavate for the benefit of your firm, the employee, and the rest of your staff:

1. HOW DO YOU THINK YOU ARE DOING? Employees know how they are doing. Their self-evaluations are usually right on target unless they are truly unaware of what their job description is. This is a thought-provoking question, and you can obtain a good sense of your employee when he responds.

2. WHAT AREAS DO YOU THINK YOU NEED TO WORK ON? Employees know what they are struggling with, and this is an opportunity for them to reach out for your help. Listen to what

they say *and* what they don't say.

3. HOW CAN I ASSIST YOU WITH IMPROVING THOSE AREAS OR SKILLS? Everyone learns differently. For example, is she a visual learner? A kinesthetic learner? Or does she learn by hearing? Does she learn by doing? By writing? This is an opportunity for the employee to inform you what method of learning something new or working on her skills will be best for her. You have made it safe for the employee to admit they need help.

Instead of making the employee feel like he was called into the principal's office to be reprimanded, a performance evaluation becomes a learning and improvement opportunity for your firm and your employee. Perhaps the employee needs help with something that could benefit all the other employees, as well. There may be an inefficient process in the office that must be addressed.

Rather than seeing this as a chance to tell your employee all the things he is doing wrong, take this as an opportunity to see the firm from the employee's perspective. This is a unique opportunity, and you might learn something!

You need not retain employees who are not performing their jobs, and employees are always free to seek employment elsewhere. Sometimes it is worth the investment in your firm and employees to make a small concession that will pay back in a big way. Like everything else, you get out what you put in.

Give your employees all the tools, feedback, and encouragement they need to perform at peak levels. Employees will often surprise you if you give them the opportunity. This can be a valuable learning experience for the firm.

CHAPTER TWENTY-TWO
HOW TO DEAL WITH OFFICE POLITICS

Believe it or not, office politics can be a problem in any size law firm—from 1000+ to as small as a solo practitioner with two staff members.

In an office, building a team requires interaction amongst the staff to develop a bond. This includes networking, provided that it does not breed negativity in the office. But there are some instances in which the word "networking" can easily be interchanged with the word "gossiping." That is office politics in the nutshell. The agenda could include promotion within the firm, a feeling of self-importance within the firm, or seeking out favoritism with managers or decision makers—anything that will somehow further the interests of the person or people involved in office politics.

Let's face it—your staff spends a minimum of 40 hours a week coexisting in the office. It is difficult for employees to isolate themselves from their co-workers, and quite frankly, isolation is not a good team building mechanism among the staff.

Truth be told, everyone likes to hear gossip every now and then. It seems to make a boring day a little more interesting. But gossip and office politics are better left to the tabloids. Zero tolerance is an absolute necessity if your staff is to work together as a team without dissension among the ranks. The message that you have to send is that no amount of office politics or gossiping will be tolerated.

What are the effects of office politics on your practice?

- They will destroy office morale. No matter what other techniques you use to build office morale, office politics will destroy it in one fell swoop. Office politics take on a life of their own.

- The effects that office politics have on the morale of your staff will naturally flow over into their work. There is nothing you can do to prevent that. We are all human beings with feelings.

- The behavior of your employees is affected by ongoing office politics. Most people aren't good at hiding their personal feelings. When employees know that their co-workers are maligning them, this behavior manifests itself in the way they conduct themselves with your clients. This can be fatal to your practice.

This is how the poison of office politics is perpetuated, and this is why you absolutely must stop it before it ever starts.

Here are some steps that firms can take to discourage office politics and encourage a healthy office environment that will not destroy firm morale:

1. Tell employees to keep their conversations with their co-workers on the lighter side. Discourage employees from discussing personal matters with everyone in the office. Because everyone in the firm is supposed to be productive and efficient, there should not be time to engage in disparaging remarks about co-workers or bosses.

2. Keep an extra eye on the office troublemaker. There is at least one in every crowd. Know who that person is, and make sure to monitor his behavior. When you see or hear him engaging in this destructive behavior, redirect him. Office politics can turn nasty, especially in a small office when an employee feels as though another employee isn't pulling her own weight. If one employee is constantly showing up late or not coming in at all, thereby forcing other employees to pick up her slack, animosity will quickly develop. Stop this early before it becomes a problem by giving each staff member specific tasks and deadlines so that you reduce the belief of the slacking employee that if she does not perform a task, someone else will eventually do it for her. If you notice that one employee is constantly slammed while another employee seems to have loads of free time, redistribute workloads before there are hard feelings.

3. Ensure that all employees understand that any aspect of employee compensation (including, not only salary, but also benefits and any other perks that may apply to one employee but not others) is not to be discussed with co-workers under any circumstances. Many firms have employees sign a confidentiality agreement to this effect.

4. Lead by example. Sometimes bosses can perpetuate office politics, often without realizing it. Do not make derogatory remarks about any staff member's work in front of other employees. This will become the topic of conversation for the next round of gossip in the office, although it may not be seen that way because it came down from management.

You cannot ask employees to isolate themselves from their co-workers. Encourage team spirit. Staff should bond with each other, support and nurture one another, and learn from each other. You cannot create a team if you don't encourage people to work together. The best advice you can offer your employees to stop office politics before they start is to take some advice from those three little monkeys—"see no evil, speak no evil, hear no evil."

ROLE PLAY ONE:
HOW TO DISCOURAGE STAFF FROM DISCUSSING EMPLOYEE COMPENSATION

Players: Narrator
Office Administrator
Paralegal
Coworker Paralegal

Narrator: Administrator overhears a conversation between two paralegals, Paralegal and Coworker.

Paralegal: (talking to Coworker, not realizing that Administrator is behind her filing something and listening) Coworker, I was just talking to one of my former classmates from school, and she was telling me that the firm she works for is paying her $30 an hour! That's nuts, right? I have the same experience and graduated at the same time, and this firm is only paying me $25 an hour. And I had better grades than she did!

Coworker: (looking uncomfortable) The firm is paying you $25 an hour?

Paralegal: Yeah. Why? How much do you make?

Coworker: I don't feel comfortable talking about this. I don't think this is an appropriate conversation to be discussing salaries with co-workers.

Paralegal: Why not? Is the firm paying you more? Are you telling me I'm underpaid?

Coworker: Well when you put it that way . . .

Administrator: (stepping into their view and interrupting) Coworker, you were right the first time. These conversations are not appropriate in the workplace.

Coworker: (looking relieved) I really felt uncomfortable talking about compensation with a co-worker in the firm. But she seemed to make a good point about having the right to know whether she is being underpaid.

Paralegal: Of course, I have a right to know! Why shouldn't I know how much she's getting paid?!

Administrator: Paralegal, this conversation is not appropriate. Not only is your coworker is not obligated to tell you, in fact, these types of conversations violate the rules in our Office Policy and Procedures Manual. Consider this a warning that these discussions are not permitted between office staff.

Paralegal: (looking annoyed) I don't understand what the problem is.

Administrator: The problem is that conversations about compensation, like all office gossip, can destroy office morale. These negative effects will naturally flow over into your work and the work of your coworkers. It harbors resentment among the staff and keeps people from working as a team.

Paralegal: I guess I see your point. But I am close with many of my coworkers because I spend so much time with them. It's hard to avoid having personal conversations with them.

Administrator: I understand, but you really must try. While I encourage team spirit, working together, and bonding amongst staff members, your conversations with one another should be kept on the lighter side. Avoid discussing such personal matters relating to your employment here. Because everyone in the firm is supposed to be productive and efficient, there should not be time to engage in gossip.

Paralegal: I guess I usually do have too much work to spend time gossiping with other staff.

Administrator: And you should especially avoid discussing any aspect of employee compensation. This includes not only salary, but also discussions about benefits and any other perks. If you check your written policies and procedures, you'll find that the penalty for violating this policy is immediate termination. It's very serious, and we therefore take it very seriously.

Paralegal: Oh, wow, I had no idea. I won't bring it up ever again!

Administrator: Thank you. We will consider the matter closed. Now get back to work!

REVIEW QUESTIONS NINE

Lawyers:

1. What is your firm's policy on office politics? Write it down.
2. How do you stress to your employees the importance of refraining from office gossip? Review your policy manual regarding same. Revise it if necessary.
3. How do you discipline employees who engage in office politics? Review your policy manual regarding same. Revise it if necessary.
4. What if an associate has a 100%-win rate, but is hated by the entire firm and casts a negative feeling throughout the firm? What if a paralegal has an excellent work product but is rude to clients and co-workers?
5. Do your employees believe you when you tell them you have zero tolerance policy for office gossip? If not, how can you change that? Brainstorm ideas and implement them. Discuss your new policies with your staff.

Law Students:

1. How do you feel when you find out that someone has been gossiping about you? List those feelings.
2. How do you feel when someone catches you gossiping about them? List those feelings.
3. Do you understand why gossip in an office environment can be damaging and hurtful? Why? List the reasons.
4. Have you ever had an experience in your life when you've lost relationships due to gossip? Were you able to mend those broken relationships? If so, how? If not, did you change your behavior going forward? Write down your experience.

CHAPTER TWENTY-THREE
HOW TO ENSURE STAFF ACCOUNTABILITY

The administration of a law firm touches on all areas of the practice, including staff accountability. Employing an operating method that ensures accountability by everyone in your law firm is imperative. Accountability will enable you to know that your clients are receiving the best possible service from your firm by ensuring that your staff is working as part of a well-oiled team to further the interests of every firm client. This includes the lawyers.

An accountable law firm starts with leaders who first hold themselves accountable and who lead by example. A leader who does not hold himself accountable to the staff can destroy the work ethic of the firm. Such behavior by a partner eventually catches up with the firm and, in the end, can financially cripple the firm with substantially reduced revenues.

There are many ways to measure accountability. In two of Liz's prior law firm administrator positions, she met once a week with the executive committee or the senior partner. Together, they would review projects the firm was working on and discuss staff issues, finances, and other administrative areas that were important to the continued success of the firm. These meetings gave the managing attorneys a good sense of what was going on with their business—not to mention it justified paying Liz.

Liz has always tried to cultivate a culture of accountability in the offices in which she works, openly holding herself accountable to the firm and to its staff as a gesture intended to encourage others to follow suit.

Meeting with staff once a week is one way of keeping everyone updated on the progress of cases and ensuring that the work is equally distributed. This prevents any one employee from being overwhelmed while others have too much free time on their hands, which leads to non-work related activities such as surfing the Internet.

However, we do not use meetings as a means for accountability by itself. When office conferences are the only tool used to measure accountability, you usually see an increase in staff turnover.

No team is perfect. Although it does not occur often, you may find that some staff members are not always honest about the progress of their work. This is the reason why you cannot rely on meetings solely to measure accountability. You must do more than take a staff member's word to prevent cases from falling apart because of tasks you thought were being accomplished. Your accountability includes monitoring cases, scrutinizing deadlines, and ensuring that your administrator reviews each timekeeper's billable hours scrupulously.

Tracking time is a very important component of accountability. With an hourly billable practice, you should set billing requirements that your timekeepers must meet every month. Some firms set an annual quota and then divide by 12 for the average hours they expect every month. Be specific that the requirement should be actual client billable hours.

To avoid any confusion, be sure that newly hired associates have a clear understanding that extracurricular and professional obligations such as bar luncheons, CLE courses, or even office administrative work are not deducted from the client billable requirement. Such professional functions, although an investment in their professional futures, are not activities that should reduce their obligation to the firm.

Your billing program will enable your firm to track timekeepers' hours on a weekly basis to make sure they are on target to meet their goal. You cannot afford to rely on the 30-day billing cycle. In doing so, you may run the risk of realizing too late that the timekeeper who should have billed 130 hours only billed 97 in the last billing period. Managing a law firm is all about the numbers, and everything in a firm can be evaluated in terms of numbers—or more specifically, of dollars and cents.

To put into perspective the importance of time tracking, let's say that an attorney's billing requirement is 130 hours, but he only bills 97 hours at $250 per hour. Your firm has lost $8,250 in anticipated revenues. Even with one or two timekeepers falling short every month, you can see how this will financially impact the firm's revenues. In a small firm, even one timekeeper who falls short of their billable requirements every month will significantly impact the firm's revenues. Over the course of a year, one timekeeper can easily cost the firm close to $100,000. Now that 33-hour shortfall takes on a different meaning, doesn't it?

When a billing cycle has closed and the month has passed, it is too late to assess the deficit in billable hours or to take remedial action. On the other hand, if your firm is ten days into a billing cycle and a timekeeper with a requirement of 130 hours has only billed 20 hours, there is still an opportunity to manage that timekeeper and hold them accountable for meeting the billing requirement. Focus on determining what the problem is, or it may become a recurring one.

If your firm handles mostly contingency cases, you can still manage time by setting metrics. In a personal injury practice, metrics could include the number of settlement demands generated every month, how many lawsuits are filed, or how many mediations are scheduled. These metrics will also help measure how a case is moving along and staff's activity in its involvement. For example, if you require that a paralegal generate 10 settlement demands per month to meet the firm's goal, and he only generates two, you will know there is an issue that must be addressed.

Resistance to accountability is a red flag. Some employees have developed avoiding accountability into an art form. They can deflect and even blame others for why something did or did not happen. Eventually it becomes obvious that the reason an employee is resistant is because she is not performing her job and is trying to hide that fact.

The common problem that arises with a lack of accountability is discovering too late that a member of your legal team is not performing. When an employee leaves a position, it can take six months or more to correct any loose ends he left behind as a consequence of his poor performance. There is no excuse, however, for failing to be aware that a member of your legal team is not pulling his weight.

The onus is on you to hold your staff accountable for the work you expect them to accomplish. You must set a protocol early in the hiring process to avoid issues with staff resisting accountability measures. Consequences arising from the failure to hold a staff member accountable can include missing a statute of limitations date, a court hearing, or a deposition, or even losing a large sum of revenue in billable hours in any given month because a timekeeper did not meet the billing requirement.

If you refuse to hold your staff accountable, there are ultimately two losers. The first, of course, is the client, but the second is you as the attorney. It is difficult to maintain credibility with a client when he repeatedly becomes aware that matters in his case are not being accomplished on time or that a legal step is overlooked, such as a hearing or a deposition.

On occasion, a client's dissatisfaction will rise to the level of a bar grievance. No one wants that.

And avoiding contact with a client is never an effective solution. Ignoring a client simply generates more telephone calls and more stress for both of you. If you have nothing to tell the client because nothing has happened or changed, be honest and tell him that. The legal market is very competitive, and clients are looking for value and good representation. That good representation includes communication with the client. The most common bar grievance filed is "he didn't return my phone calls."

As mentioned, you, as the attorney, are the other loser. When a client files a bar grievance or other complaint, including a lawsuit, you cannot blame your staff. You are the one with the bar license.

One of the more common complaints of clients who file bar grievances against their attorneys is that an attorney missed an important scheduled event. Employ a checks and balances program in your firm in which the paralegal who sets up the file also calendars the important dates, and then the attorney who works the file checks to ensure that all dates were calendared correctly. Having another set of eyes on important deadlines will not take up too much additional time, and it will allow you to avoid the serious issue of missing a critical event.

Discuss these tactics with your staff during your weekly meetings to ensure that they proceed as they should and that they are living up to the high standards that you have set.

How do you establish a culture of accountability in your office, without singling out any particular individual?

- Conduct regular staff meetings to discuss the status and progress of cases.

- Review your docket and deadlines, including the all-important statutes of limitations, and know what issues need immediate attention. Don't wait until the week of a hearing to discover that there has been no preparation for it or that you have missed important deadlines relative to it.

- Stay a month ahead. Determine what is coming up, what is needed, and who is expected to provide it. Ensure that he or she knows that you have that expectation.

- Follow up.

- Make sure there is coverage for everything on the calendar so that no hearings or depositions are missed or overlooked.

- Review billable hours for each timekeeper on a weekly basis until there is no longer any concern whether a timekeeper will meet the billing requirement.

- Even if your timekeepers are routinely meeting their billable hour requirements, be sure to always review billable hours at the end of a billing cycle to make sure that they continue to meet your requirements.

- Initiate and participate in the culture of accountability with your staff.

- Inform potential employees during the interview process that accountability is part of the firm's culture. Ensure that you obtain "buy-in" before they are even employed. Doing this will result in little or no resistance later.

Establishing a culture of accountability in your office will build confidence with your staff and let them know that you are working on being part of the solution with them. Your name is on the door—don't employ a hands-off approach.

Be sure that you yourself are doing a good job, and be accountable. Your staff will follow your lead.

CHAPTER TWENTY-FOUR
HOW TO RAISE MORALE *AND* YOUR BOTTOM LINE

Over the course of Liz's career, she has worked as an administrator in law firms that varied in size from solo practitioners and small firms to those having 500 attorneys. Joryn, too, has worked in small, medium, and massive firms, as well as in a government office and in a law school environment. To this day, it never ceases to amaze us that attorneys do not recognize the importance of morale and team building in the office and how it impacts efficiency and productivity.

We can just hear some scrooge-like attorney mumbling to himself, "They get paid, don't they? Isn't that enough?" The short answer is, "No, it isn't." Sure, the staff gets a paycheck for their work. Most firms provide at least health insurance, and some firms provide additional benefits. However, attracting great employees with a decent salary and benefits is not enough.

Operating under the premise of "doing more with less," it is more important than ever that there is a team spirit in the office that draws the staff together to work as a cohesive team. Bringing that culture into the office is the job of the attorney, firm administrator, or HR. Employee attitudes have changed over the years. Good, loyal employees want more than a paycheck and health benefits. Studies have shown that compensation does not even rate in the top five factors of what makes an employee happy with her job. Salary is what attracts an employee to the job; it is not usually what will keep her there.

We firmly believe in and promote the philosophy that "happy employees are productive employees." You would be surprised how very little can really go a long way to turning morale around and motivating employees to go the extra mile. When a paycheck is all that is holding an employee at your firm, there is no surprise that someone would make a move to another position for an extra $25 a week. Of course, your employees are there for the paycheck and the health benefits, too. That's essentially the reason why we are all working. Money is a necessary evil, and for most of us, the only way to get it is to work. But does it really have to be in a morgue-like atmosphere where employees come in like mechanical drones, sit down, do their work, go to lunch, come back, do some more work, and then go home?

We are not talking about a raise, although there's no doubt that every member of your staff would eagerly accept that. But that will *not* promote morale or team building. We are talking about indirect financial rewards or perks that will make employees feel appreciated longer than a raise does. The glow of getting that raise wears off in a few weeks, and then it becomes "just" their paycheck again. We have seen time and time again how giving employees as much as a 20% increase in their salary wears off quickly. Then the employees are back to complaining about something else.

Not so long ago, Liz had an opportunity to work at a firm where the morale was zero. (It was less than zero, but because that is hard to imagine, we will call it "zero.") Employees came in and did their work. They did not speak or look at each other unless they had to. It was a big firm where multiple attorneys were assigned to one legal assistant. There were six legal assistants and some other support staff. If a legal assistant was out, the staff was supposed to cover for each other. There was no team spirit, so Liz had to make assignments of coverage because the legal assistants would not volunteer to help each other, even if they had the time to read a book. Liz knew this when she accepted the position, and it was high on her agenda of issues to address.

The first week she was there, Liz told the staff they were having a staff lunch. One person asked if attendance was mandatory, and if it was, wanted to know if they would be paid overtime for attending. Long story short, after a few lunches, including a taco day when the staff brought in everything we needed to have a taco bar with fake "margaritas," morale turned around, and they began acting like a team.

Now, when a legal assistant is going to be out, there are e-mails flying around with everyone volunteering to provide coverage for the attorneys. In addition, two legal assistants who had not spoken to each other for years, for reasons which neither of them could even remember, were talking to each other once again.

Liz's only holdout was a legal assistant who had been demoted from office manager to paralegal. But without anyone in the firm wanting to admit it, it is probably that attitude that got her demoted in the first place. Malcontents will always find something about which to complain.

Here are a few things that will boost morale and help build a cohesive team that every firm can do without breaking the budget:

- Breakfast together once a week. We recommend Fridays. We are not talking about an elaborate three-hour breakfast where everyone stands around the break room and loses valuable billable hours. We are talking about a pot of coffee and a dozen bagels and cream cheese. A few minutes talking in the kitchen as everyone gets his or her bagels and coffee is not a bad thing. It promotes team building and company spirit. It doesn't have to be bagels, and it doesn't have to be the firm providing breakfast. If you set a budget, have staff members take turns bringing in the breakfast, and reimburse them for the expense. You'd be amazed at how creative some people can be and how hard they will try. With her efforts at that big firm, Liz even had attorneys bringing in cakes and treats that they had baked at home to share with the staff. It becomes contagious and spreads throughout the firm.

- Occasionally cater an office lunch. A couple of sandwiches and drinks or a few pizzas and sodas won't bust the budget that you prepared, especially if you budgeted for morale building lunches (which is certainly worth doing). The goodwill goes a long way. The staff will eat together. Eat with them, and share some downtime. Learn a little more about your employees and share a little of yourself with them. It will make them feel more connected to the firm.

- Have a potluck lunch for a holiday. Have a barbecue-themed lunch in the summers around the 4th of July, Memorial Day, or Labor Day. The firm pays for the barbecue, and the staff participates by bringing in side dishes and dessert. Even if you have a small firm with a few employees, you can put together a lunch that everyone will enjoy. Here, it is not just about the lunch, it is about everyone working together to plan a menu and work out who will bring what.

- Bring your legal assistant or paralegal a cup of coffee. Sound silly? Maybe to you. You would be surprised by how much it will be appreciated, and someone will notice that the boss brought a staff member a cup of coffee. Don't be surprised when employees start paying it forward with a colleague or co-worker.

- When an employee does a really good job on a project, leave a sticky note on her computer thanking her for her hard work.

- Celebrate employee birthdays by getting a cake. Fifteen minutes in the kitchen or conference room to sing "Happy Birthday" and have a piece of cake won't affect the billable hours that much. Yes, we are all about those billable hours, but your employees will go back to their desks and make sure their work gets done and their billable hours are met. They will also know that you cared that it was their birthdays and took the time to acknowledge them.

- Send your staff a motivational e-mail in the morning. Liz had gotten in the habit of doing this. One day she got busy and forgot. The senior partner sent her an e-mail asking where her inspirational e-mail for the day was. One of our favorites is, "We take care of our employees, and they take care of our clients." It takes less than one minute, but people *do* notice.

- In smaller firms, buy a $25 gift card for each employee every so often. Something they can use to put gas in their car or to go out to lunch on occasion. Joryn often brings small gifts to her staff that she knows they will enjoy, like used books, handmade jewelry, and homemade treats. She once sent out an e-mail asking what their favorite color was, what their favorite mythical creature was, and what their favorite symbol was so that she could tailor Christmas gifts to their liking. And when she travels, whether for fun or a speaking event, she always brings back something from that far away destination to let them know that she was thinking of them while she was gone. Such attentiveness cost little but lets her staff know that she appreciates them and has taken the time to learn what they enjoy.

Human resources and administration are all about relationship management. We could make an endless list of the gestures that cost little or no money but go a very long way in terms of creating goodwill.

Consider offering creative perks for your employees based on their specific interests. For example, Joryn's long-term associate was extremely motivated by fitness. Joryn enjoys Pilates, so, rather than taking classes at a studio, she hired her instructor to teach a mat class at her firm a couple of times per week. Not only was it a nice perk for her staff, but it provided a couple of invaluable hours each week for the two lawyers, Joryn and her associate, to discuss cases, if necessary, or to just get to know one another and bond even more. It also provided employees a much-needed hour away from their desks to regroup and come back re-energized.

Joryn also had a client who was unable to pay her legal fees. She was a nail technician, so Joryn invited her to come to the office each week to do the employees' nails. Not only did it give Joryn's staff an hour of free (to them) pampering, but it was also a way for the client to pay down her debt to the firm.

With every attorney or firm with whom Liz works, she encourages a culture of team building and good morale. It is the backbone of a solid organization in which everyone works together for a common goal—to provide outstanding service to the client.

Someone reading this is shaking his head and thinking, "I do not have to stroke my employees' egos, encourage them, or do more for them than give them a paycheck and the benefits that I agreed to provide." You are absolutely correct—you don't have to give them more than a paycheck and the benefits you agreed to. Remember, however, that you get what you give.

The reality is that employees want to do a good job and be appreciated, and the return will trickle down to outstanding service to your clients. Because the practice of law is all about good service to your clients (so they will be repeat clients or send you referrals), this is a win-win for your firm. What goes around really does come around.

One of Joryn's clients recently brought a doggie bag to the office loaded with goodies for Hachi, Mack, and Sam, the three office dogs. Another stopped by with a gift bag loaded with sweets for the staff. Neither gift was terribly costly. But have no doubt, they each made a tremendous impact on Joryn and her staff.

Still not convinced? We leave you with one final thought. *How did you feel the last time a client went the extra mile with a heartfelt thank you for doing a good job—the job you got paid to do?*

ROLE PLAY TWO:
HOW TO THANK EMPLOYEES FOR A JOB WELL DONE

Players: Narrator
            Lawyer
            Paralegal
            Secretary

Narrator: Attorney Lawyer stops at Paralegal's desk with a cup of coffee. Secretary is sitting at the computer next to Paralegal, listening in.

Lawyer: (handing the cup to Paralegal) Paralegal, I brought you a caramel macchiato from Starbucks. That's your favorite, right?

Paralegal: (looking surprised and taking the cup) It is! Thank you so much!

Lawyer: I just wanted to compliment you on the wonderful job that you did on that motion for summary judgment. The research you did and the compelling argument that you crafted helped me to win in court today. The client is going to be very happy. Great job!

Paralegal: Well, thank you so much! I like doing a good job, but especially when I'm appreciated for it.

Lawyer: Keep up the good work! (Walks away)

Secretary: (leaning toward Paralegal) Wow, I can't believe the boss bought you coffee! And I can't believe she noticed what your favorite coffee is either. She's really paying attention to the little things. I have to say that I've never seen that happen. That must've been some motion.

Paralegal: I know. When I worked at other firms, my bosses never did stuff like that. I always felt under-appreciated. But you're going to *love* working here. Lawyer takes the time to tell us when we've done something especially well. It makes me want to work even harder. I enjoy making her happy, and I *really* enjoy when I've helped her win for our client!

Secretary: I agree. I can't wait until I give her a reason to bring me coffee! I'm going to work extra hard on this letter she asked me to draft for her!

CHAPTER TWENTY-FIVE
HOW TO AVOID HIRING AN EMPLOYEE WHO DOES NOT FIT

From time to time, your firm will need to hire a new member of your legal team. You post your position in an ad under "legal" for a legal assistant/paralegal. Your post is really specific about what you are looking for in terms of experience and skill. The job market is so flooded with applicants these days that you receive resumes from cashiers and file clerks with aspirations to fit into a position they do not have the skills for. These applicants are enthusiastic enough to send a resume even though your ad says, "If you do not have three years' legal experience, please do not apply." We, ourselves, have tried including that language in ads that we have posted. It doesn't prevent candidates who are not qualified from sending in their resumes.

When we receive these resumes, the first thing that we wonder is whether this person can actually follow directions. The second is that we have to admire the enthusiasm of someone applying for a job knowing she does not have the requisite skills or experience.

After reviewing a few dozen resumes, they all start to look alike, and you realize that no one has *exactly* the experience you need. After searching for the perfect candidate that seems impossible to find, you need a warm body to get the work done. Right about now it probably seems like *someone* would be better than no one. After wading through an endless sea of resumes, you relent and hire someone you think might actually work out, but who has a bigger learning curve than you wanted. The candidate tells you that all word processing and case management software is the same. She's never filed in federal court, but she has filed in state court, so isn't that the same? Litigation is litigation. So even though her experience is in foreclosure work, and you do criminal or personal injury, it's all litigation, right?

Before you hire the wrong person, ask yourself, "*What will this hire cost my firm?*" If this wrong hire doesn't work out, then in many respects, you are worse off than you were before. The big problem with hiring the wrong fit is *clients do not like to see a lot of turnover in their attorneys' staff.* It makes them wonder why employees leave so often. They call one week and speak to Mary and call two weeks later and speak to Lisa. Two months down the road, there is yet another new employee. It makes a client question the stability of your office and the continuity of their work.

Clients do not want to bear the brunt or the cost of downtime in your office while new employees get up to speed on their cases and learn your systems. We have known clients who refuse to speak to new employees, insisting on speaking to the attorney every time because there is so much turnover in a firm. News travels fast in the legal community, and sometimes the word gets out to potential candidates that there is a problem with this firm or that one. It makes it difficult to attract good employees.

With an associate, the cost of getting up to speed is higher because your firm cannot charge a client while a new associate learns the details of a client's case. The associate cannot work on the case without knowing those details. Calculate even a minimum of one hour per file in your office for an associate to become familiar with a file, at $250 per hour for 200 files. That is a $50,000 investment for the new associate to become familiar with the files in the office and is a huge financial investment. The same holds true for any timekeeper in the office. You cannot pass on the cost of this learning curve to the client.

For the sake of the continued success of your office and the satisfaction of clients who will refer you new business, hiring the wrong employee is an expensive mistake that you cannot afford to make. Your firm needs someone who will hit the ground running and be productive on the first day. With the right person, that is not as unreasonable as it might sound. There will always be a learning curve, but it should not be about the fundamentals of how to be an attorney, paralegal, legal assistant, or firm administrator.

There are three important things to consider when hiring legal staff for your office:

1) Does she have the relevant experience to do the job?
2) How current are her technology skills?
3) How professional is the candidate?

Attracting the right candidate for a position can be hit-or-miss. Even hiring a headhunter or recruiter will not necessarily bring you better candidates because she is pulling from the same pool of applicants to send you potential candidates to interview. Her ads are on the same job boards where you post for open positions. If you assign an administrator or someone else in your firm to assist with the search for a new staff member, ensure that it is someone who has actually performed that job and who can ask very specific questions.

A potential litigation paralegal, for example, should be able to answer these types of questions without any hesitation:

- How many days does a defendant have to file an answer to a complaint?
- What is the deadline for filing a response to discovery served with the original complaint?
- How many days do you have to set a motion for rehearing after an order has been entered?
- How many days before a pretrial hearing does the pre-trial memo have to be submitted?
- When preparing an appellate brief, what is the font type and size that should be used?

Above all, keep in mind that every staff member you hire, be it a legal assistant, paralegal, or attorney, is a representative of *your firm*. She is in contact with your firm's most precious asset—*your clients*. Make sure that the person you hire is capable of carrying out the responsibilities of the position and is someone you want representing your firm. Everything matters in a law firm, and everything that your firm does for your clients is tied to the people you hire. Make sure it's a good fit *for everyone.*

ROLE PLAY THREE:
HOW TO AVOID HIRING AN EMPLOYEE WHO IS NOT THE RIGHT FIT

Players: Narrator
Lawyer
Administrator
Applicant

Scene I

Narrator: Lawyer, a lawyer in a small firm, discusses with her paralegal, Paralegal, that it is time to hire a second paralegal.

Lawyer: Administrator, please place an ad in the Bar Journal, on my LinkedIn page, and on Craigslist for a paralegal with three years' experience in family law. Applicants should know how to research on both Westlaw and Lexis, should understand how to put together financial affidavits and mandatory discovery, and should have a basic understanding of family law. Anything else you can think of that I ought to include?

Administrator: No. But it's going to be hard to find someone with that much experience who will work for $20 an hour.

Lawyer: I think you can find someone. I want you to do the first round of interviews for me. As you're interviewing applicants, keep in mind that there are three important things to consider when hiring legal staff:

1. Does she have the relevant experience to do the job?
2. How current are her technology skills? and
3. How professional is the candidate?

Administrator: I'll keep all that in mind.

Lawyer: Please let me know when you have a couple of applicants who might be a good fit. I would like to do the final interview and hiring. But I'll leave the initial ad, resume review, and interviews up to you.

Administrator: I'll see what I can find.

Scene II

Narrator: Administrator is performing the initial interview of Applicant.

Administrator: [shaking hands] Hello, Applicant. I'm administrator for the firm. As you saw from the ad that you answered, we are looking for an experienced paralegal. I see from your resume that you just graduated from school six months ago. What have you been doing during that time?

Applicant: Well, I started working for a worker's comp attorney, but they expected me to come in to work before 8 a.m. and leave after 6 p.m. on most days. I just can't do that. I have a young daughter, and I need to be home around 5 p.m. on most days.

Administrator: We certainly understand that. Although there are some times, like right before a trial, when we will need you to put in longer hours, that doesn't happen too often here. I'm more concerned with your lack of experience. We are specifically looking for someone with at least three years of family law experience. You don't have any family law experience, right?

Applicant: I don't. But I did work for the worker's comp attorney for six months. How different could it be?

Administrator: Actually, it is very different. Family law is its own beast. The law is very specific, the attorneys know each other well, and the clients need to be handled more gently than regular clients. When you worked for the worker's comp attorney, did you put any discovery together?

Applicant: A little bit. But he mostly had me doing research.

Administrator: Okay. Was research a fulltime job at the firm? Did you use Lexis? Or Westlaw?

Applicant: Actually, I used Best Case. The attorney I worked for refused to pay for those other websites. But I did learn to use both Westlaw and Lexis in my paralegal certification program, and it hasn't been that long since I graduated, so I'm sure I can still use both of those apps.

Administrator: Hhhmmm. Okay, what about trial prep? Did you do any of that?

Applicant: A little bit. The attorney was a bit of a control freak, so he would let us do portions of trial prep, but he never just handed over full responsibility to us.

Administrator: Do you know how many days a respondent has to file an answer to a petition for divorce?

Applicant: Umm, a couple of weeks?

Administrator: Actually, he has 20 days. What is the deadline for filing a response to discovery served with the original petition?

Applicant: A couple of months?

Administrator: No, 45 days. How many days do you have to set a motion for rehearing after an order has been entered?

Applicant: A week?

Administrator: Ten days. When preparing an appellate brief, what is the font type and size that needs to be used?

Applicant: Times New Roman 12? But I can look all those answers up in the rules, right?

Administrator: Yes, you can, if you *know* that you need to do that homework. In fact, the primary paralegal always double checks all of that anyway, because the rules change all the time.

By the way, you were close. It's Times New Roman 14.

[sighing] Okay, well, as you know, you don't have the experience that we're looking for. But it's been almost a month, and we haven't had many fully qualified applicants. We have way too much work, more than we can handle, so we need to hire someone ASAP. I like you, so I'm going to recommend that Lawyer interview you. [standing and putting her hand out to shake]

Applicant: That is terrific news! Thank you for giving me a chance.

Scene III

Narrator: Administrator and Lawyer are discussing the possibility of hiring Applicant.

Lawyer: So, how is the applicant search going? With that huge trial coming up, we really need some help soon.

Administrator: Believe me, I know! I know your paralegal is sick of working ten hour days. I'm afraid we are going to burn her out. But I just don't know that we have the right person yet. The best applicant we have is Applicant. I'm recommending that you interview her, although she only has six months' experience as a paralegal. And it was for a control-freak worker's comp attorney who didn't give her much responsibility. She didn't even have access to Westlaw and Lexis.

Lawyer: We can't hire someone like that!

Administrator: But I really like her, and we don't have any other options.

Lawyer: I know that you're anxious to hire someone. I am, too. But as you're weeding through applications, you need to consider what a potential applicant is going to cost the firm. If Applicant doesn't work out, in many respects we are worse off than we were before.

Administrator: Why do you say that?

Lawyer: Clients do not like to see a lot of turnover in their attorneys' staff. It makes them wonder why employees leave so often. It makes a client question the stability of our office and the continuity of our work. Additionally, clients do not want to bear the brunt of downtime while new employees get up to speed on their cases and learn our systems.

Administrator: I guess that makes sense.

Lawyer: And news travels fast in the legal community. If the word gets out to potential candidates that we have a high turnover rate, it will be difficult to attract good employees.

Administrator: True.

Lawyer: Also, I cannot charge a client while a new paralegal learns the details of their case. The paralegal cannot work on the case without knowing those details. Calculate even a minimum of one hour per file for a paralegal to become familiar with a file, for 50 files. At $20/hour, I'm out $1,000 and over a week of her time. But at $100 per hour that I could have been billing her out at, for those 50 files, that's a $5,000 investment.

Administrator: That is expensive.

Lawyer: For the sake of the continued success of this office and the satisfaction of our clients who will refer us new business, hiring the wrong employee is an expensive mistake that we cannot afford to make. We need someone who will hit the ground running and be productive on the first day. With the right person, that is not as unreasonable as it might sound. There will always be a learning curve, but it should not be about the fundamentals of how to be a paralegal.

Administrator: Since it is so important, maybe we should consider hiring a headhunter or recruiter.

Lawyer: That's an idea, but I don't want to do that just yet. I would have to pay the headhunter, and she would not necessarily bring any better candidates because she would be pulling from the same pool of applicants. Her ads would be on the same job boards where you posted for a paralegal.

Administrator: I see your point. Are you sure we shouldn't just go with Applicant? I'm really slammed! I don't even have time to interview applicants!

Lawyer: Keep in mind that if I hire her, she will be a representative of this firm. She will be in contact with our most precious asset, our clients. We need someone who is capable of carrying out the responsibilities of the position and someone who we want representing this firm. Even though Applicant sounds like a nice gal, I think that it is important that we wait longer for a better fit.

Administrator: I suppose you're right. But can you at least increase the hourly rate you are offering so that we get better interest? And maybe we should post to the paralegal programs? Even though we're looking for experience, sometimes graduates return to the school placement program for help?

Lawyer: Both good ideas. Hopefully they will make the difference.

Scene IV

Narrator: One month later, Administrator walks excitedly into Lawyer's office.

Administrator: Great news! I just found the perfect applicant! She has five years of family law experience, knows how to use Westlaw and Lexis, has prepped for 16 trials, has tons of discovery experience, and looks and acts extremely professionally!

Lawyer: That is wonderful! I'm so glad that we waited for the right applicant. [high-fiving Administrator]

Administrator: Me, too! She is the perfect fit for this firm. I've already scheduled her in to meet with you.

CHAPTER TWENTY-SIX
HOW TO FIRE AN EMPLOYEE

When anyone asks Liz to tell them her least favorite thing she does as an administrator, her answer never changes—she hates it when she has to terminate an employee's service. And she has never had anyone tell her that dismissing an employee is fun. It is an unpleasant experience for the one who has to do the terminating. And it is not much better for the individual being let go.

Most employers are really bad at firing employees. Liz recalls an attorney who used the phrase "I'm going to set you free" when she was terminating an employee. This gal's theory was that she was doing the employee a favor by setting him free to pursue career endeavors for which he was better suited. Liz always thought it was just her way of making herself feel better about what is usually just a business decision.

Liz watched another employer doing such a poor job of managing this discussion with an employee who was being discharged that the employee had to ask if he was being let go. That attorney's firing phrase was "Things just aren't working out," which was supposed to be the hint that the employee was being discharged.

When Liz hires someone, she is very thorough in all aspects of the hiring process. So much so that the need to terminate an employee is always due to something that could not have been discovered during the interview process. And that happens rarely. Generally, it is due to something that no one had any way of knowing and something that would not become obvious until they were deep into the employer/employee relationship.

The need to disengage an employee is not an event that suddenly happens one day. It is a process that cultivates itself over time, especially when skills or expertise are so lacking that it makes it impossible for an employee to meet the expectations of the position. Thus, once an employee is in a position, do not only track performance through performance evaluations that involve observations by his direct supervisors. You must also track the employee's accountability through update meetings and timekeeper records.

Sometimes an employee who is having difficulty measuring up to the firm's expectations is willing to work on correcting the problem. You should then invest the time and effort to re-train, educate, and mentor that employee with the goal being to help him develop the skills needed to meet the expectations of the position.

The timetable you should use is between 60 and 90 days. Once you have worked with the employee for a period of time and there has not been a noticeable improvement, the employee will probably know that he will be discharged because he has participated in trying to rectify the situation. Termination actually comes as a relief to the employee who has tried to learn the skills or expertise lacking to perform the duties of his position and is simply unable to do so.

Liz worked with a paralegal a few years ago whom she had interviewed and hired. He came from a large firm that had a reputation for doing volume work. He was articulate and personable, and he said all the right things. When Liz called for a reference, they told her that he was punctual, rarely missed time from work, and was diligent about his duties.

What neither he nor the former employer told Liz was that, although he had the paralegal training and knew what had to be done, his work habits were such that they had to change his job description and narrow the scope of his work to scheduling only. Liz worked with him for three months in an effort to help him develop the skills he needed for the paralegal position for which he had been hired.

At the end of the three months, when she had to fire him, he admitted that he knew he could not perform the work that the firm required. It was particularly difficult to terminate this employee because he had a good attitude, a good work ethic, and was well-liked by the employees of the firm. He had so much integrity right to the very end of his employment with the firm. He not only thanked her for all the efforts she had made, he also shook hands with the senior partner and thanked him for giving him an opportunity to make the position work.

Even in situations when discharge is a relief to an employee who cannot meet the firm's expectations, this is never a pleasant situation. The firm is losing an employee and will spend time, money, and effort, as well as endure another learning curve when it hires a new employee. The now former employee has to deal with the humiliation of being terminated, apply for unemployment benefits, tell their spouse/family, and look for another position.

Before your termination meeting with the employee, prepare for the meeting with the following:

1) Have any COBRA information available so the employee can navigate the system to make sure that he will have health insurance if he can afford it after separation from the firm.
2) Provide the former employee with his final paycheck.
3) Give the employee a written termination letter. This may assist him with securing unemployment benefits or the COBRA benefits.
4) With today's economy and the job market being what it is, if an employee has not stolen from the firm, harmed a client, or performed some act that went against the best interests of the firm, consider bringing a severance check with you to that meeting.

What is the best way to have this conversation with an employee who must be relieved of his position with your firm? Here are some suggestions:

- Obviously, have this conversation in private behind closed doors with the employee. Consider having a witness who you can trust present.

- Do not berate the employee by attacking him with all the things that he has done wrong in his position with the firm. Because he is being terminated, unless this is a downsizing or rightsizing, he knows he has done something to warrant termination. Instead, simply discuss what the employee already knows were performance issues and mention that the remedial efforts he made were appreciated but unfortunately not sufficient to enable him to meet the expectations for the position. Never destroy someone's self-esteem because the position did not work out for the firm.

- Explain that, while the skills that he has do not mesh with the needs of the firm, or that he may have been unable to live up to the performance expectations of the firm, there is likely a position with a firm where his skills would apply that might be better suited to the employer's needs.

- Being very connected to the legal community, Liz suggests other positions within that community that might be better suited to the employee's skill level.

- If the employee has not committed some act that negatively impacted the firm or a client, and your firm can afford it, provide the employee with two weeks' severance pay. For some people who have luck finding jobs or whose salary expectations are at or below the market, these two weeks' severance pay may be enough to carry them through to their next position or until unemployment benefits kick in.

- Consider whether you really want to challenge his claim for unemployment benefits. The amount of compensation provided by unemployment is usually so small an amount compared to a salary, that unemployment is a last resort for some employees. It is really just enough to get by for some people until they can find a job.

  In fact, the percentage of payment for unemployment benefits paid by you as the employer is so small that it is probably not worth the risk of the employee deciding to fight the firm to collect his benefits. We have seen situations like this turn really ugly when the former employee retains an attorney and sues for wrongful termination. Regardless of whether there are actually grounds for the suit, this is a headache that you just don't need.

- Do not allow other employees of the firm to speak badly about the former employee, no matter what. This kind of office politics is inappropriate *regardless* of the reason why an employee was discharged. Things like this get around, and the last thing that a former employee needs is to have gossip spread throughout the legal community that could impede his ability to get another job. Your current employees should know you don't permit such things to be said about a former staff member, not to mention that your firm does not need to be sued for slander.

The transition for the firm is often not an easy one either. Probably never as difficult as it is for the terminated employee, but nevertheless, your firm now has to go through the hiring and training process all over again. Unless the discharge was a spur of the moment decision, and for us it never is, consider beginning the search for a replacement even before the discharge occurs. If you are working with an employee, and, a few weeks into it, it does not look like he will work out, post an ad for the position, and begin reviewing resumes and pre-screening potential candidates.

We have both done this in the past; it gives you an idea of the candidate pool that is out there and what kind of salary and experience is available. Do not rush the process and take just anyone because you need a warm body in the chair. Hiring mistakes are costly, not only in terms of dollars and cents. Terminating the employment can be quite costly, as well.

In the end, the easiest way to avoid having to fire someone is by doing your homework before you ever hire him. Not only should you trust your gut regarding whether you feel the person is a good fit for your firm, but you should also always call his references and perform background checks. There is a wealth of information available on the Internet. Not only can you find out if the person has been arrested, but you can research his social media accounts to get a better idea of his personality.

We also like to have potential job candidates take the Myers-Briggs Type Indicator to make sure that they are a good fit for the rest of the staff at the firm. This is especially important in a small firm where you will spend more time directly with the person and where having a variety of personality types who complement one another is necessary.

CHAPTER TWENTY-SEVEN
HOW TO OUTSOURCE (AND WHY)

Law firm staffing has taken on a very different look from even 10 or 15 years ago. Liz and Joryn both remember law firms not only having a receptionist but also employing a "relief receptionist," as well. (We were never quite sure from what the receptionist needed to be relieved.) Gone are the days when a receptionist could read a book as she waited for a call to come in. Today, a receptionist in a firm must enter time slips, do the mail, and scan or e-file documents with the court—in addition to interacting with clients.

All staff members must be more efficient than ever. No firm can afford the luxury of having someone standing around waiting for the next thing to do. It is not cost-efficient. With today's clients wanting more value for their legal fees, law firms must find ways to provide high-quality services to their clients without draining firm revenues on positions that generate no direct billable hours.

Not long ago, the legal profession frowned upon the concept of virtual, outsourced, or independent contractors. Back in the 1980s, Liz worked as an independent paralegal, and it was difficult to convince attorneys that she would not lose their files. (This was back before firms went paperless.) Firms had so many issues with outsourcing their work, it was difficult to convince them of the benefits.

Now, many positions in law firms are, in fact, virtual, outsourced, and independent contractors. Many firms, especially the solo and smaller ones, are learning to delegate administrative tasks. Lawyers who are performing accounting, writing basic motions, and shopping vendors or supplies are neglecting the important task that lawyers must accomplish: *billing time for their legal services*. Any timekeeper accomplishing work that is non-billable is a waste of the firm's resources.

There are so many ways to outsource both administrative and even legal work in the office because, surprisingly enough, those positions previously held by full-time employees are not necessarily full-time positions when the work is delegated to efficient and productive independent contractors.

Virtual paralegals have become increasingly popular over the years. With remote access and paperless firms, paralegals can gather records and write settlement demands from home. Law firms pay an hourly rate to paralegals who work part-time in positions formerly held by full-time paralegals. The firms pay no benefits, no parking expense, and no taxes, and they do not have to provide a place to work. As an added benefit, because they pay by the hour, they only pay for work that is actually performed. There is no pay for downtime.

As an independent law firm administrator, Liz can work more efficiently and productively for a firm than a full-time administrator employee can working in the office by working just a few hours a week in the attorney's office, and then being available remotely the remainder of the time. For many firms, an administrator is not a full-time position—or a full-time luxury they can afford. Billing, if it is being done correctly, is accomplished once a month. Pre-bills are run and edited, reviewed by the attorney, finalized, and transmitted to the client. Trust funds are transferred, replenishment retainers requested, and client ledgers updated. Payroll is accomplished bi-weekly or semi-monthly. Bills are paid on a schedule, bank accounts reconciled, HR issues handled, etc. Items that must be handled in-office are handled in-office, and everything else can be handled remotely with remote access.

Here are some more benefits of outsourcing law firm work:

You Pay an Hourly Rate Rather Than a Salary

Whether paralegals are paid salary or hourly, they are paid to be in the office even when there is a slow-down in work. Downtime is a loss to the firm, but the paycheck to the paralegal continues. By outsourcing paralegal work that can be accomplished on a subcontracted basis, such as preparing settlement demands, the paralegal is paid on an hourly basis, instead of salaried. In this way, compensation is only for work actually performed.

You Avoid Paying Benefits

These days the cost of benefits is astronomical, but firms continue to offer either 100% paid health insurance and related benefits or they require employees to make a contribution. With outsourced contractors, law firms need not provide benefits because they are not employees of the firm.

You Avoid Paying for Parking and a Workplace

Most cities in our country, especially larger cities, charge for parking these days. With outsourced employees, the firm does not have to pay for parking, nor must it provide a place to work. Because the outsourced employee works remotely, even a law firm that has no space for another employee can add to the productivity by outsourcing work. Increased productivity adds to the bottom line revenues of the firm.

You Have an Extra Attorney When You Need One

Some lawyers today work as independent "appearance" or hearing attorneys, handling specific parts of cases or attending hearings and depositions on a stand-by basis for other attorneys and their firms. This is a cost-efficient way to add a lawyer to your staff when the calendar is booked without incurring an additional regular paycheck. There are lawyers today whose practices consist of working as outsource attorneys. You can establish a regular relationship with an outsource attorney whom you pay only for actual work he performs. He will become familiar with your firm, your clients, and the way your firm operates.

There are precautions you must take to protect your firm and your clients when working with outsourced help. If your firm utilizes outsourced employees, always ensure the following:

1) The fee for the subcontracted work is reasonable. If the outsourcing isn't cost-effective and efficient for the firm, then there is no point. There are rules that differentiate the differences between a contractor and an employee, and individuals interested in outsourcing should familiarize themselves with those regulations to ensure adherence. There have recently been lawsuits (against Uber and Amazon, in particular) brought by contractors who believed they should have been given employee benefits because they were treated as employees, and not as independent contractors.

2) The client is informed and agrees to the relationship with the outsourced employee. This only applies to attorneys, paralegals, or members of the legal team who will be working on client files. Your clients need not approve administrative functions, IT, HR, and payroll.

3) Many outsourced employees work for several firms. Be sure that you know which firms an outsourced lawyer works with. You should not ask him to perform work on a case if another firm with which he works represents a party to the case. And, if it happens, be sure to put up a Chinese Wall to protect the files.

4) Paralegals do not commit the unauthorized practice of law. We have known paralegals over the years who *almost* crossed the line of practicing law, especially when not supervised in the office. Responsibility for this will fall back on your firm.

5) Accountability is still important. A supervisor in your firm should oversee the work of the outsourced contractor and ensure that the quality of work is of the same caliber as the law firm itself requires and performs.

Many firms are still opposed to outsourcing. But given the need to reduce expenses and still provide quality work and representation to clients, outsourcing is a viable and workable option that can be cost-effective.

Not only do law firms profit from outsourcing employees, but the outsourced employees benefit, as well. They are afforded much more flexibility in their work lives and are better able to work as much as they can when they can, even if it is not during the weekday hours between 9:00 a.m. and 5:00 p.m.

Joryn's associate of ten years became an independent contractor for her firm a couple of years ago when she had her first child. Now, she is able to earn a living and stay connected to the legal community while also remaining at home and raising her child. She saves an hour and a half every day because she no longer commutes to the office. It is an ideal relationship for them both because she does not lose out on valuable time with her child, and Joryn still benefits from the diligent work that she originally trained her to do and that she performs for Joryn's firm.

When seeking outsource help, look to your own network. Ask other professionals if they have anyone to recommend. Search professional networking websites like LinkedIn for possible candidates. See whether your professional associations can recommend someone. Like Joryn, consider prior employees who have moved on to different stages of their lives. If all else fails, a professional headhunter or temp agency may be able to provide you with acceptable options.

Regardless of where you find your outsource help, always be honest with them about the kind and amount of work that you will need. The hiring process is just as important for an independent contractor as it is for a salaried employee. Open communication is even more important as you may not work with these individuals on a regular basis, and it may take longer for them to get accustomed to your desires. There is no excuse for sub-par work because your staff is a representation of yourself. But if you find the right folks, you will save money while having more time to focus on other matters and clients.

CLIENTS

CHAPTER TWENTY-EIGHT
HOW TO MANAGE YOUR MARKETING
AND CLIENT DEVELOPMENT

Do you take your watch to your auto mechanic when you need to fix it? No doubt you are shaking your head right now, thinking "What?" Some firms hire someone who knows as little about law firm marketing and client development as your mechanic knows about fixing your watch.

Every aspect of managing a law firm, including marketing and client development, which contribute directly to the bottom line, is different than it is for any other type of business. Some law firms have bigger budgets and more revenue to fund marketing campaigns to bring in new business. Smaller firms often have budgets that are just a fraction of what big firms earmark for marketing. In the larger firms, a marketing manager handles the firm's marketing and client development. The law firm literally throws thousands of dollars a month (sometimes tens of thousands of dollars) towards television and newspaper ads to attract new business. All good when it seems there is an endless budget for that kind of marketing. Not so much when you are a smaller firm.

Some firms, rather than retaining someone with actual law firm experience to develop a true marketing campaign, will hire people who know nothing about law firms. It is always a good idea to find out how much actual law firm experience someone has before you hire him to develop your marketing strategy.

Liz had an interesting experience a few years ago in a law firm that did hourly work for its clients. This attorney worked with a business consultant who had made his mark by working with large corporations unrelated to the legal industry. His suggestion was to pick 20 of the firm's top clients and to send each client a letter thanking them for their business.

As he rambled on about this letter, Liz wondered where he was going with his idea. The very next words out of his mouth were, "To thank you for being such a good client and in the hopes that you will refer us five new clients, enclosed is a $50 gift card to go to dinner as a way to show our thanks for being our client and the consideration of sending us new business." As she sat quietly in her chair, waiting to see how the partner would respond, the first thought that came to mind was that The Florida Bar would not condone that kind of blatant trolling for clients.

Just as she was about to say something, the senior partner slapped both of his hands on the table, shaking his head violently, saying, "No, no, no, that won't work. The bar won't allow it."

That's right; the bar won't allow it. Had this business consultant been a true *law firm* business consultant, he would have known more about the rules and regulations of The Florida Bar.

Here are some things to consider when developing a strategic plan for marketing and client development:

1) IDENTIFY WHAT IS UNIQUE ABOUT YOUR FIRM. There is so much marketing going on these days. Some areas of law are more saturated than others, especially, for example, the area of personal injury. Clients shop law firms just like they shop for anything else. The retailer who offers better value, service, and a superior product is the one who gets the business. Does your firm handle some business litigation matters on a contingency fee basis rather than hourly? Do you have fee structures aside from hourly such as flat fee, value billing, or a combination of flat fee and contingency? Do you have special training or experience that makes you more qualified? For example, are you a lawyer who has a medical degree and who handles medical malpractice cases? Clients are looking for that special something that will make one firm stand out over the rest.

2) IDENTIFY YOUR MARKETING GOALS. This would seem pretty obvious. Your goal is to get more business. But you have to identify what your goals are to achieve them.

3) DECIDE WHO YOUR TARGET MARKET IS. Unless you are a true general practitioner who will take anything that walks through the door (you joke that you practice "door law"), your marketing plan should be developed with the intention of attracting clients in whatever area of law you practice.

4) DETERMINE YOUR BUDGET FOR YOUR MARKETING PLAN. Look at your budget, and decide what percentage of revenues your firm can afford to invest in a marketing plan without shortchanging other expenses. If you prepared a budget at the end of last year, even if you didn't have a marketing strategy in place at the time, you should have allocated revenues for marketing. As we've already mentioned, a firm with no marketing plan will fail. So, budgeting something for marketing is essential.

Finally, like so many other aspects of managing your law practice, do not manage your marketing or client development campaign yourself. That is not your area of expertise. And, financially, it does not make sense to lose precious billable hours to do something that you can assign to a law firm administrator or to someone who is a member of the executive management team of the firm. You can retain someone outside the firm to assist with this, provided that it is an individual with legal experience who can strategize a client development/marketing campaign, write your newsletter, maintain your website, and manage your social media. Make sure it is someone with some law firm experience who will use creative and innovative ideas to help you expand your client base and attract and retain new clients.

Now is a good time to put a strategic marketing plan in place that will help you get the most out of your marketing budget and hedge against the competition. Keep in mind that every satisfied client is the best source for referral of new business. The marketing budget for that is zero.

Before you do anything else, though, consider putting a process in place that actually suggests that your happy clients send you new business. When Joryn completes a case, she always sends the client a "close file letter" thanking the client for the work and asking that he refer his friends and family to the firm. She also requests a testimonial and permission to use the testimonial in her marketing.

When marketing for your law firm, remember Joryn's five fortes of successful legal marketing: pitch, publish, present, profile, and partner.

Pitching allows you to share your vision with potential clients and colleagues.

Publishing frequently on a subject gives the author credibility. Credibility is the ability to write clear and compelling blogs, articles, tweets, and books that people will read, relate to, and share with others. Writing helps you learn and understand your subject better, which again leads to credibility because you will come across as more knowledgeable when you discuss your subject.

When you present often, people begin to think of you as an expert in your field. Also, like publishing, the more that you present, the better you will learn the topics.

Your profile should be conspicuous, visible, and easily identifiable, both online and in traditional media. It should reflect your brand, mission, and vision.

Finally, form strategic alliances with referral sources, with first responders, with colleagues, and with other influencers.

These fortes should be a part of every lawyer's marketing plan.

CHAPTER TWENTY-NINE
HOW TO PREPARE TO GROW YOUR CLIENT BASE

Liz is what amounts to a "solo" practitioner as an independent law firm administrator. She does not have a large staff of her own or high overhead. Her only concern is to provide outstanding administrative services that will help attorneys manage the business of practicing law. In order to do that, she must keep in check the management of her client base and make absolutely sure that she provides each attorney the best possible service so that all of her clients will remain her clients.

Growing her client base without ensuring that she is prepared to continue to provide outstanding services to her existing attorney client base is self-defeating. What is the point of having more clients if she hasn't given enough forethought to how she will continue to give every attorney outstanding service? What happens if she takes on more work than she is prepared to handle and she suddenly has unhappy clients? Every professional knows that once you have lost a client, it is difficult to get them back.

Many law firms want to grow their client bases, and eventually their practices, without developing a strategic plan. You must be sure to continue to give each client outstanding service, not only to attract new clients but also to retain current clients. Retaining current clients is as important, if not more so, than attracting new ones. We have seen many firms whose client bases consisted of a plethora of "one hit wonders." They represent a client once, do not satisfy the client in service or in results, and never see the client again and, worse yet, never obtain a referral.

Many years ago, there was a plaintiff personal injury practitioner in Tampa who was known for having huge client turnover and no repeat business. We always wondered how he stayed in business. Developing a strategic plan on how you will handle new business is as important as your marketing plan. Once your marketing plan starts yielding a return, you must be sure you are prepared to handle the business.

Recently, Liz worked for a firm that had arranged to receive referrals of collections work from another law firm in a very specific area of law in which the firm did not specialize. In the first couple weeks, they received two or three referrals each week. The firm was promised as many as 20 cases a month or more. Before the number of referrals rose even to a total of five or six per week, the partner was preparing to add another attorney and additional support staff to handle the onslaught of cases he was certain were coming his way.

Everyone's first thought was, "Great! Awesome! Additional revenues for the firm and new business." You know what Liz's first thoughts were?

1) How long will it take to get to those 20 or more referrals a month, and how long will it take for them to pay off?

2) When we do get to that many referrals per month, how sustainable will that work be?

3) Will we just receive a rash of new cases and then the business will die off?

4) Do we have all the forms for this kind of practice: letters of representation, collection letters, complaints, discovery, etc.?

5) How long will it take for us to gear up to be ready to efficiently handle these cases, including setting up all the forms and templates?

6) How will we fund the overhead expense of the additional staff until these cases settle and start generating revenues for the firm? (These were contingency cases, which would not pay off anytime soon unless a collection letter did the trick and the defendant settled. The expectation of that happening was remote, at best, so the firm was in for protracted litigation. There would likely be no fees generated until the end of each case.)

7) Where will we put these additional staff members when our office space is nearly full to capacity?

8) Along those lines, because these are referrals, how much revenue will the firm actually realize, considering we are carrying the expense of the additional staff, but paying out a percentage of the fees on referrals?

9) Who in this firm will handle these cases as the area of law is outside the area of specialty of the firm?

As she voiced all of her concerns, Liz's boss thought she was being a bit under-enthusiastic about these referrals. He was quite vocal about the fact that she was not as excited as he was about this new business.

But, although Liz thought, "I'll believe it when I see it," she was not trying to rain on his parade. There were several things that needed to be considered. For her, it was not a question of whether they should accept the referrals, although she was concerned that no one in the firm had any experience in this area of law. She was more anxious about preparing the firm for the potential onslaught of new cases and what would happen when they really *did* need to expand staff. To her, it just made good business sense to consider these things.

The partner, however, was taking care of the practice of law, while she was taking care of the *business of practicing law*. In this situation, they went together, and the business end of things needed to be considered because it was the means to getting the work done.

When client development and marketing strategies do come to fruition, and new business comes to the firm, you must consider the sustainability of the new business. Do not run out and add an attorney and additional staff to handle the influx of new business until it has been sustainable for six to twelve months. Wait until you really get that busy that you are stretched to the point at which you cannot provide good service to your clients without adding someone to the firm's payroll, i.e. when everyone starts putting in 12-hour days, but before people start making mistakes because they are overwhelmed, or when there is a possibility that other clients' work begins to suffer.

Even then, before hiring a new full-time associate to whom you will have to pay a salary and benefits, try to find an independent contractor to help with the overflow from an influx of new work. That way, you will only pay for additional help as you need it, and you will have time to gauge how steady and income-producing the new work will be before committing yourself to new staff.

When you do make the decision that it is time to add new staff to handle the work, add what you need, as you need it. Hiring one attorney to start and another legal assistant makes more financial sense than hiring half dozen additional employees if there is not yet that much work.

If this is a new area of law to the firm, strongly consider hiring someone with experience in that area of law because even an associate and paralegal with similar experience will be very advantageous.

The new business must generate the revenues to cover the added expense of additional staff for the firm to continue to be profitable. If the new business is not generating enough revenues to cover the added overhead costs, and you are spending profits from other areas of your practice, then something is not working. Re-examine the whole process, and identify where there is a breakdown. New business should not be cutting into the existing profits of the firm.

Be sure that your forms and templates are up-to-date and in usable form. Do not allow your staff to find a motion they need, make changes to the old one, and then re-save it. You don't want to miss a name or some other information that your client will be sure to find. Ensure your processes and systems are in place so that the firm can be efficient, productive, and cost-effective. Think through the business aspect of taking on new business. Don't just look at the revenues it will generate. Look at what the cost will be to the firm.

Because the management of the practice of law is a business, an uncomplicated business strategy aimed at expanding your client base and growing your firm will go a long way. Preparing for success will help you achieve it!

A sample retainer agreement is included in Appendix One.

REVIEW QUESTIONS TEN

Lawyers:

1. How do you market yourself so that you get as many good clients as possible? List the ways.
2. Do you have an elevator pitch? How often do you give it? To whom? Give it to someone, NOW! Do so at least once a day.
3. Do you present? How often? To whom? List the presentations you have given in the past year, and to whom you presented. Also, list how you felt before, during, and after each presentation.
4. Do you publish? How often? On what subjects? Brainstorm new subjects on which to publish.
5. Have you written a book? List the books that you have written.
6. Do you blog regularly? List the blogs you have written in the past six months. Brainstorm new topics. Now get writing!
7. Do you write articles for magazines and journals? List the articles you have written in the past year.
8. Do you maintain a social media presence? Do you handle it, or have you hired someone to do it for you? What are the advantages and disadvantages of doing so?
9. On what social media websites do you have pages for your firm and for yourself? List your social media accounts, recording how often you visit each site in the upcoming month. If you are neglecting some of those sites, how can you rectify that?
10. Have you partnered with other professionals in your community? List your partners.
11. How did you determine with whom to partner? List the new partnerships that you would like to develop. Brainstorm ways to establish those new partnerships.
12. Have you ever had a bad partner with whom you had to cut ties? If so, how did you do it? What effects did it have on your reputation? Journal that experience.

Law Students:

1. Have you taken marketing courses in college or law school? If so, do you still have your notes and/or the course book? If you do, take a look at them.
2. Do you know what an elevator pitch is? Have you written one? Have you practiced giving it to people? Write your elevator pitch, and start giving it at least once a day.
3. Are you comfortable presenting? If not, register for a course, like public speaking, so

you become more comfortable presenting.

4. Do you fancy yourself a good writer?

5. Have you written for your Law Review?

6. Have you ever been published? Brainstorm new subjects on which to publish.

7. Do you blog regularly? How often? On what subjects? List the blogs you have written in the past six months. Brainstorm new topics. Now get writing!

8. Do you maintain a social media presence? On what social media websites? List your social media accounts, recording how often you visit each site in the upcoming month. If you are neglecting some of those sites, how can you rectify that?

9. Do you appreciate the importance of partnering with the right types of people to increase your chances of being successful both professionally and personally? List your current partners. List the new partnerships that you would like to develop. Brainstorm ways to establish those new partnerships. List the advantages and disadvantages of partnering.

10. Have you ever had a bad partner, friend, or acquaintance with whom you had to cut ties? If so, how did you do it? What effects did it have on your reputation? Journal that experience.

CHAPTER THIRTY
HOW TO DECIDE TO TURN AWAY A CLIENT

When you are planning and executing your marketing strategy, the goal is to attract potential clients who will convert to paying clients. At no time in developing your marketing strategy does it ever occur to you that one day you will find yourself trying to decide whether to turn away a potential client. Especially if you are a solo or smaller firm practitioner, you may think you need to practice "door law"—that is, take whatever business walks through the door. After all, turning away a client means turning away revenues. Doesn't that seem a little counterproductive?

It takes time to realize a return on the investment of marketing dollars. This is not easy as you sit at your desk, knowing that your firm is spending money to bring in business and you have to wait for a return on those dollars. At some point, however, your marketing strategy starts working. The telephone is ringing and potential clients are calling to schedule consultations and retain your firm. When you enter into a contract with a client to represent him, it is with the implied understanding that you will zealously represent his best interests—no matter what.

Right now, you may be thinking, "Who would ever make the decision to turn away a client? I'll take that client!" Not so fast.

Every client is *not* the perfect client, or more importantly, *the right client*. The client consult is a two-way street. The client interviews you to decide if he wants to retain you. You interview the client to see if you want to be retained and represent him.

There have been times when Liz's attorney clients have taken on representation of a client even though something did not seem quite right. Sometimes, the warning signs can be obvious that a client is going to be a problem client. However, when a client sits in front of you waving a retainer fee and the payroll needs to be paid, it's easier to overlook the warning signs than to turn the client (and his retainer fee) away. You think to yourself that with your lawyer skills and people skills, you will be able to manage the situation and the client's expectations. Everything will be just fine, right? Wrong.

A family who had been in a car accident contacted a personal injury attorney with whom Liz works. The case involved representation of two adults and one minor child. Liz was not involved in the consultation, but after getting involved in the case, she felt that the warning signs of a problem client were apparent, at least to her. The clients had previously been represented by four different attorneys, and they had discharged three of them. The other attorney had terminated representation of the clients. Furthermore, only one of the four prior attorneys had filed a lien in the case against the settlement proceeds. The other three had waived any fee. Just a few months later, the clients became very difficult and unreasonable. They were unwilling to accept offers that were made and were calling, texting, and emailing the attorney during the days, evenings, and weekends. Shortly thereafter, Liz's attorney client was terminated, and the clients moved onto attorney number six.

The best decision you can make is to turn away a client if something doesn't seem right because it may be the best money you never made. There are some warning signs that potential clients may be more trouble than the retainer fee is worth.

1.   The client tells you about the problems he had with his prior attorney or that he has had more than one prior attorney. This is a huge red flag, and it will be one of the first things a client discloses as he describes to you the circumstances of his pending case. Be especially wary of this if you know the current attorney through the profession. What the client tells you may not mesh with what you know about the other attorney. If that is the case, you now know that the client's perception is not always accurate.

2.   The client wants you to do something you consider unethical or a violation of bar rules. Under no circumstances should you ever compromise your ethics or morals to further the interests of a client. Your bar license is an expensive investment, and it took a lot of your time and effort to pass the bar. Never risk your livelihood or your bar license for a client. *Never.*

3.   The client tells you that he has been "lawyer shopping." He has consulted with two or more other attorneys before consulting with you, and none of those lawyers would take the case. Delve into some information about the other attorneys the potential client consulted. If the area of specialty was not quite a match to the client's case, there is some latitude here. If the client tells you that the other lawyers wanted too much money, the fees were too high, or that they wanted a retainer and a cost deposit, these are all indicators that you have a potential problem client sitting across the conference room table from you.

4.   While explaining his case during the consultation, the client is unwilling to hear the advice you are giving or argues the law with you. Clients do not have law degrees; that is the reason the client is sitting in your office. Lay people often have misconceptions about the law or do not interpret the law as well as an attorney for obvious reasons. If after explaining a client's rights to him under the law, he refuses to listen and starts arguing with you about interpretation and what his rights should be, he may be a difficult client to represent. He may be unwilling to listen, to follow court orders, or to participate in his case. This will make it difficult for you to represent them.

5.   The client tells you that he is not worried about how much you will charge to handle his case. The likelihood here is that you are going to have trouble getting paid. People who don't worry about how much legal fees are or how much you are going to charge by the hour will become slow or no payers. Even corporate clients want to know what your hourly rate is, what the retainer will be, what costs are involved, and a projected long-term idea of

how much the case will cost. Anyone who acts like he is not concerned with cost probably isn't because he isn't going to pay you.

6.   You and the client don't seem to click. Personality conflicts that are obvious during a consultation will magnify exponentially during representation. Not everyone can work together. If you spend enough time with a potential client at a consultation and really hear what is being said, you should have a good grasp on whether you can work with this client. First impressions are often quite intuitive, and while you may not know everything about a potential client from a first meeting, you should be able to decide whether you can work together. If you realize there is a personality conflict, you are doing yourself and the client a disservice by accepting representation. Better to turn away the client than have to figure out how to withdraw from the case later on.

7.   If the client's situation is something that is outside the area of expertise of your firm, refer the client to another attorney. To be successful in this competitive market, it is best to find an area of law and specialize in it. The "jack of all trades, master of none" general practitioner is rare. The demands of the client require that you provide high-caliber legal services in your specialty area and that you do it efficiently and cost-effectively. No matter how badly you might need that retainer check, refer the client to someone who specializes in that particular area. Getting a referral fee is better than taking on a case in an unfamiliar area and risking harming the client and yourself if the client files a Bar grievance.

8.   The client does not have the money to pay you. When you have a potential client sitting across from you and you ask for a $2,500 retainer, the client winces. He tells you that his last attorney terminated representation because he did not have more funds after paying the initial retainer fee. He tells you he is broke, that he can pay something in two weeks when he gets paid, or asks if you will take weekly payments or will take the case on a contingency. No one wants to work for free. If you are willing to enter into some kind of alternate fee arrangement with a client, make sure you are willing to wait it out until you get paid, possibly never. A reduced hourly fee agreement with a contingency component is not that unheard of today. However, do not just consider the retainer that you are going to receive when the client cuts a check. Consider the hours that you will have to put in, the staff that you will have to pay who will work on this case rather than working on another paying client's case, and dealing with the client when that retainer runs out. Consider all the time you will be working towards a settlement offer so the client will settle and you can get paid. Remember, too, that settling a case is always at the client's discretion, not yours. You will be at the mercy of the client to accept a settlement offer that will result in fees to your firm. If a client does not want to settle, no matter how hard you work on convincing him to settle, it will still be the client's decision. The client will not take into account the fact that you have been working and waiting to be paid. The client will do what is in his best interests, and if you really try to sell him on the idea of settling, he may try to renegotiate the fee to give you even less money. In the end, you may, in fact, agree to reduce your percentage just to get the case settled. By the time all is said and done, you will be surprised at how much representing this client has cost

FROM LAWYER TO LAW FIRM: HOW TO MANAGE A SUCCESSFUL LAW BUSINESS

your firm.

9.   The client is dishonest or has done something dishonest. Clients are very savvy today and they all know about attorney/client privilege. During a consultation, a client may feel safe discussing with you something that he has done which is dishonest or vindictive. Generally speaking, if this is something he has done once, his honesty filter may not be working well, and there is no guarantee that he will not do something dishonest or even vindictive again in the future. Next time, you may be the target. Stay focused on the ethics and morals of a potential client. Do not put yourself in the position where you are ethically bound to keep your client's dirty little secrets. It will impede your ability to represent him because his actions are against your moral compass.

10. The client has unreasonable expectations. Ask the right questions at the consultation. Come right out and ask the client what his expectations are and what he wants to accomplish. Some clients want payment of attorneys' fees to be part of their compensation in a case, even when statutes or case law don't provide for attorneys' fees. A client might want a business that wronged him to be put out of business. In all likelihood, that is not going to happen. You have to manage a client's expectations throughout the representation. If at the consult, it is obvious that the client's expectations are more than the law will ever allow, this may not be a good fit. It is always a good practice to under promise and over deliver. This is a recipe that will never fail.

The negativity of representing a difficult client will impact you, your staff, and indirectly, the work for other clients. The stress and time involved in representing a difficult client, regardless of his ability to pay, will be counterproductive, both financially and emotionally. So, while the decision to turn a client away is not an easy one, it may be a financially sound decision for your firm.

CHAPTER THIRTY-ONE
HOW TO AVOID THE ACCIDENTAL ATTORNEY-CLIENT RELATIONSHIP

In this book, we cover many of the issues that are obviously implicated when it comes to law firm administration, issues that include accounting errors, ineffective marketing, staff management and retention, and the like. But one issue that is often overlooked in books on law firm administration is that of the accidental attorney-client relationship.

What *is* the accidental attorney-client relationship? This is a relationship that forms with a potential client when the consult leaves the attorney's office mistakenly believing that the lawyer has taken his case. The key to this inadvertent relationship is that the attorney-client relationship has commenced in the understanding of the client, therefore imposing certain professional responsibilities on that attorney.

But, you ask, "How can that be? If the potential client has only paid a consult fee, or sometimes, not even that, and has signed no retainer agreement, how is this possible?"

Unfortunately, it is. So how does one determine that the attorney-client relationship has commenced?

Restatement (Third) of The Law Governing Lawyers §14 (ALI 2000), states:

> [A] relationship of client and lawyer arises when (1) a person manifests to a lawyer the person's intent that the lawyer provide legal services for the person; and either (a) the lawyer manifests to the person consent to do so; or (b) the lawyer fails to manifest lack of consent to so do, and the lawyer knows or reasonably should know that the person reasonably relies on the lawyer to provide the services . . . .

So, okay; that's not so bad, is it? That seems like a pretty simple test to overcome. Well, maybe not.

In Florida, one court explained,

> [T]he test for determining the existence of the fiduciary relationship is a subjective one and hinges upon the client's belief that he is consulting a lawyer in that capacity and his manifested intention is to seek professional legal advice.

Bartholomew v. Bartholomew, 611 So.2d 85 (Fla. 2d DCA 1992).

Is it possible that an attorney-client relationship can sometimes be created purely in the mind of the client? If so, the attorney can then be held liable for his failure to act on behalf of the client, usually in the form of missed deadlines and the expiration of the statute of limitations, unless he can show that he specifically told the client that he had not been retained.

So, no written retainer agreement is necessary to form the attorney-client relationship. Surprisingly, there are plenty of cases that demonstrate that a formal retainer agreement or engagement letter is not required in order for the attorney-client relationship to commence. In one such instance, the court held that an attorney-client relationship can be created through just an initial interview between a prospective client and an attorney.

As with any legal issue, there are also countervailing cases that hold that the commencement of the attorney-client relationship occurs only when both the attorney and the client have consented to the relationship. These courts explain that the relationship is contractual in nature and can only be commenced by a retainer agreement or a fee being paid to the attorney. These cases make it seem that the attorney-client relationship must exist in the mind of the attorney *and* the client and there must be a document or a fee paid to represent the commencement of the relationship.

Thus, contrary to popular belief, the lack of a signed retainer agreement or engagement letter may not be determinative of whether the attorney-client relationship exists. But what about the failure to pay a retainer fee? Can an attorney-client relationship exist even when no fees have been paid to the attorney by the client?

Sadly, the answer is "yes." In most instances, the client's failure to pay the attorney a fee does not necessarily mean that an attorney-client relationship has not commenced. In explaining this policy, the Florida Supreme Court stated that "if a fee were required to establish an attorney-client relationship, a lawyer could never perform work *pro bono* for a client." *Florida Bar v. King*, 664 So.2d 925 (Fla. 1995). Additionally, in certain cases, such as a personal injury case taken on a contingency fee, a client may not be required to pay any fees up front and the attorney-client relationship can certainly still be commenced.

All of the foregoing scenarios might combine (i.e. the relationship has formed in the client's mind, no retainer has been signed, and no fees have been paid), and an attorney-client relationship might still commence. So how can your firm avoid the pitfalls and potential malpractice associated with the accidental attorney-client relationship?

1) After every consultation with a potential client, explain and ask the client to execute a document (the "not retained" form) that clarifies that the client has not retained the law firm to represent him. The "not retained" form should also indicate that, should the potential client subsequently decide to retain the law firm, a written retainer agreement or engagement letter must be executed by both the potential client and the lawyer and, if appropriate, the client must pay a fee before representation commences. Provide a copy of the "not retained" form to the consult prior to his departure, and maintain it with your potential client files or conflict management files. See Appendix Two for a sample "not retained" form.

2) If you consult on the phone and cannot have the consult execute the "not retained" form, then send him a letter that indicates that your representation will only commence after he signs a retainer agreement/engagement letter and, if appropriate, pays a fee. Again, maintain a copy of the correspondence in your potential client files or conflict management files.

3) If you have advised a current client on an issue unrelated to the matter for which the client retained you, then send a "not retained" letter to the client regarding the unrelated issue. Such correspondence should specify the issue discussed and reiterate that the client has not retained the law firm to represent the client in the matter.

4) *Avoid* providing "casual" legal advice to clients, friends, family, and strangers. A two-minute phone call from a family friend regarding their son's DUI arrest can result in the commencement of the attorney-client relationship. An offhand remark at a cocktail party regarding a legal dispute in which the host was involved can create the attorney-client relationship.

Be aware of the possibility of creating an accidental attorney-client relationship. Be mindful of the casual legal advice you might provide in your everyday life. Arm your law firm with the tools necessary to protect you from any liability associated with the accidental attorney-client relationship; put a "not retained" form in your arsenal, and stash a stack of them in a convenient place where you usually conduct your consultations. Ensure that your staff is aware to follow up on your phone consultations with a not-retained letter.

Chapter Thirty-Two
How to Ensure Clients Feel Welcome

Consulting with a lawyer is one of life's biggest stressors. This is especially true for someone who has never needed a lawyer before. It does not matter why he is in your office.

While you cannot do much to change the way a client feels about having to be in your office, there is a great deal your firm, including your staff, can do to make the visit a pleasant one and to reduce some of the stress. It will not only put the client at ease but it will also make it a better experience and make it more likely he will tell his friends and family.

The appearance of your office makes a first impression and sets the tone for the client as he walks through the door. The décor is important. Your office should not be sterile and antiseptic feeling. Make sure the furniture in the reception area is comfortable. Sit on it! If you don't think it's comfortable to sit on for five minutes, your clients will not think it's comfortable if they have to sit on it for 15 or 20 minutes. Some clients tend to come early because they are unsure of how to get there or find parking. And sometimes lawyers run five or ten (or more) minutes late.

While on the subject of sitting in the reception area, you should offer a variety of reading materials for visitors. It is certainly appropriate to have pamphlets about the firm and to provide clients with reading materials on successes you have had or the ways the firm has helped the community. You want potential clients to know as much about the firm as possible so they will feel they are hiring the right attorney for them.

If you plan to have magazines and newspapers for clients to read while they wait, make sure they are current. What would you think if you went to someone's office and wanted to read something while you waited, only to find a magazine that was out-of-date by more than a year? Your first thought would probably be, "How hard is it to keep your reading material up-to-date so it's interesting while I have to sit here and wait? And if you can't pay attention to that, what else are you neglecting?"

There is a lot to be said for office plants. Many of us never think about that, especially if we're not plant people (mostly because we cannot keep them alive). Thankfully, silk plants and flowers were invented for those of us who have brown thumbs. Live plants are preferable, but if that does not work for your office, silk plants are a good option.

Liz once worked for a firm where the senior partner brought fresh flowers every Monday morning for the reception area. Combined with silk plants, fresh flowers are a nice bright touch that brings some life to the office. Plus, if they are cared for during the week, they should last until Friday. Make sure to remove them when they reach the point at which "they've seen better days," even if they don't make it until Friday. Dead flowers give the wrong impression.

Staffing also affects your environment. Hire a receptionist who loves her job! We cannot emphasize enough that the receptionist is truly your "director of first impressions." A happy-to-be-here receptionist sends all kinds of positive messages to your clients. It tells them you have hired an enthusiastic person who wants to help them and who is happy to be working there.

The same firm with the fresh flowers at one time had the most wonderful receptionist Liz had ever met. She was so positive, so kind to the clients, and really took care of each and every one of them. On the occasions when clients had to wait, sometimes up to 30 or 45 minutes because the lawyer was delayed in court, the clients did not care. The receptionist talked to them the entire time they were there, brought them coffee or other refreshments, soothed their stress, and kept them informed of the status of the delay. Liz went out to the reception area once because she knew clients had been waiting an extraordinarily long time, and they told her, "Oh, we don't mind at all. Your receptionist is keeping us entertained, and we just love talking to her!"

Be sure to have refreshments like coffee, tea, fruit juice, water, and soda on hand for clients while they wait. One or two bowls in the reception area of hard candy or even fresh fruit is also a nice touch. When the fruit starts to turn, make sure someone throws it out.

Inviting smells put people at ease. When Liz and her husband were selling their home, Liz would make a pot of vanilla coffee and bake a few loaves of banana bread whenever they had a showing. In the rooms where the smells did not penetrate, she placed vanilla or other scented candles. In the winter, they turned on the fireplace. Even though the coffee was always made for the aroma, there was that one person who actually asked for a cup of coffee—and he and his wife bought the house! We love the smell of lightly scented candles, and your clients will too, even if they're not consciously aware of the scent in the air.

Working in the legal profession is stressful for your employees, too. You must do an exceptional job of vetting employees who will interact with your clients. Being frustrated at their desks and feeling pressured to get work done and to meet time deadlines is one thing. Meeting a client and giving off a vibe of "Hurry up, I have work to do and you are wasting my time!" is a sure-fire recipe to lose clients. If you think clients don't or won't know when your staff feels that their time is being intruded on, you are mistaken. Help your staff be mindful of the fact that the clients are the reason why they all have jobs.

If you hire staff who do not have good people skills and who cannot shield your clients from the stress and pressure they are feeling, then you must employ new staff. Don't think, however, that it is easy for a staff member to change her ways. It is hard for anyone to change her personality. That kind of attitude towards your clients will cause your firm to lose clients. Unhappy clients talk—a lot.

Many attorneys we know do not concern themselves with client comfort or how the client feels about the office. A lawyer's primary concern is those precious billable hours. We get that. Anyone in management gets that, and anyone who wants a paycheck should get that. But making your clients feel welcome and at ease in your office is actually a continuation of your marketing plan.

Your marketing plan does not end when the client calls your office, makes an appointment, or comes in for a consultation. Your marketing plan morphs itself over the course of the attorney/client relationship. Having a signed retainer agreement does not guarantee that the attorney/client relationship will last forever.

To sustain a successful practice, you must build an ongoing relationship with each client that survives long after the retainer agreement is signed. Think of this as a marriage. Having been happily married for many years—with our share of ups and downs—we can tell you that a marriage takes work every single day.

Do not ever take the attorney/client relationship for granted. Never allow your clients to feel unwelcome in your office or like they are intruding on the firm's time. If you make your clients feel welcome when they come to your office and like they matter, they will remain clients.

In Joryn's own small firm, if her associates or paralegals are meeting with a client and she is not needed, she still makes the effort to poke her nose in to say "hello" and to share a brief conversation with the client. Clients must feel like you value them, and this small gesture goes a long way.

Also, Joryn, like many of Liz's clients, brings her dog to work with her. Hachi (short for "Hachiman," which means "divine protector," in Japanese) does indeed provide comfort to many of Joryn's clients. You would be amazed at her ability to get the toughest of clients to open up as she sits on their laps while they pet her, soothing themselves and spilling their most personal goals and interests to Joryn, a necessary aspect of the divorce practice Joryn runs.

You might not feel comfortable setting the ambiance for your office and making the environment stress-free and inviting. However, it is important for your clients to feel welcome, so delegate this task to someone who has a talent for it.

CHAPTER THIRTY-THREE
HOW TO MAKE A GOOD FIRST IMPRESSION

As the saying goes, you never get a second chance to make a first impression. Therefore, it's important to consider what judgment calls your clients are making about your firm's efficiency and professionalism based on their first impression of you, your staff, and your office.

Balancing a client's perception of your firm's success and its competency can be a double-edged sword. Back in the early 1980s, Liz asked a partner if he thought it was time to replace his worn-out briefcase because it was looking a little shabby. He responded that clients thought his worn briefcase meant that he worked hard, and, if he bought a new briefcase, it might make clients think he was not very busy because his briefcase looked so unused.

Somewhere there is a fine line on which you can balance a client's perception with reality. First impressions do matter to clients, and, if you think a client will overlook anything, the only person you are fooling is yourself.

A few years ago, Liz was the administrator for a law firm in New Port Richey. The firm only did hourly work. As a result, the senior partners were always very conscious of the appearance of the office and how the staff was dressed. In fact, the somewhat timeworn policy and procedures manual stated that women were not allowed to wear pants suits in the firm's dress code.

There were one or two staff members who were always campaigning for "Casual Friday." But Liz's first problem with Casual Friday is that it starts out as Casual and turns into Sloppy. The second problem is that the firm had an "open door" policy with its clients, and the clients knew they were always welcome to drop by. The senior partners were rather old school and believed that hourly clients did not want to see the staff in Casual Friday attire.

Good intentions on the part of the staff to wear nice dark, washed jeans with shoes and a shirt and blazer will, in a few weeks, become torn jeans, sneakers, tank tops, t-shirts, and even worse—flip-flops. Liz once had a potential employee show up for an interview wearing flip-flops. Liz's initial reaction was, if she is wearing flip-flops to the interview, what happens next?

There are several ways to leave a good first impression with your clients that will matter in a big way and that will affect whether you can attract and retain them.

1) Clean up your desk. Disorganized stacks of paper and clutter will not impress a client. It will likely make him wonder how you can possibly

manage his case if you cannot keep your desk organized. A client who is tech savvy may believe that the reason you have such a cluttered desk, besides being disorganized, is that you are not tech savvy. Clients know that many companies, not just law firms, are becoming "paperless." How do you explain the mess on your desk if your firm is paperless?

2) Take a look at the reception area. Make sure that your receptionist always looks and acts professionally. The way that your receptionist speaks to clients on the phone and to visitors in the office will leave a very distinct impression.

3) Give your office décor a second look. Thirty or forty years ago, law firms had heavy mahogany or oak furniture, leather sofas and chairs, and artwork with meaning that was worth collecting. Those days are gone. Your office décor should reflect that the firm is successful but not so successful that clients wonder how expensive it will be to hire you. On the other hand, avoid the eclectic "I got my furniture at a yard sale or flea market" look.

4) Is the furniture comfortable and inviting? Not sure? Go out there and sit on it for a while. Sit on it for as long as clients will wait in your reception area to be seen by someone. If the furniture is not comfortable enough for you to sit on for a reasonable period of time, get new furniture.

5) Show nothing. Confidentiality is very important to clients. If there are confidential client documents left out in the open and unattended, especially if the receptionist leaves her desk or if clients have to walk by work areas to get to your office conference room, the client will question whether her own confidentiality will be protected by your firm. Make it a policy that papers and files are kept out of sight of clients.

6) Dress for success. This applies to both your lawyers and your staff. While many law firms are now "business casual," ensure no one forgets about the "business" part. In some firms, that means that khakis and a jacket are acceptable business casual dress.

Liz worked at a law firm years ago in which the senior partner forgot that he was scheduled to meet with clients and was walking around the office without wearing his jacket. His clients showed up for their appointment. Because they saw him, he greeted them and then said, "Let me get my jacket." The clients, of course, said not to worry about it, but the partner replied, "No, you are paying me to be your lawyer, and you should get a lawyer." He came back with his suit jacket.

First impressions do matter. Even if a client does not outwardly react to a loud and messy reception area, a disorganized desk, and jeans and a polo shirt, he is subconsciously formulating an opinion of you and your law firm. Call it "lawyer profiling." Should clients judge a lawyer or his firm on appearances and relate that to the kind of service he will provide? Probably not. But when you are trying to attract and retain new clients, why risk it?

As we have mentioned, Joryn practices primarily family law. Clients are understandably very nervous when they come to see her for the first time. It is likely that they have never needed to hire a lawyer before. Not only are they sad and stressed about their personal issues, but they may be intimidated by the idea of meeting with an attorney. Rather than wear stuffy business suits, she and her staff dress more casually to put them at ease. Women wear dresses or slacks, and men wear khakis and polos. The more comfortable we can make a consult, the more readily the client will open up about her personal matters, and the better we can guide her.

Nevertheless, our "casual" attire is stringently enforced. We don't allow torn jeans, shorts, bathing suit tops, low-cut blouses, etc. So, if "relaxed" is the rule, be sure to define what "relaxed" is and everyone will be happy.

CHAPTER THIRTY-FOUR
HOW TO ANSWER THE PHONE

A significant percentage of law firms invest large sums of money on client development and marketing—be it online through social media, through the firm's website, via television advertising, or otherwise. The universal goal among these firms is to encourage potential clients to pick up the telephone and to schedule appointments to procure the firms' services. Do you think that's the end of a successful marketing plan? Do you think that attaining that initial phone call to obtain services marks the termination of your successful marketing plan? If you do, this might be a good time to rethink your marketing strategy and to relearn at what point your marketing plan really ends.

When *does* your marketing plan end? The truth is that your marketing plan continues throughout the entire representation of your client, and beyond—hence, your marketing strategy is never really over. The marketing strategy simply changes direction as it morphs into the client retention strategy of your plan.

Retention is the marketing that takes place after the initial telephone call, after the client comes into your office, and after she signs your retainer agreement. What happens between the time when a potential client calls your office and when she signs your retainer agreement can mark your marketing strategy a complete success or a total failure.

In other words, the way your firm's phone is answered can make or break your marketing plan.

The staff member primarily responsible for answering the phone for your firm should *never* sound as if he has been interrupted from doing something more important than answering the phone. He should not sound overstressed or be unable to connect with the caller. If he does, he is impeding a crucial element necessary to bringing your marketing plan full circle.

The prospective client on the phone does not want to talk to someone who:

1) Is distracted because he is doing something else or is unfriendly;
2) Forgets the client's name while he is speaking to the client or doesn't address the client by name during the conversation;
3) Doesn't know how to transfer a call without disconnecting the client;
4) Doesn't know how to schedule a consultation; or
5) Takes too long to answer the phone, causing the call to be sent to voicemail.

These all give the caller the impression that her phone call just isn't that important. If her first call isn't that important, she will wonder how important her case is to the firm. The call will end with the client deciding not to schedule an appointment, or, worse, not showing up for the appointment she managed to schedule.

What just happened here? All the time and money invested in the marketing strategy designed to get new clients to call was wasted. That person will never call back. She will probably also tell her friends about her experience with your firm.

Here are three things that you can do to ensure that, when your phone rings, the caller knows how important her call is:

1) Write a script of how you want the phone answered; include what to do, what to say, and what information the receptionist must obtain from the caller.

2) Require the person who is primarily responsible for answering the phone to run through the script several times, and make sure he does not sound like he is reading what he is saying.

3) Call the office yourself (block the number or call from another phone), and verify how your staff handles the call.

An example of the ideal way to answer the phone:

> *Good morning/afternoon. Thank you for calling the _____ law firm. This is Sandy Jackson. How may I help you?*

A lot of positive information is conveyed in that greeting. The name of the firm, the name of the person with whom the caller is speaking, and that the firm wants to help the caller. Even if your firm has caller ID and you know that Jim Smith is calling, the receptionist should answer the phone the same way every time. After a potential new client is identified, the person answering the phone should record the client's full name and telephone number. When asking for this information, Liz always adds, "just in case we get disconnected."

Callers often ask receptionists for legal advice or for their opinions about a case. Ensure that your receptionist knows how to politely divert this type of inquiry.

Joryn gives her receptionist a script of how she would like him to answer the phone and how to respond to many frequently asked questions. Every so often, she will conduct training for everyone in the office on this script, to ensure that everyone is on the same page and answers the phone the same way. Her staff has become so good at explaining the seven courtless divorce options to a caller that, by the time the prospective client comes into the office for her consult, she already knows all about her process choices.

In addition:

1) Ensure that the phone is always answered during business hours. If the phone rings more than three times because the person primarily

responsible for answering the phone cannot pick it up, tell everyone that they must pitch in to pick up that phone. If there is a live person in office to answer the phone, don't let it go to voicemail. When someone calls a business during the day and is sent to voicemail, he will often hang up without leaving a message, and usually, won't call back. He will also assume that, if he cannot reach a live person during business hours, the chances that he will reach someone at night or on the weekend if he must speak with someone right away are slim to none.

2) Pay attention to the way the phone is answered in your office. Listen to what your employee says to a caller and what her demeanor is. Does she convey to the caller that his telephone call is the most important thing she has to do at that moment? Make sure that she does. At that moment, that call is the most important thing to the client, and the only thing that matters is the client's perception.

3) Train the person answering the phone to do what she can to turn prospective client calls into new client consultations. Do not make a client wait more than 48 hours to come in to see an attorney if scheduling permits. If it is not possible to have the client come in within 48 hours, you must get on the phone and talk to the client before his consultation. While clients understand that a firm has more than one client, for most, there is a sense of urgency. If you cannot accommodate them and they are really desperate for advice or to retain someone to help them, they will keep dialing until they find someone who can see them sooner rather than later.

Once a prospect becomes a client, the telephone is still an important marketing tool. Liz will answer the phones for some of the attorneys for whom she works when the phones are exceptionally busy and she knows the person tasked with answering the phone is tied up with someone. So does Joryn. When current clients we have come to know call the firm, we both make sure to do more than perfunctorily answer the phone. We inquire how they are and how their family is doing. Clients want to know that your firm cares about them—everything about them—not just their case or their money. It makes clients feel that they have a special relationship with the firm, and it goes a long way toward building a good attorney/client relationship with that client.

On a client's contact page, record notes about the names of his spouse and children, his special interests, etc. That way, when a client calls, the receptionist will be able to mention specific personal details as though she is remembering them by heart if, in fact, she cannot.

Anyone who answers your law firm's telephone really is the "director of first impressions" at that moment. We cannot say it enough, and this applies to every area of your practice that involves client contact, *you never get a second chance to make a first impression.* Make sure your firm's first impression is the right impression.

ROLE PLAY FOUR:
HOW TO ANSWER THE PHONE

Players: Narrator
            Lawyer
            Receptionist

Scene I

Narrator: Lawyer discusses with Receptionist the importance of answering the phone correctly when a potential client calls.

Lawyer: Hello, Receptionist. I hear you've been doing a wonderful job your first couple of days, and now that my trial's over, I wanted to discuss with you our office protocol for answering the phone, especially when a potential client calls to schedule a consultation.

Receptionist: Thank you. I'm happy to follow the firm procedures. No one gave me any input until now.

Lawyer: Clients are our most important asset. The firm spends a lot of time and money on marketing strategies and without our clients, we are nothing. When a client calls the office after seeing one of our ads or browsing our website, the goal is to get a consultation scheduled. We want to get the client into the office through the telephone call and get her to sign a retainer agreement. So the way you answer that initial phone call can make or break us.

Receptionist: I understand.

Lawyer: When answering the phone, no matter how busy you are, never sound like you have been interrupted from doing something more important than answering the phone. Although it may be difficult, never sound overstressed or unable to connect with the caller.

Receptionist: That makes sense. I always try to sound welcoming. I know that it is often hard for someone to call a lawyer, so I try to make it as easy on them as possible.

Lawyer: That is terrific. Remember that the client on the phone does not want to talk to someone who is distracted because he is doing something else or is unfriendly. You are the first representative of this firm that a potential new client talks to so the way you respond to the client means everything and will make all the difference.

It's important to call the client by her name once she has introduced herself. This shows her that you are paying attention and that she matters. If it's the first time she has called, write down the name immediately, and confirm that you got it and the spelling of it right. Take notes (preferably on the computer) during the conversation so that you can "remember" what the caller told you the next time she calls.

And make sure that you understand how to transfer calls without disconnecting the client. Do you already know how to do that?

Receptionist: Yes.

Lawyer: Never give the caller the impression that her phone call isn't important. If her first call isn't that important, she will wonder how important her case will be to the firm. The call will end with the client not scheduling an appointment. Once a client hangs up without scheduling an appointment, it is unlikely that we will ever hear from her again.

Receptionist: Okay.

Lawyer: (handing a paper to Receptionist) I have written this script that you should follow when someone calls. You can see that I have included how I want you to answer the phone, what to do, what to say, and what information you should get from the caller. Please run through the script several times first thing in the morning so that you don't sound like you're reading it.

Receptionist: (reading script) Okay. This is a lot to remember, but I'm sure that with practice, I'll have no problem with it.

Lawyer: Never take too long to answer the phone. Calls should not be sent to voicemail because then that potential client might just call another attorney, and we could lose our chance with her. Please don't allow the phone to ring more than three times. I understand that is not always possible to get to it that quickly, so everyone in the office knows that if they hear your phone ring more than three times and you are unavailable, they will need to pitch in and answer the phone.

If there is a live person in office to answer the phone, it should never go to voicemail. I don't know about you, but when I call a business during the day and get voicemail, I hang up without leaving a message. And, usually, I never call back. If I cannot reach a live person during business hours, what are the chances I will reach someone at night or on the weekend if I need to speak with someone right away? Do you know what I mean?

Receptionist: I do. I'm the same way.

Lawyer: Always come across to the caller like her telephone call is the most important thing you have to do at that moment. Because, at that moment, that is the most important thing to the client, and the only thing that matters is the client's perception.

Receptionist: I always try to do that. I agree that it is so important.

Lawyer: Good! You should do what you can to turn new client calls into new client consultations. Do not make a client wait more than 48 hours to come in to see me if in any way scheduling permits.

Receptionist: Okay. But what if that's just not possible? Lawyers get really busy.

Lawyer: Good question. If it is not possible to have the client come in within 48 hours, set a time for me to at least talk with the potential client before her consultation on the telephone. I'm always happy to do an *initial,* initial consult on the phone.

Remember, if she is really desperate for advice or to retain someone to help her, she will keep dialing until she finds someone who can see her sooner rather than later. We want to avoid her reaching out to another attorney.

Receptionist: That makes sense. Is there anything I should do differently once the client retains us?

Lawyer: Once a potential consult becomes a client, the telephone is still an important marketing tool. Make sure to do more than perfunctorily answer the phone and transfer the client. Inquire how she is and how her children are. Make sure you know, or can have at your fingertips, the crucial information about this client's personal matters, whatever's relevant to her, whether it's her parents, her kids, her business and whether it's about her health, problems in school, or the new office admin she just hired.

And you should know what *is* relevant to her. Clients want to know that we care about them – everything about them – not just their case or their money. It makes clients feel like they have a special relationship with the firm, and it goes a long way toward building a good attorney/client relationship with that client.

Receptionist: Okay, I can do that!

Lawyer: Just remember that, as our receptionist, you are the "director of first impressions" at that moment. You never get a second chance to make a first impression.

Scene II

Narrator: Lawyer calls the office, blocking the number, to see how Receptionist answers the phone.

Receptionist: (phone rings twice) Good morning. Thank you for calling Johnson Law. This is Receptionist. How may I help you?

Lawyer: Hi, Receptionist. My name is Susie Smith. I caught my husband cheating last weekend, and we need to get divorced.

Receptionist: Hi, Susie. I am sorry to hear that. We can certainly help you with that, as long as there is no a conflict of interest. What is your husband's name?

Lawyer: His name is Scott Smith.

Receptionist: Okay. I do not believe there is a conflict of interest, but I will make sure after we finish talking. Let's not talk about your situation until I make sure there's no conflict. In the meantime, let me get some basic information from you. Is that ok?

Lawyer: Well, I want an attorney representing my interests, which is why I am calling. I have a friend who recommended your firm. But I need to see a lawyer right away. I want to know my rights!

Receptionist: Okay, Susie. I'll schedule a consultation for you with Lawyer regarding all of your options. Are you available to come in this afternoon or tomorrow?

Lawyer: I can come in this afternoon. That's great that the attorney can see me so quickly.

Receptionist: Well, our clients are a priority. I'll set your appointment for this afternoon at 2:00. We'll see you then!

Scene III

Narrator: Lawyer meets with Receptionist again.

Receptionist: Lawyer, we had a new client call this morning while you were in court, Susie Smith. She wanted an appointment right away, and you were available at 2 pm today, so I scheduled her to come in.

Lawyer: Receptionist, I don't know if you realized it, but I was the potential client, Susie, who called in this morning.

Receptionist: Oh, wow, I didn't even realize it!

Lawyer: Well, you did a great job. You answered the phone just as I hoped you would. You made a great impression and made the client feel like she was important. Great job!

Receptionist: Thanks!

Lawyer: You can clear that appointment from the calendar for this afternoon.

CHAPTER THIRTY-FIVE
HOW TO GIVE YOUR CLIENTS A LITTLE EXTRA

The legal market is very competitive, and some law firms spend more money on advertising than other firms earn. Client marketing and development is obviously important because you must attract new clients. After you do, however, the question for the client becomes "What can you offer me that I cannot get anywhere else? And how much will it cost?"

It really does come down to how does your firm can stand out. The nuts and bolts of handling a case—any case—are virtually the same. The process is the same no matter what attorney the client retains. Set aside the process, and perhaps the years of experience or skill level of the attorney, and this is where the similarities end.

Clients are looking for value in their legal representation. With the right firm, they can find it. Even large corporations with seemingly bottomless pockets are looking for value for their legal fee dollar. Clients for whom legal fees are inconsequential are looking for value. Value billing and flat fee billing are becoming more prevalent because many clients cannot afford huge legal fees, and sometimes, they do not feel they are justified.

Here are three important things that you can incorporate into your law practice that will enable your firm to give your clients value:

- BE EFFICIENT. Do not reinvent the wheel every time you handle a case that is similar to one you have handled before. As already mentioned, ensure that your forms are in order, up-to-date, easily retrievable, and ready for immediate use. No one in your office should have to read through forms and remove other clients' or parties' names, change statutory time periods or amounts, etc. If your forms contain information from other cases, your forms are not ready for use. Using forms this way leaves a lot of room for error in the name of a party, or an amount, or other pertinent information. Even if your staff misses it, you can be sure that your client won't. This is a big time-waster, and your client does not want to pay because your firm cannot function efficiently.

Along those lines, all aspects of the procedures of handling a case should be *pro forma* and your staff should know what they are. File a lawsuit, get an answer, do discovery, set depositions, set a mediation, etc. Make sure all information for calling court reporters, contacting opposing counsel, and setting hearings is easily accessible for everyone.

If your procedures are a little scattered and you have not been able to fine-tune them so that you are efficient, consider getting some help with legal project management. Also, ensure that your technological systems are integrated into your workflow in a manner that helps alleviate stress and ensure productivity.

- KEEP THE CLIENT INFORMED. Give clients personal service. While every client would like to win every case, they do know it is not always possible. In fact, they sometimes know that their case is not winnable, but for whatever reason, want to bring it anyway. The "giving the client something extra" here is keeping him informed every step of the way. Make it as simple as e-mailing or snail-mailing the client a copy of pleadings or any correspondence prepared or received.

This process adds almost no additional work but can go a long way to keeping the client informed. Send regular status letters or e-mails to the client. When the information highway to the client becomes predictable, clients feel they are getting value and that they are valued. Keep in mind that the more information that you provide to your client on a regular basis, the fewer telephone calls or e-mails he will make to you asking about the status of his case.

The most common complaint to the bar grievance committees is that the grievant's attorney did not communicate with him. While handling lawsuits is commonplace to a lawyer, each case is unique and stressful to that particular client. Each client requires a certain amount of handholding to remain content with your services. This may mean daily communication. It may mean monthly communication. It depends on the client. You and your staff should always strive to respond to clients within 24 hours, even if it is just to say that you are busy with another matter but will look into their question and get back to them as soon as possible. This is not difficult to do, and it will make your clients so much happier with your services.

- FOCUS ON BEING COST-EFFECTIVE. This is part of being efficient and keeping your client informed. As we've said before, flat fee and value billing have become more common as clients try to keep legal costs under control and get more value for their legal dollar. To remain profitable, law firms must operate cost effectively. Liz calls it "lean and mean."

With good time management skills, experienced staff, effective legal project management procedures, good organization, and easy access to information, clients will have the metrics they need to measure whether they are getting good value for their legal dollar.

Following these guidelines, you can work to streamline the processes in your office and to give every client great value and outstanding service. Your marketing dollar cannot buy better advertising than a happy client.

CHAPTER THIRTY-SIX
HOW TO ENSURE A SATISFIED CLIENT

Law firms spend a significant percentage of their annual revenues on marketing, also known as new client acquisition. In the process of attracting new clients, many firms neglect the importance of retaining current clients. From a financial standpoint, client retention is as important as acquiring new clients. Plus, it's more profitable and less expensive.

Undoubtedly, at some point during the attorney-client relationship, clients will be unhappy. However, client unhappiness should be the result of legal issues and not the service they receive from your law firm.

Take an objective overview of the attorney-client relationship that your firm has with its clients, and see things from the client perspective. There are some things that you can do to help build healthy client relationships and a solid foundation for client retention.

1. WRITE A FIRM NEWSLETTER. It is an easy and inexpensive way to communicate with all of your clients on a regular basis regarding success stories on cases (make sure you get permission from your client or write the story without mentioning names), changes in the firm such as new staff, upcoming events, and the like. You want to generate a positive impression of your firm. Clients want to hear that their lawyers have had successful outcomes and that they have won awards or been recognized by their peers for some exceptional achievement. It builds the confidence that the clients have in you and your firm. Post your newsletter on your website or do an e-newsletter and e-mail it to your clients. Clients do not just want to hear from your firm when it is time to pay the bill or talk to them about their case. See each client as the person she is and you will develop a long-lasting bond with that client.

2. PARTICIPATE IN SPECIALTY ACTIVITIES. If your firm specializes in a specific practice area, participate in organizations related to it. It gives your firm publicity and enforces the concept with your client that you really care about what you do. Be present in the community. Make sure people know you care about more than the success of your law firm.

3. COMMUNICATE WITH CLIENTS. Maintain a good relationship with your client. This relationship begins with the consultation and continues with open communications, updating your client regularly on the status of her case, doing client surveys, and being involved in community activities (and writing about it in your newsletter).

4.   Aggregate Information and Then Share Your Wealth. Be a resource for information your clients need or can use. Include this information on your website. It may include links to court websites, information regarding support groups, or other resources. Clients will appreciate that your firm shares information that is important and relevant.

5.   Make Time to Meet with Your Clients. Having an in-person office conference with your client should not be seen as an inconvenience but as a necessity to build and maintain a relationship with your client. Sometimes there is nothing to say to a client, but the client needs to feel that her relationship with her attorney and the firm is important enough that someone will take time out of their day to meet with her.

When your receptionist does schedule an in-person client appointment, be sure she reserves a reasonable amount of time for you to meet and talk with the client and to answer all her questions. Because she is paying for your time, do not rush her out the door before you know that she is satisfied and has had all of her questions answered.

6.   Listen. Listen to your clients if they tell you that they are dissatisfied. In this situation, it is their perception that matters, not your reality. If clients believe they are unhappy about something, ask how you can improve. Sometimes all they want to do is vent. Maybe they are not really dissatisfied with your firm; perhaps they are upset because their case is not going well and they just want some support and reassurance. Many lawyers find that annoying, but the reality is that attorneys who spend actual "people time" with their clients develop and maintain a solid attorney/client relationship, often long after the initial services are performed and paid for.

7.   Have Some People Skills, and Use Them. Or make sure that someone in your office does. Clients like when you remember that they had an anniversary or birthday, or notice that they were sick, that they had a death in the family, that they had a new baby, etc. Remembering something personal makes them feel like they really matter to you. Don't let a client think that you are so disconnected from him on a personal level that he doesn't matter to your firm except when it is time to pay your bill.

Some of Joryn's best friendships grew out of her relationships with former clients. Especially as a family attorney, she sees good people during their worst, most stressful times. Joryn is often the only shoulder on which they have to cry. Once their case is finalized, they often continue their personal relationship with her.

This sounds pretty basic, doesn't it? Yet so many firms neglect the significance of building and maintaining an attorney-client relationship. Perhaps the most important thing to remember is to treat your clients the way that you would want to be treated.

With a little objectivity, really look at the overall picture of your firm. Now, ask yourself, *"If I were the client, would I be satisfied with my firm?"* If the answer is anything but "yes," you must go back and reread this chapter, and then give some thought to implementing new processes to ensure client satisfaction.

REVIEW QUESTIONS ELEVEN

Lawyers:

1. How do you and your staff welcome clients and other professionals to your office? Prepare a script for your staff to use when welcoming clients to the office.
2. Do you, your staff, and your office make a good first impression? List the ways that you make a good first impression.
3. In what areas could you improve? List those areas and brainstorm how you can improve. Now get to it!
4. Do you go the extra mile to make sure your clients feel satisfied? How? Do you offer rewards to your clients for referrals? Do you treat them to lunch once in a while? Do you send holiday cards? Do you follow up with them when you know they are sick or going through something especially stressful? Brainstorm other ways to make your clients feel special. Now implement them.
5. Do you have many return clients and referrals? List the return clients and referrals you've had in the past six months.
6. If not, what could you do differently to change that? Brainstorm ideas, and implement them.

Law Students:

1. When you enter a business, what does the staff do to make you feel welcome? List those things.
2. Have you ever entered a business and not felt welcome? Why not? Were you not greeted with a smile, or perhaps not greeted at all? Did the exterior and interior design of the office leave something to be desired? List those times where you didn't have a good experience with a business.
3. When you have an ongoing relationship with a certain business, why do you continue going to that business? List the reasons.
4. What are some of the reasons why you stop going to certain businesses? List the reasons.

CHAPTER THIRTY-SEVEN
HOW TO DETERMINE WHEN A RETAINER IS REALLY NON-REFUNDABLE

Although creative fee arrangements like flat fee and value billing are becoming more common, driven by the client's demand for reduced legal fees, many firms still bill by the hour. Not only do attorneys typically bill for their time, but also paralegals, and even law clerks. As discussed in this book, your retainer agreement must specifically state that the client will be billed by the hour for services rendered by the firm. It should also set forth the hourly rates billed by each timekeeper.

Like other professionals, lawyers deserve and need to be compensated for work done for clients. To ensure payment of the fees, most law firms require an upfront fee retainer that is usually deposited into the trust account. Every month when a billing cycle occurs, the firm draws against those funds to pay the invoice generated for the client that month.

When quoting a retainer fee, some firms require that a client post a "non-refundable" retainer. The highly-debated ethical dilemma that every attorney will eventually face is determining when it is appropriate for a non-refundable retainer to actually be non-refundable.

A fee is not earned simply because it is designated as non-refundable. Some courts have held that a non-refundable retainer is truly an *advance fee*. Therefore, the client should receive a refund of unused retainer monies at the conclusion of a case. The Professional Ethics Committee for the State Bar of Texas has opined that a true retainer "is not a payment for services, it is an advance fee to secure a lawyer's services, and remunerate him for loss of the opportunity to accept other employment." (Tex. Comm. on Prof'l Ethics, Op. 611, 2011 WL 5831792.)

The issue of refundable versus non-refundable retainers is a slippery slope, and most jurisdictions err on the side of caution and protect the client. The written retainer agreement is intended to protect the client and the law firm. You must explain in your written retainer agreement in terms that a layperson can understand all terms concerning retainers, billable hourly rates, fee retainers, and cost deposits. Remember that ambiguity in a contract is always interpreted in favor of the party who did not draft the agreement. This will be particularly true in a retainer agreement where the drafter is you, the lawyer. Be sure to include the following language in the retainer agreement:

1) Clearly identify the amount of the retainer to be paid, and specify whether the retainer is refundable or non-refundable. Keep in mind that a retainer

is not payment for services, it is payment in advance of services being rendered.

2) If you are requesting a non-refundable retainer, be sure to specify that it is a "non-refundable retainer," and include language that states the retainer fees are earned upon receipt.

3) If the retainer being paid is for a flat fee case, be specific and clearly state that the fee to be paid is a flat fee and not an hourly fee.

4) Outline the hourly rate of each timekeeper who will be working on the client file: partner, associate, paralegal, and law clerk. Each rate should be set forth as a line item that is clear to read and easy for a layperson to understand.

5) Be sure to include in your retainer agreement that retainer funds (regardless of whether they are specified as refundable or non-refundable) will be billed against at each billing cycle and that the client agrees that the firm is to be paid monthly from those funds.

6) To protect the firm, request a cost retainer for anticipated costs. State the amount to be paid as a cost retainer. Indicate that client costs incurred will be paid to vendors or others on the client's behalf and that those costs expended will be accounted for on the billing statement.

Deposit all client funds, whether they are refundable or non-refundable retainers or cost monies, into your trust account. Do not deposit any fee retainer or cost retainer monies into your operating account.

If an attorney/client relationship goes bad, you must protect yourself in writing and be as thorough as possible. Consider all scenarios that could happen which are case specific to that client matter. Draft your retainer agreement to contained clear language which identifies retainer monies as up-front compensation for your availability and lost opportunities.

Keep in mind that it is your responsibility to protect your client's best interests. Consider whether the representation for which you are being engaged truly warrants a non-refundable retainer.

The retainer agreement is as much for your protection as it is for your client. Do not inadvertently commit professional misconduct. The attorney/client relationship will be a better one if you make sure that everyone understands what is expected.

CHAPTER THIRTY-EIGHT
HOW TO USE CLIENT SURVEYS AND TESTIMONIALS

For many years, Liz and Joryn were each the consumer who would be the first to voice their displeasure in goods or services they received if they did not think they were getting value for their money or if a service or product somehow fell short of their expectations. Over the years, we both realized that feedback of any kind is important; it helps a business to ensure that its clients, now and in the future, are happy.

Now, we try to be as conscientious about paying a business a compliment as we are when we have a complaint. Not surprisingly, businesses are very appreciative to receive compliments about their services or employees. It actually makes them aspire to do even better.

As business owners ourselves, we are interested in what our clients have to say, whether they feel that they are getting value for their money and if there is anything we can do better. This kind of relationship builds goodwill with Liz's attorneys and Joryn's divorce clients because we know that they appreciate our desire to do an exceptional job for them and to not only meet but exceed their expectations.

Some things are hard to hear. No one wants to hear that a client is disappointed or unhappy with the work he received. However, getting this valuable information helps to change the way we approach the work we do and improve the service to clients.

Client surveys are still very under-utilized by law firms as a benchmark for whether they are meeting their clients' needs and giving value for the fees they receive. Considering the economy, the clients' need and desire for value is more important to them than ever. With the competition in the legal market, a client survey is a tool that is a relatively easy way to obtain feedback. Remember, though, the information a client provides on a survey is all about the client's perceptions and her needs. It does not necessarily mean there is something "wrong"—but it can help you assess how the administration and every day function of your law practice is meeting the client's perceived needs and helping you to build a sustainable client base.

Ideally, client surveys should be utilized throughout the pendency of handling a case for a client. The feedback that these surveys provide is priceless, and clients' observations and opinions can be used to enhance client service. Here are some of the added benefits that your firm can derive from client surveys:

1) Develop practice strategies to improve on areas of client service or office procedures;

2) Keep your client contact information updated;
3) Market other services that your firm offers to clients directly on the survey, asking if they would consider utilizing other services; and
4) Ensure that your firm stays competitive with other firms offering similar services.

There is no one way that is more effective than another to encourage a client to complete a survey. Here are some suggestions:

GIVE YOUR CLIENT A SURVEY TO COMPLETE WHEN HE SIGNS THE RETAINER AGREEMENT. Of course, there is a good chance that by the time the client's matter has concluded, he will have lost or misplaced the survey. But giving a client a survey at the time when he retains the firm will show the client from the beginning that your firm cares about him, cares about his concerns, cares about his suggestions, and that your firm wants to know his opinion about how he feels he has been treated by the firm. From the outset, the client will know that the firm cares what he thinks. To a new client, this is very important.

PUT YOUR SURVEY ON YOUR WEBSITE. Be sure to tell the client that there is a survey on the website. If your survey is on the website, there is little more work involved in obtaining a survey from the client. In this instance, you might encourage the client to complete a survey at any time during the pendency of his case, not only at the conclusion. In this way, if there is something that happens that makes the client dissatisfied, you can make an effort to remedy the situation during the representation, before it becomes a big issue that may interfere with the attorney/client relationship you are trying to forge with that client.

ASK YOUR CLIENT TO TAKE AN ONLINE SURVEY. When you've finished the job you were retained to perform, include the link to the survey on your website in the e-mail. Be sure to tell the client that his feedback is valued and suggest he take five minutes to open the form, complete it, and submit it. This will probably be the most effective way to get responses to client surveys.

ASK YOUR CLIENT TO TAKE A PRINT SURVEY. At the conclusion of the client's matter, when you send that closing letter, enclose a written survey, and ask the client to complete it and return it to your office. It is likely that you will only receive a very small percentage of the surveys you send because clients will put it aside, forget about it, or lose it, but every client opinion counts and the client will appreciate that you asked.

ASK FOR A CLIENT TESTIMONIAL. Happy clients will give you the most amazing testimonials. And amazing testimonials are how you will bring in new clients. Ask those clients for permission to put their comments on your website or marketing materials. Potential clients will feel more comfortable retaining you if they see that former clients were happy with your services. When asking for a testimonial, be very specific as to exactly what information you would like the client to provide. Ask questions like:

- What was frustrating you that caused you to retain our services?
- Describe the moment you knew you had made the right choice with our services.
- What was your biggest fear prior to retaining us?
- What worked well for you once you retained us?
- Did anything scare you during the process?
- What difference did using our services make in your life?
- What did you like about our services?
- What did you dislike about our services?
- Did anything happen during our services that made you feel great? Tell me about that.
- Did anything happen during our services that made you feel awful? Tell me about that.
- Did you learn anything from our services?
- Did anything surprise you about our services?
- Do you have any critique of or compliment for our services?
- What did we do to prove to you that you were getting real value from our services?

A positive testimonial can be the best form of advertisement. Here's a review that was posted on February 18, 2017 on AVVO for Joryn's law firm, *Open Palm Law*:

> Best caring lawyer!!!!
>
> When I went to Ms. Jenkins' office, I was expecting another blood-sucking lawyer, I was ready to set my demands but once I met the team I was shocked. After meet with 4 other lawyers which non of them explain the system, what are my options or how can I save money and time, how to try to approach this unknown I was heading to. Ms. Jenkins explain everything by stages of the divorce, my options, the amount of money they all involve and how can I do my portion of the process and they would fill in where we can't or aren't able. Ms. Jenkins was caring which I never had from a lawyer, problem solving skills are superb. Their office is set up more to a familiar approach which it made me feel like home. She will be my lawyer and defend me and my family. Thank you, Ms. Jenkins. I told my family and friends about Ber [sic] already.

Nine days later, on February 27, 2017, Joryn received this wonderful compliment:

> As a new business owner I made the same mistake that so many

business owners make. Neglecting thier wives, the ones that have supported them the most, and my marriage was on the brink after 18 yrs. I went to see Joryn and she explained to me that there were options to ending the marriage and one of them was "Collaborative Divorce." Since my wife and I still cared about each other, and had just grown apart, we still wanted the best for each other. I figured that collaborative divorce would be the best option for us to have a peaceful seperation for the both of us. It was days later while making plans to go through with the collaborative divorce when Joryn reached out to me and GAVE me a copy of *The Five Love Languages* to read. (she could sense that my marriage was not ready to be ended) She suggested that I read it. I did . . . and it has changed my life. I quickly read the book and applied what I had learned. I am happy to say that applying what I have learned has allowed me to have another chance at saving our marriage. We are currently working things out through counceling and it looks as if our marriage with some work will survive. Hopefully another 18yrs +. Thank you Joryn for your compassion, knowledge, and insight. Because of you I have a chance at turning this around and I now have the knowledge I need to make our marriage work and stand the test of time.

These are the kinds of testimonials for which we hope, in part because of the wonderful advertisements they are for the firm, but also because it is amazing to hear that our hard work and compassion is appreciated and making a difference. There is nothing better. Testimonials are important because people tend to follow other similarly situated people.

If a client provides information on a survey that is confusing or the firm feels is somehow inaccurate, contact your clients and speak to them or even schedule an in-office meeting (free of charge). Sometimes there is a misunderstanding in the client's perception, and a few minutes on the telephone or in-person might be well worth the investment of time to clear up a misunderstanding and salvage a client relationship. Clients will remember that you took the time to contact them and discuss any perceived misconceptions they might have had.

Client surveys are inexpensive and indispensable marketing tools. There is no better way to improve on services for future clients than to know how current clients feel about the work you have done for them. Retain current clients by keeping them happy. Attract current clients with referrals from happy clients. It's a win-win for everyone!

FINANCES

CHAPTER THIRTY-NINE
HOW TO GET IN TROUBLE WITH THE BAR
(FIVE TRUST ACCOUNT ERRORS)

Let's start with the most critical financial element of the law practice that distinguishes it from nearly every other business—*the trust account.*

The last thing an attorney needs is a subpoena from the bar association for a trust account audit. Bar associations have specific rules with which attorneys must comply, including handling of trust monies, maintaining client ledgers, and reconciling the trust account. All bank accounts should be reconciled every month. Reconciling your trust account and maintaining accurate client ledgers is not optional—it is absolutely mandatory.

Some lawyers cannot be trusted with a client's money. Our experience, of course, has been that those lawyers are the exception and not the rule. Most trust accounting problems are merely the result of errors, such as mistakes in transposition or a lack of knowledge of the specific rules and regulations that apply to the handling of client trust monies

Over the course of her legal career, Liz has attended three trust account audits. Only one of those instances was precipitated by a banking error. The law firm was cleared in the trust audit. In the other two cases, the lawyers involved made calculated decisions to "borrow" monies from client trust accounts with the knowledge that they were taking other people's money.

In one instance, an attorney who was always interested in investing in real estate but who never really had the cash flow to do it borrowed the monies from an estate account to buy property. Liz remembers the family calling month after month, wanting to know when the estate would be closed and the funds distributed. The lawyer could not close the estate because he had borrowed over $100,000, which was a lot more back then than it is now. He continually asked the court for extensions on the deadline to provide a final accounting and close the estate. The court granted his repeated requests until he ran out of excuses and was more than a year late to file an accounting or to ask for another extension.

His lack of response triggered a bar audit. The bar examined his account and asked him to explain the unaccounted funds. He responded that he was investing the estate monies to ensure the family a higher yield on the return of their money than the bank would afford them. He forgot the part about how he did not notify or get the approval of the family—or that when he bought the real estate, he titled the property to himself without any kind of mortgage payable to the estate.

Fortunately, the estate was made whole because the court ordered the attorney to purchase a bond at the time he had opened the estate and was appointed the executor. The bonding company, however, initiated a criminal prosecution against him to recover the monies it had paid out on the bond.

The other attorney for whom Liz attended a trust account audit was a bit more brazen. He had drafted a will for an elderly client. In the process, he had convinced her to appoint him the executor and the trustee for a trust she wanted to set up for her long-time caregiver and live-in companion. When the client passed on, this attorney "borrowed" the money from the trust to buy himself a burnt orange Corvette convertible. He gave no explanation whatsoever for taking these funds.

When the bar audit uncovered the missing trust funds, this attorney, too, was criminally prosecuted. Unfortunately, the beneficiary of the estate died before the attorney was sentenced. He never received the restitution the attorney was ordered to pay to him. Fortunately for potential future victims, however, the attorney was subsequently disbarred.

Attending these trust account audits was not a pleasant experience, though you certainly learn everything about trust accounting regulations you always wanted to know but were afraid to ask.

There are five specific activities involving trust accounts that will give probable cause for a bar audit.

1. DRAWING ON FUNDS TOO EARLY

Monies of any kind, with the exception of cash (which rarely, if ever, changes hands these days), cannot be drawn on when deposited until they clear the bank. Do not draw on trust account monies thinking that deposited funds will eventually clear the account and that, in the meantime, there are other client funds in the bank to cover the disbursements. This is a common violation of trust accounting regulations. The account will remain "out of trust" for however long it takes the deposit to clear your account.

If you know in advance that you will need to draw on deposited funds as soon as possible, monitor the account to verify when the funds have cleared. When in doubt, or as a precautionary measure, contact your financial institution to confirm that specific funds have, in fact, cleared.

Always be exceedingly careful when drawing on trust funds. If the funds that you deposited are returned for any reason, the account is "out of trust," and you have misused funds that are the property of another client. This is definitely a trust account violation. Because your financial institution *must* notify the bar association that a check has been returned, you are guaranteed to at least receive a letter of inquiry by the Bar, if not a full-blown audit.

2. FAILING TO MAINTAIN SEPARATE CLIENT LEDGERS

You must maintain an individual ledger of some kind for each client who has funds in your trust account. We both remember the days before accounting software when we kept handwritten ledger cards for each client. Each individual client ledger was required to reflect every deposit, withdrawal, and balance in the account for that client. The accounting software available today maintains client ledgers for you if you set up your software appropriately and enter accurate information.

If your firm's accounting and billing software are linked, you will be able to make one entry and thereby avoid errors in transposition. If your accounting and billing software are not linked, be sure that whoever handles your bookkeeping is painstakingly accurate and rechecks her entries to avoid clerical errors. While even a clerical error is not permitted according to bar trust account regulations, it is not viewed as seriously as outright theft of funds. It is, nevertheless, a violation that will be picked up by an auditor in the event of a trust account audit. And there will be consequences, even for inadvertent errors.

3. Failing to Reconcile Trust Accounts

All bank accounts *should* be reconciled but, without exception, your trust account *must* be reconciled every month. Having a check returned on an operating account, while not actionable by the bar for an audit, creates headaches. Failure to reconcile your trust account every month is a violation of bar regulations that will give you far more than a headache.

Perform a full trust account reconciliation every month—not just of the bank balances and of your check register. Reconcile the bank statements with each one of your client ledgers and your check register every month. The total amount in the trust account must match the total amount of each client ledger. If all your accounting processes are in order, reconciling the trust account should not consume much of your time. Your billing program should also be keeping an accurate accounting for each client with monies in trust. Every deposit and withdrawal should be recorded in your accounting program and should match the ledgers and the bank statements. If you perform all of the necessary recordings when you make the deposits and withdrawals, everything should fall into place easily when it comes time to prepare your monthly reconciliation.

Create a binder for every year of reconciliations for the trust account with 12 tabs for the year—January to December. Create four tabs under each month in which you will place the following:

- A copy of the month's bank statement that you are reconciling;
- A copy of the register for that month showing all deposits and checks/withdrawals;
- A printout of the summary for each client from the billing program showing the funds for each individual client; and
- The actual spreadsheet of the reconciliation of the account.

If the Florida Bar audits any of Liz's attorneys, the reconciliations are up-to-date and in order, ready to be turned over to the auditor at a moment's notice. The expediency with which records are turned over is an indicator to the bar that reconciliations are being accomplished on a monthly basis. When the bar serves a subpoena for a trust account and the law firm requests an extension to produce these records, the bar knows that the reconciliations are not up-to-date. That sends up a red flag before the actual audit ever gets started.

4. Allowing Credit Card Merchants to Debit Trust Accounts

Everyone uses credit or debit cards these days. Few of us write checks by hand anymore. Law firms have kept up with this trend, and we personally do not know of any law firms who do not accept credit cards as a convenience for their clients. Joryn certainly does. But accepting credit cards for trust account funds can be a bit tricky.

If your firm accepts credit cards, be mindful that some merchants only allow you to deposit to the operating account or to the trust account. If you deposit all credit card payments to trust, the merchant will likely debit the trust account for the credit card fees. Unless you absorb the cost of the credit card transactions for your client, a $750 retainer fee can become $739 after the merchant deducts its fee. You must give credit to the client for the entire $750 retainer, and the $750 must be credited to the client in full. However, once a merchant takes the fee, there is no longer $750 in trust for that client. There is only $739 in trust for that client.

On the other hand, having the merchant deposit the monies to the operating account and moving it to trust becomes a bookkeeping headache. If you receive $750 into your operating account, even though the merchant charges $11 for the transaction, you must transfer $750 to trust because that is the amount the client paid. As you can imagine, this scenario is also just a mistake waiting to happen.

Find a merchant who will allow you the option of depositing to operating or trust, depending on what the funds are meant *for*. There are merchants who will give you the option of depositing to either account. They will then only debit any fees from the operating account once a month for all the transactions to both accounts. This is the best way to proceed because the entire amount deposits into trust and the client receives credit for that total. The fees are taken out of operating so there is no money debited from the trust funds.

You must determine the best way to charge the fees to the client. Most firms Liz works with absorb the fees as a cost of doing business. (Joryn does.) The amounts are usually negligible. Furthermore, when you weigh paying a few dollars versus the possibility of the client seeking out another attorney who will take credit cards and absorb the fees, it might be worth it to eat that expense. Tell your clients that you accept credit cards as a convenience and that your law firm absorbs the credit card fees as a courtesy.

5. Paying Fees to Operating Without a Proper Statement

If you take retainers that are refundable, these must be deposited into your trust account. The retainer is not "earned upon receipt." The unused proceeds are to be returned to the client at the conclusion of the matter with an accounting of how any trust monies were spent for fees or costs. This information should be provided on your monthly billing statement as you withdraw funds from your trust account every month to pay the current invoice.

Every time you apply money from the trust account to pay a client invoice, send the client a statement reflecting what the firm has charged for fees and costs. You will need this accounting detail if your firm is ever audited. As previously discussed, taking client fees from the trust without justifying the transfer is a red flag.

Some law firms take "non-refundable retainers" which need not be deposited to the trust account. Many firms include language in their retainer agreements stating that non-refundable retainers are "deemed earned upon receipt." Ensure that your retainer agreements clearly state, "Any unused funds will not be returned."

When you disburse trust funds to your operating account to pay a firm for fees, perform a client-by-client transfer in the specific amounts owed to the firm. For example, if Mr. Smith's bill is $1,306.24, transfer exactly that amount in a separate transaction from the other. Move every client transaction separately so it is identifiable on your bank statement.

We know some attorneys who will move money throughout the month to their operating accounts in ten or twenty thousand dollar increments. When monthly bills are generated, they calculate the amount of fees owed that month to the firm and subtract whatever they have already transferred throughout that month. They then deposit the difference to the operating account. At that point, they break down the unidentified monies they took that month and assign it to clients.

There is so much room for error with this procedure, not to mention the fact that they may not have been entitled to take ten or twenty thousand dollars at the time they moved the funds to operating. Do not do this!

Be sure to include in your retainer agreement that the client agrees that you are permitted to pay the firm out of the fee retainer in trust for any statements for services that are generated. If you do not have a client's permission to move the money, get it before you withdraw money and pay your firm. Clearly outline the fee arrangement in your retainer agreement so that, in the event that a client files a grievance with the bar regarding retainer fees held in trust and disbursed, you will have protected your firm.

SIMPLY PUT – THERE IS NO ROOM FOR ERROR

Trust account regulations are designed to protect clients from the misuse of their funds. Even if the error is a simple bookkeeping mistake such as the transposition of a number, the bar has little appreciation for the level of error.

Whoever handles your trust account and performs the monthly reconciliation must be familiar with all that is involved in preparing a reconciliation that complies with the bar rules *to the very letter*. Perhaps surprisingly, most CPAs or bookkeepers are not familiar with the detailed bar regulations governing trust accounts. Keep in mind that any bank activity on your trust account that causes a check to be returned for any reason will trigger notification by the bank to the bar association that there is a problem with the account. This will initiate an inquiry at the very least, and, at worst, a trust account audit.

It has been our experience that a technical violation will not result in suspension or disbarment of an attorney. Those extreme measures only occur when there is the potential for financial harm to the client. However, a technical trust violation may give rise to the firm being required to hire an accountant or to designate someone to reconcile the trust account every month for a specified period of time and turn those reconciliations over to the bar for review.

Whoever you designate to manage and reconcile your trust account on a monthly basis must ensure your firm is in compliance. No matter what the outcome, a trust account audit really is an expensive headache that generally results from a mistake that could have been avoided. The bar does not consider ignorance of the rules an excuse for trust account violations. Remember, it is your name on that bar license.

During the time Joryn served on *The Florida Bar Professional Ethics Committee* and the *Grievance Committee 13-A*, twice as chair, she was shocked by how frequently attorneys got into trouble for trust account violations. Of course, she hadn't yet opened her own practice back then. To that point, she had mostly worked in law firms at which she wasn't involved with the trust accounting. That was the concern of the partners and the law firm administration, and she trusted them to take care of it.

It seems commonsensical that an attorney should never misappropriate his client's funds, and yet, time after time, she saw attorneys being reprimanded and even disbarred for such trust violations. Obviously, malicious theft is worse than theft by mistake, but the bar takes both very seriously because, ultimately, clients need protection in both situations.

If you find yourself needing "to borrow" your clients' funds, get help. If you notice that you often make mistakes in your accounting, hire someone to perform that function for you. If a member of your staff performs this critical task for you, check her work often to make sure that she is accomplishing it appropriately. Only have a staff member perform this task if she is well versed in the rules of the Bar, has a meticulous personality, and is dedicated, without question, to your firm's well-being.

Joryn once represented an employer whose bookkeeper embezzled funds while theoretically performing her job. Thank goodness, the only victim of the crime was the small business (it was not a law firm) and its owner; no clients suffered. The bookkeeper was ordered to pay restitution, however, many years later, she had still only repaid a minuscule portion of the money she had taken and spent.

Well known for her ethics work, Joryn was asked to represent a law firm that was victimized by one of its own partners. When she got the call, it was urgent. Would she walk the partner off the property? None of the partners wanted to do it. She agreed to do so. Would she figure out how to tell the clients of the firm that the partner, who had a developed a gambling addiction, had targeted all of them and negotiate the least painful resolution to the problem? Yes, she would.

Ultimately, Joryn was able to negotiate a solution that included absolution by The Florida Bar and complete repayment *by the law firm* of the missing funds to the clients. But do not doubt the fear that this caused all twelve of the innocent owners, who should have been paying closer attention to what their law partner was up to. After all, it is always your reputation, and your license, on the line.

CHAPTER FORTY
HOW TO RECONCILE YOUR OPERATING ACCOUNT

Want to know your liquid assets? Most lawyers do. After all, revenue is the lifeblood of your business. Without revenue, you have no law firm because you have no telephone, no office, and no staff—you get the picture. So how, if your business depends on revenue for everything, can a law firm manage their revenues without reconciling their accounts?

Unlike the trust account, there are no bar association regulations mandating that an operating account be reconciled on a monthly basis. That old joke, "*I must have money because I still have checks*" is not grounded in reality.

The revenues collected by a law firm are deposited into its operating account. These monies are fees earned, and they comprise the liquid assets of the firm. Why would anyone *not* want to know the exact balance of the firm's liquid assets? Yet making it a point to reconcile the operating account is something that escapes many law firms.

Working as an independent law firm administrator, Liz was recently asked by a firm to handle its bookkeeping. After one month, Liz realized that its bookkeeping transactions, including deposits, checks, and client ledgers, were only being updated once a month instead of contemporaneously or even once a week. Handling bookkeeping transactions in this once-a-month fashion leaves a lot of room for error; something will surely be overlooked. While generally not as important for the operating account, client trust ledgers and funds *must* be updated as transactions occur, rather than monthly. There is just too much room for error resulting from an oversight.

If you do a good job with your accounting software, all debits and deposits to an account are entered into the register, and your balance should be quite accurate. However, operator error can still occur. The transposition of a number or the failure to deduct a bank charge or other debit can render the register balance inaccurate.

Reconciling the operating account will ensure that all adjustments are made. It also serves as a double check that all entries have been properly entered. If proper procedures are followed every month, accurate entries made, and bank charges accounted for, reconciling an operating account is fairly easy and does not take too much time.

A reconciliation statement includes the following information:

- The firm's record of account balance (usually the check register which is part of every accounting software program);

- Addition of all deposits;
- Subtraction of all expenditures; and
- Any adjustments, such as outstanding checks or deposits.

The purpose of reconciling the account is to make sure that all records (once adjustments have been made) will balance to each other and that the total amount of available funds is accurate. Transposition errors occur easily, and the smallest errors are usually the hardest to find. Reconciling regularly can help you spot any errors early on.

Some attorneys may avoid reconciling their operating accounts because they fear that their liquid assets are far less than they should be considering their expenses. But to be successful in business, it is important to know where you stand. You may find out that you are better off than you expected. Or you may come to realize that cutbacks are necessary.

Just as it's critical that you contemporaneously capture the time you spend on a client with a record in the client's file, it's also imperative with the issuance of checks with your check register and reconciliation statements.

CHAPTER FORTY-ONE
HOW TO PREPARE YOUR BUDGET

How much fun is preparing your law firm's budget? Not much. Who wants to see how much it will cost to run your law practice and where the revenues will come from? The answer should be . . . everyone!

How important is preparing your law firm's budget for next year? *Critical.* Your budget is a footprint of where your firm is headed and how you plan to get there over the next 12 months. No doubt it seems like there are more important items on the agenda. Perhaps, more accurately stated, there are other things you would rather do. Maybe you have no desire to think about what it will cost to maintain your overhead and pay your staff for another year. Put this important planning strategy off until the very end of the year, and the holidays are suddenly right on top of you. The last thing you want to deal with then is figuring out how much money everything will cost next year while also trying to fund the holiday season bonuses and parties.

Preparing a budget for the coming year will be the most important thing you can do for your practice. On January 1st, you will know exactly where your firm is headed and how you will get there.

As a former office administrator with a 500-attorney firm, it was important for Liz to know what the annual (and monthly) budget was for expenses like office functions, office supplies, rent, etc. In January of each year, the firm gave her the annual budget, which she divided by 12. Being more frugal with other people's money than she is with her own, it was always her goal to spend less each month and get more value. The more she could save on an expense, the more revenue there was to accomplish something else for the firm and the employees.

There are multiple ways to save money. Vendors are very competitive and they all want your business. No one should sacrifice quality for cost. After all, it is your money. Just because you *can* afford to pay more for quality, does not mean that you *should*. Both Liz and Joryn are avid negotiators. So, negotiate.

What is the easiest way to come up with the numbers to prepare next year's budget? Use your previous year's income and expenses. This will give you a general idea of expenses for the coming year. You can plan for growth and look at what you must do to be on target to achieve your firm's goals. Anything—and everything—can be accounted for or related to dollars and cents. Money is, after all, a universal language; everyone can relate to it!

Here are some simple steps that you can use to budget and forecast for the financial health and wealth of your firm for the next year.

1) Run a year-to-date total of all expenses that your firm incurred during the year through the end of November. Take the totals in each category and divide each total by 11. This will give you a baseline average of what your expenses cost you each month: rent, employee salaries, utilities, equipment leases, benefits, office supplies, etc. Be sure to include every category of expense that your firm incurred during the year. While the totals will not be perfect for a year, they will be close to accurate.

2) Review the expenses from the previous year that you have now broken down into different categories. This is where you can tighten the budget. Look for excess spending, perhaps by shopping vendors for office supplies, process servers, equipment, etc. Unless you are eager to overpay for services, it does not make sense to overspend for vendors or supplies or equipment. You might also include a miscellaneous or "slush fund" category if you really want to prepare for the unexpected. If your firm has a pay-for-performance bonus program, you must include it as part of your annual expenses. That amount will likely fluctuate because it is tied to income, but it will give you an approximate amount with which to work. You can use a prior year as a guideline when planning for bonuses. Employees who are motivated by incentives will usually meet or exceed their performances from a prior year.

3) Prepare a strategy outline of where you plan to take the firm in the next 12 months in terms of growth. Are you planning to add an associate or two? Do you need to expand your support staff? Will an office move over the next 12 months increase (or decrease) the rent overhead? Maybe it is time to invest in purchasing a building. Project what you will spend on an annual basis for any growth that you are anticipating and divide by 12. This will give you an idea of the added cost of growth.

If you calculate the monthly totals from #1 and #2 above in each category of expense and make adjustments for growth or future anticipated expenses in #3, this will give you a rough budget for the coming year.

With this budget of projected expenses for next year, and looking at your income for last year, you will have a snapshot of where your firm will be in the coming year. At the end of every month, review your expenses and income, and compare it to the budget that you prepared. You can then make adjustments for the following months accordingly.

Remember, a budget is only good on the day when it is written. Things change so quickly that on any given day, income or expenses will change. If you modify your budget—not for the minutia, but for big items like the purchase of office equipment or hiring a new employee—your budget should be pretty accurate within a few dollars.

Once you have your annual budget worked out, you can use it to prepare a strategic budget for your firm. The strategic budget will help you determine partner salaries, bonuses, expanded marketing plans, and capital expenditures.

Every law firm accounting software gives you the ability to easily generate the reports that you will need to prepare a budget. Typical reports would include general ledger, income and expense, profit and loss, billing reports (to assess future income based upon recent billings), and the like. Some accounting software programs allow you to customize reports for specific budget purposes.

Financial planning is an important part of managing the business of practicing law. There is no excuse not to work with a budget. It does not take that much effort. Do not fly by the seat of your pants. Get your administrator or someone who is in touch with the firm's finances to prepare your firm's budget on a regular basis. It's your law firm's money; there is no excuse not to be connected to it and be aware of what it is doing.

In law school, we are taught to be good lawyers, not good business people. But many lawyers eventually hang their own shingles, so it is necessary to understand how to run a business. You can be the best attorney in town, but if you can't efficiently manage your practice, you'll never be as successful as you could be. If running a business just isn't your thing and you want to be able to focus your energy on being a great lawyer, then hire someone who is competent and trustworthy to handle managing the business of practicing law.

REVIEW QUESTIONS TWELVE

Lawyers:

1. Does your firm prepare an annual budget? Is it in writing? If not, prepare one now.
2. What kinds of expenses are listed on your budget? List them. How well do you typically adhere to it?
3. Do you monitor your income and expenses each month to make sure you are working within your budget? If not, begin doing so. Set a monthly reminder on your calendar.
4. Is your forecasted annual budget typically accurate? Or do you find yourself spending beyond your budget each month?
5. What do you do when you spend beyond your budget in a certain month? Do you adjust your budget for the next month?
6. What happens if you spend beyond your annual budget?
7. Where does the money come from to pay those extra expenses that were underbudgeted or not included in the budget? List possible places where you could obtain those additional funds.
8. If you underbudget one year, how do you make up for it the next year? List your strategy.

Law Students:

1. In your personal life, do you prepare an annual or monthly budget? If not, why not? Prepare one now.
2. If so, do you find that it helps you manage your spending? List how it is helpful.
3. Have you ever compared your spending in months when you did prepare a budget and months when you didn't? What did you find? Did you spend more money during the months when you did not plan a budget? Prepare a comparison analysis now.
4. If you do prepare a personal budget, how successful are you at adhering to the parameters of your budget?
5. What do you do if you go over your budget? Do you cut back in the next month? List possible places where you could obtain additional funds or where you could cut back, if necessary.
6. Do you understand the importance of preparing a budget once you begin your own firm? Why would it be helpful? List the reasons.
7. What kinds of expenses would you list on your firm's budgets? List them.

CHAPTER FORTY-TWO
HOW TO CUT COSTS WITHOUT CUTTING CORNERS

After much resistance to change, lawyers are accepting the reality that the *business* of practicing law is separate from the practice of law itself. What exactly does this mean? *It means that a law practice is a business, and from a management standpoint, it must be run as such or it will fail.*

There are more attorneys competing for the same clients than there were 20 years ago. Clients are "shopping" for legal services that appeal to their individual situation and need. They want fee structures that include value billing, flat fees, reduced hourly billings, and discounts. Clients today review their bills more closely than ever to ensure they are not paying for unnecessary services. This means that law firms must take a good hard look at their financials and operate more efficiently and cost-effectively than ever before. There is no more excess—clients will only pay for services they see as valuable, regardless of the size of the firm.

Here are some crucial cost-cutting strategies that will add to your firm's bottom line.

RESTRUCTURE YOUR LEGAL STAFF. Examine the job descriptions and individual tasks performed by attorneys and staff members. Review the nature of the tasks and determine whether a lower level legal staff member is capable of performing the task. For example, can a paralegal schedule an expert deposition instead of the associate? Can the receptionist schedule a new consult and provide the paperwork to the client instead of the paralegal?

The goal is not to shortchange the efficiency or the quality of the work that is performed but to ensure that the associates perform the higher skill level tasks. Don't waste their time on scheduling depositions. For defense firms, this is particularly important because insurance carriers will spend hours scrutinizing a bill and slashing time from an attorney if they think a paralegal could perform the same work at a lower hourly rate. Everyone is cost conscious these days.

REDUCE YOUR LEGAL STAFF. This is an option that will likely be vetoed by your legal staff—both the ones being "right-sized" out and the ones left behind to undertake the "extra" work. The reality is that rightsizing is becoming a reality in law firms. Gone are the "legal teams" of years ago that consisted of a partner, a junior partner, two or three associates, a paralegal, and at least two secretaries. With software, process improvement, and better problem solving, rightsizing is becoming an efficient and cost effective way to reduce overhead expenses and to increase productivity.

Legal assistants who can bill for their time are replacing legal secretaries who were formerly part of the "clerical overhead" of a firm. Paralegals are being substituted for associates to perform many tasks that do not involve the actual "practice of law." Even insurance companies are jumping on the bandwagon, and, in many instances, may be the precipitators by refusing to pay an associate's hourly rate for work that can be performed by a paralegal.

This staff reduction or rightsizing can be implemented in such a way that it does not sacrifice efficiency and good service to the client, but instead makes each member of the firm a productive, timekeeping, and income-generating member of the team.

REDUCE COMPENSATION. Pay-for-performance and incentive pay is becoming increasingly popular in law firms. Paying people simply for showing up for work is not cost-efficient and does not contribute to the bottom line of a firm—it just does not show up in revenues. Alternatively, compensating—and by that we mean rewarding—employees for meeting their billable quotas, for scheduling a specific target number of depositions or mediations, or for preparing a certain number of settlement demands is becoming the rule rather than the exception.

Paying employees incentive bonuses in addition to their salaries is a way for firms to reward the performers. Attorneys, for example, are often paid bonuses for meeting and/or exceeding billable hour requirements, not to mention the added incentive of working up to partner status. Why not the rest of your employees?

When an employee is reluctant to accept employment in which "pay-for-performance" is part of the compensation package, beware. That employee may have no ambition, initiative, or enthusiasm. He is not driven. Conversely, an employee who is motivated by an incentive plan as part of her compensation will be a producer for the firm.

Be sure that if pay-for-performance is part of any employee's compensation, the employee receives her bonus. Plan for this expense in your budget. When employees perform according to the parameters you set, they must be recognized for their performance on time. With increased performance levels, the revenues should be there. Make sure they are.

OFFER EMPLOYEES DIFFERENT HEALTH INSURANCE OPTIONS. For some employees, the need for benefits outweighs the need for a specific amount of paycheck compensation. The costs for health insurance and other benefits have soared out of control, and some coverage premiums have more than doubled in the last few years. We all know too well that illness can financially devastate an individual or a family if they are without health insurance.

Many employees are disgruntled because of downgrades to insurance policies with higher deductibles and bigger co-pays necessitated by higher premiums. Employers who provide paid health insurance can balance their desire to provide and an employee's desire to have health insurance and at the same time provide a better option for health insurance with lower deductibles and co-pays.

Employers should consider offering at least two health insurance options: one option for which the employer pays 100% and one for which the employer pays up to the amount of the first option for a better policy and to which the employee makes the contribution for the better coverage with the lower deductible and co-pays. In this way, the employer is contributing exactly the same amount to the employee who chooses either policy and the option of receiving better coverage at his own expense exists for the employee who wants or needs the better coverage.

REVIEW OFFICE LEASE AND SPACE REQUIREMENTS. Real estate markets are very competitive, and in some places, there are thousands of square feet of empty office space. Office buildings of all sizes in all areas are sitting empty because the market is saturated with real estate. If you need more office space or want to reduce your rent overhead, you might consider looking at the inventory that some landlords are carrying.

Some of the larger office buildings here in Tampa will rent space to the first few tenants in the building at a reduced per square foot rate, which will generate significant rent savings. They use these first tenants to entice more renters to a building. Often a realtor can rent space more easily in a building that is partially occupied.

Remember, everything is negotiable. Review your current lease situation and compare space in surrounding buildings. Attempt to renegotiate your lease if you prefer to remain in your current location. Raising your current landlord's awareness of other options and great deals that are available in the real estate market might be an incentive for him to renegotiate a better deal with you. No one wants to lose a paying tenant.

However, if for any reason that is not workable, find more than one space that would satisfy your firm's space needs, and begin negotiating one rental agent against the other to negotiate the best deal for your firm.

Above all else—*negotiate.*

ENGAGE VENDORS IN BIDDING WARS. The bottom line when it comes to office supplies is that, with few exceptions, all supplies are the same, regardless of the source from which you obtain them—a case of paper is a case of paper, and a highlighter is a highlighter. Vendors and suppliers know that the market is competitive. Do not be afraid to shop vendors and engage them in a bidding war to obtain the best deal for your firm. Ensure that whoever is negotiating with your vendors and suppliers is really looking out for your firm's bottom line.

Liz works with a shredding company in Tampa that does not charge to pick up documents for shredding. They provide the bins and come twice a month (or more frequently if you need them) to empty the containers. The prior shredding company charged $43 a month to shred documents. By replacing that shredding company, the firm's shredding is now free.

In addition, she buys paper from the shredding company for just $19.99 a case. Some vendors charge as much as $42 for a case of paper. Thus, for every two boxes of paper she purchases for the firm from this company, she is getting one for "free."

Remember—everything is negotiable. Unless someone has a particular affinity for a vendor, you can always use the deal you have to negotiate a better deal somewhere else.

REVIEW NON-LEGAL BACK-OFFICE FUNCTIONS. There are many administrative functions in a law firm that can be locally outsourced to independent contractors. There are outside vendors who can perform these functions more cost-effectively than an in-house employee is able to do. Services such as law firm administration, business management, IT, HR, accounting, billing, and client development/marketing are all necessary non-attorney functions. Consider outsourcing or downsizing these services.

The resulting benefit here is not only efficiency of cost and productivity but also an increase in competency. Your firm may not have the resources to attract and retain competent and experienced full-time professionals whom you'd need to entice with other employment benefits. Having the flexibility to hire from an array of contractors and outside vendors makes it more affordable for your firm to obtain the services specific to its needs at the highest level of competency.

Employ a Mindful Marketing Strategy. It is a new world since we began our careers—that goes without saying. And because the legal market has become so competitive, not marketing is a sure-fire way to be out of business in three months. However, "in your face" marketing without a marketing strategy and with no method for tracking conversion of prospects to new clients is a waste of money and will likely not be very successful either.

The way to ensure that you are getting the most value for your marketing dollars is to track the conversion of *potential* client traffic to *actual* clients. Who is a "potential client"? A potential client is one who visits your firm's website, contacts your firm with inquiries, or even one who interacts with current or past clients.

So how long must you track this information? Six months is a reasonable amount of time to track the return on investment (ROI) on marketing dollars. This is the same amount of time that it should take, on average, for a prospect to become a client if your marketing strategy is effectively in place.

Six months later, if your marketing plan is not paying for itself with enough resulting new clients to cover its cost via the additional revenues to the firm, it is not working. And, if your marketing strategy is not working, then it is time to move on to the next step, with a change in delivery, source, or platform.

We make it a point when entering into any kind of contract for marketing services to negotiate an "early-out" clause. An early-out clause will give your firm the opportunity to abandon any strategy that proves to be unproductive to the purpose of the contract.

Recently, Liz worked with a client who had signed a contract to have billboards posted around town. Because Liz did not believe that the billboards would attract the high-end clientele the firm wanted to engage, she returned to the advertising company and renegotiated a "30-day early out" clause. The original contract was for 39 months, and, after ten months, it allowed you to cancel upon 30-day notice. Had they had to wait that ten months, the firm would have spent $15,000 on ineffective advertising. Instead, Liz negotiated a "30-day early out" clause with the company that allowed the firm to cancel the contract if, for example, after three or six months, the ROI on those marketing dollars had not justified the expenditure. It is always best to cut your losses as inexpensively as possible.

Similarly, do not use your marketing strategy on the general public unless your firm provides general practice services. Before attempting to engage a marketing strategy, identify your target client. When you advertise to everyone, missing your target client, you waste your marketing dollars. Such broad-based "marketing" does not constitute a functional marketing plan.

   If your firm does not have a marketing strategy, be sure to read the chapter on client development and marketing.

   INSTITUTE LEGAL PROJECT MANAGEMENT AND PROCESS IMPROVEMENT PROTOCOLS. Legal project management services establish and institute the procedures that dictate how to handle cases. This is the method by which your firm gets work accomplished in the business of providing legal services to clients. While many firms have not yet instituted this concept, it is becoming increasingly popular in law firms working under alternative fee arrangements with their clients, including fixed or flat fees, value billing, cost limits, and success bonuses.

   Even for firms that are still working on an hourly fee arrangement, legal project management protocols can increase the efficiency of legal services by designing a plan or timeline for handling cases. While you cannot control a case entirely with legal project management because you cannot control opposing counsel or the court system, legal project management will enable you to exercise some control over the case itself—which, in turn, will allow you to have some control over the cost.

   In handling a litigation matter, for example, you might institute timelines that will allow cases to move along as follows:

- Prepare, file, and serve complaint;
- If no answer on the 21st day after service of complaint, file for default;
- If answer received, follow up on discovery;
- 30 days after discovery is completed, set depositions to be completed in 30 days; and
- 30 days after depositions and all discovery are completed, schedule mediation.

   These legal project management protocols will provide a step-by-step timeline to help move a case along. While there may be deviations depending on the type of case, each procedure will nonetheless keep a case moving forward. Using these protocols will also help monitor staff accountability.

   Legal *process* management affects efficiency and productivity and is the companion to legal *project* management. Assess legal process management by measuring the performance of all processes running in your practice:

- Define the problem;
- Measure the current performance of the process currently in use;
- Identify the problem; and
- Control the problem by implementing solutions designed to eliminate the problem and improve the process.

If you or your staff notice an inefficient procedure in your office, take the time to fix the inefficiency sooner rather than later. To encourage this practice amongst your staff, reward them with small gifts like $25 gift cards or by allowing a staff member to leave an hour early while still being paid. You'll be surprised how much these small gifts will mean to your staff. Beyond the gift, they will feel appreciated and valued for their hard work. Your gratitude serves as encouragement to continue excelling.

The most important components of a business strategy designed to improve the bottom line of a firm are:

- To increase revenues and
- To reduce expenses.

The focus of the business of practicing law is on revenue and expenses—to increase one, while decreasing the latter. There are many things about the typical law practice that must be changed to accomplish these goals for your law firm. Your firm administrator or business manager is the best candidate for effectuating these changes, but there has to be support from the partners, or any effort you make will be futile. This is an all-or-nothing proposition. The survival of your law firm depends on it!

ROLE PLAY FIVE:
HOW TO ENGAGE VENDORS IN A BIDDING WAR

Players: Narrator
             Administrator
             Paper Salesman
             Paper Saleswoman

Narrator: Administrator calls the paper supplier to discuss prices.

Administrator: (dialing number on phone)

Salesman: Dunder Mifflin. This is Salesman.

Administrator: Hi, Salesman. This is Administrator from Johnson Law. I am shopping paper vendors and would make a switch from my current supplier if you can make it worth my while. I want to discuss prices with you.

Salesman: Wonderful. I am happy to discuss that with you. Our prices are quite competitive, so we should be able to work something out. What are you currently paying for your paper needs?

Administrator: Ha, ha – I know how this works. The first one to mention a dollar figure loses. I need you to quote me a price first and let me see whether you are really competitive with what we are paying now.

Salesman: Certainly. But first I need to know more. What type, size, quality, and amount of paper would you like to purchase?

Administrator: Well, I need 8 x 11 computer paper of standard quality. We are in the process of going paperless, but we still have hard files that require quite a bit of paper, approximately 2 cases each month.

Salesman: Okay. We also provide additional services, like shredding. Do you currently have a shredding provider?

Administrator: We do, but I am willing to consider going with a different company if the price is right.

Salesman: Well, we do offer paper by the case for $22.99. But, if you purchase at least ten cases in a six-month period, the price goes down to $21.99.

Administrator: Well, that is more expensive than I am currently paying.

Salesman: Really? That's surprising because our prices are quite competitive. What do you pay?

Administrator: I pay $21.50 per case, and there is no minimum case requirement for me to get that price.

Salesman: I'm surprised. How heavy is your paper? It must be thinner than our product.

Administrator: It is 70lb.

Salesman: Oh, well, that's the same as ours.

Administrator: Is there anything we can do to get the cost lower than what I am currently paying?

Salesman: Yes. I actually have the authority to price match if you can send me a receipt for what you are currently paying.

Administrator: Well, that's great, but it doesn't make sense for me to change providers if the price is just going to stay the same.

Salesman: We may be able to work out a better price if we bundle your paper products with another one of our services, like shredding. How much are you currently paying for shredding?

Administrator: We pay $100 per bin that we drop off at the shredding company.

Salesman: Well, if you commit to purchasing at least one case of paper per month at the price match rate of $21.50, then I could charge you $85 for one bin to be shredded each month and $40 for additional bins. And we come to you to pick up the bins.

Administrator: That is much cheaper! At the very least, we'll save at least $15 per month, and likely $75 per month since we usually need two bins to be shred. Plus, the time and money of paying an employee to drop off the bin at the shredder. This is wonderful! I'm so glad that I contacted you.

Salesman: I'm glad that we could meet your paper needs. I will email our contract to you.

Administrator: Fabulous. (hangs up phone)

Administrator: (sits a moment at desk thinking out loud) That went better than I expected it would. I thought that it would be a waste of time. But, I really like my current vendor. She always talks with me like we are old, good friends. I hate to switch to a new vendor who I don't really know. Unfortunately, business is business, and it is my job to manage the expenses of the office, personal relationships aside. Now that I have this quote, I wonder if my current vendor could meet it. Or better!

Administrator: (dials number on phone)

Saleswoman: (answering phone) Best Paper Ever, Inc., this is Saleswoman. How can I help you?

Administrator: Saleswoman, I wanted to discuss our current contract. Do you have a moment?

Saleswoman: For one of my favorite clients, absolutely! How can I help you? By the way, how are your adorable kids? And your husband? And your precious little doggies?

Administrator: They are all doing wonderfully. Listen, Saleswoman, I'm going to be up front with you.

Saleswoman: What is it?

Administrator: Well I enjoy our relationship, but I had heard that I could purchase paper at a cheaper rate. So I contacted Dunder Mifflin, and sure enough, they are willing to price match your prices, as well as include shredding for only $85 for the first bin each month and $40 for every additional bin. And they will pick up the documents to be shredded right from my office. This is just so much cheaper and less time-consuming than my current services that I don't see how I cannot choose to switch to this new company. That is, unless you can offer me something similar? (looking hopeful)

Saleswoman: I must say that I am surprised. Our rates are so competitive, I didn't think that you'd be able to find anything cheaper. But we also have a price match guarantee, so as long as you provide documentation of Dunder Mifflin's offer, I can meet that price for both your paper and shredding needs.

Administrator: That would be wonderful. I really felt bad about switching companies, but I have to go with the company that offers the best deal.

Saleswoman: I understand. And since you have been a customer for so long, I also have the authority to reduce your paper case cost by additional 50 cents – so we can actually beat the quote that you got. How does that sound?

Administrator: That's wonderful! Thank you so much! Just email me our new contract, and I'll get it back to you asap.

Saleswoman: Will do. Have a nice week!

Administrator: You too. (hanging up phone) Well that was easier than I thought. Everything is so expensive these days. If I can save the firm money, I can use those savings to do some morale boosting events for the staff. It all adds up. I think I'm on a roll. I'm going to call our print cartridge provider to see about lowering those rates!

Chapter Forty-Three
How to Avoid Debt

Twenty years ago, Liz owned a paralegal business that outsourced contract work with attorneys who specialized in personal injury services and medical malpractice work. She recalls one of those attorneys giving her advice that she will never forget—that a law firm should be run *"lean and mean."* As a law firm administrator, Liz continues to pass this advice on to attorneys who want to secure a credit line to pay bills.

When it comes to debt, less is always more. Going into debt to finance a service business simply doesn't make sense.

Lawyers sell their time, not widgets. And money should only be borrowed to produce widgets— never borrowed to sell time.

Borrowing money to finance a law practice opens the door to unending debt that will self-propagate as the borrowing and repaying become a vicious cycle of cash flow problems and crunches, in addition to regularly occurring firm expenses that must be paid. When you borrow money to cover everyday expenses and the overhead that you were already stretching to pay, you create a revolving credit line with more debt hanging over the firm like a black cloud. Your monthly expenses increase because of the payments on the credit line, and now you find yourself going back to the credit line to borrow more money each month. Eventually, you tap the credit line out, and you now have another expense with no more resources.

This is financially counterproductive and is surely a recipe for financial disaster.

Here are some ways to minimize the firm's debt and to avoid the downward spiral of incurring debt for your firm:

- PREPARE A BUSINESS PLAN BEFORE YOU OPEN YOUR PRACTICE. First, consider what area of law you want to practice. Second, explore how competitive that area of the market is. Next, determine how you'll bring in business to support your practice by determining your client development and marketing plan.

Finally, once you have this information, record it by writing your strategic business plan. Include client fee structures, an affordable rent budget that is mindful of times when revenues are not at their maximum potential, and what you expect your monthly operating expenses will be. It is much easier to achieve goals having a plan that delineates not only *where* you want your practice to go but also *how* you plan to get it there.

- INVEST IN A FINANCIAL PROFESSIONAL. Employ a business or financial manager or an administrator with a financial background to handle the revenues of your firm, including billing and collections. Many attorneys lack management and financial skills. Investing in a financial professional is a way to avoid incurring debt. A savvy financial expert with some objectivity can see what you can't. Honest feedback about your firm's shortcomings and management of the finances can be difficult to digest, but it is a necessary evil. If you are unwilling to hear the truth about the areas in which your firm's finances or spending habits can be improved, you will never be able to bring your firm's finances under control.

- AVOID BORROWING TO FINANCE LAWSUITS. Borrowing money to finance lawsuits is a risk. Years ago, many law firms handled hundreds of the Dow Corning breast implant cases. Some firms opened credit lines to finance the expense associated with those cases. They advanced the costs for medical evaluations and medical reports to enable claimants to be assigned to classes. In the end, the fees generated in those cases did not justify the debt some of those firms took on. Consequently, those firms likely paid off those credit lines for many years or dissolved.

- AVOID BORROWING TO FINANCE FIRM'S DAILY EXPENSES. Do not borrow money to cover day-to-day operating expenses. If you must borrow money because you cannot cover the day-to-day operating expenses of the firm, you have another problem. Incurring additional debt on top of what you already cannot pay will not solve the underlying problem—it only creates more debt. Someone should take a good, hard look at the financials of the firm, determine where the leak is, and take immediate remedial action. This includes reviewing expenses, reducing overhead, and ensuring that timekeepers are meeting their goals, fees are being collected, and the finances are being managed. The budget you created in your initial business plan would come in handy right about now.

- DO NOT RELY ON MONEY YOU DON'T YET HAVE. Do not spend funds you have on hand in anticipation of receiving money that is owed to you to cover expenditures. There is too much risk involved in spending future money with no guarantee that it will ever be received. *If it is not yet in your operating account, you do not have it.* And that includes waiting for deposits to clear.

- CONSIDER OUTSOURCING TO A PAYROLL COMPANY. Pay your payroll taxes through a payroll company. Not paying your 940/941 payroll taxes every time you run a payroll is creating another debt that will eventually catch up with the firm. The IRS and the Department of Revenue do not forgive payroll taxes. It may seem "cheaper" to simply run payroll now and worry about the taxes later. Be warned that when *later* comes (and it will), the notices in the mail can be for thousands of dollars because of the interest and the penalties that accrue. It is much easier to pay taxes in small amounts as payroll is due than to allow it to add up and to pay one huge lump sum. Avoid putting yourself in a financial situation in which the temptation develops to borrow money to pay the taxes. It is wise to outsource your payroll through a payroll company, pay your taxes and 401k contributions every pay period, and avoid those additional financial obligations.

- DO NOT HIRE NEW STAFF BEFORE THE BUSINESS TO PAY THEM IS GENERATED. Don't borrow money to add staff in anticipation of new business. The new business has to generate enough revenues to cover the cost of additional staff. Until the new business has been sustainable for a minimum of six to nine months—and preferably twelve—do not add staff that will not have enough work to do to do to justify their compensation. You must manage your firm with the staff you have until you ascertain that your new firm business will last, pay for itself, and generate sustainable revenues for the firm.

- DO NOT EXPAND YOUR SPENDING ACCORDING TO YOUR INCOME. When your firm is doing well financially, do not spend revenues simply because the funds are available. This is a good time to invest in a money market or other form of financial account to save money for potential cash flow deficits in the future.

Prosperity is seldom constant. There are always dips and waves in the economy. It is wise business practice in times of prosperity to save for times when the economy plummets or for times you may lose a big client. Such occurrences are unavoidable, but if you prepare for them, you and your firm will have a far better chance of making it through unexpected financial downturns. Afterward, your firm's goal ought to be to "pay back" money borrowed from investments when the cash flow allows.

- DON'T USE YOUR OPERATING ACCOUNT AS YOUR PERSONAL SLUSH FUND. Don't use your firm's operating account for personal purposes. Attorneys in solo or small firm practices tend to fall into this habit because they do not have partners to ensure they are accountable. The attorney acquires a debit card on the operating account, and suddenly, purchasing or personal spending spirals out of control. The problem intensifies when it is time to reconcile the account at the end of the month. It is difficult for the administrator or a bookkeeper to keep up with and reconcile an account when there are debits constantly being made to it. There is no way for them to know what will show up on the bank statement and no way to cover your overdrafts. This could result in overdraft fees being assessed against the account—and that is simply wasted revenues.

Keep in mind that any operating funds spent on personal expenses will be considered personal distributions to the attorney at year-end. These personal distributions, which have not had any taxes withheld, can create a personal tax liability for the attorney. In addition, attorneys using the firm debit card must be careful not to use funds that have not yet cleared. Doing so is a recipe for disaster.

The best option to avoid intermingling of expenses is to get a corporate credit card and dispense with the debit card. While we do not endorse debt, a corporate credit card will help to avoid incurring penalties for the overages of unexpected charges.

Make it a habit to pay the corporate card statement every month *in full.* Doing so will also help put into perspective the depth of your spending. Avoid using the corporate credit card as a source from which to borrow. Otherwise, when the card taps out, there will be yet another debt to pay and no resources from which to draw.

There are many ways to handle finances and avoid the need to borrow. Manage the firm's income and expenses, *do not let the finances manage the firm.*

Attorneys often do not have the time to manage the firm's finances and also may lack the objectivity to do so. Sacrificing an attorney's time to manage the firm's financial future really does not make sense if he can bill that time to paying clients. It is best to hire an administrator or a business manager who has the necessary professional services experience. The return on hiring such an expert will be well worth the investment—in fact, it's one you can take to the bank!

Chapter Forty-Four
How to Manage Client Billing and Collections

Billing and collections are pivotal components to the financial success of a law firm. Your billable hours generate the revenues that comprise the financial foundation of the practice and make everything possible. Without billable hours, there is no law firm.

How effective are your law firm's billing procedures? You can measure the effectiveness of your billing and collection procedures with the percentage of receivables that are collected from your clients every month. Generating revenues and the efficient management of a law firm is all about *managing the business of practicing law.*

Nothing strikes a nerve with clients more than having to pay legal fees. Why do clients think it is acceptable to expect lawyers to work for free? Doctors and other professionals are not expected to work for free. No one asks for a discount for a bypass or appendectomy. In fact, it would be deeply disconcerting if a doctor offered "discounted" surgical procedures.

In today's economy, the client wants to reduce his legal expenses and still receive good service and achieve satisfactory results. This is the "have your cake and eat it too" phenomenon. Value billing and flat fee billing structures are becoming more prevalent.

But even in today's economy, you still get what you pay for.

The Realities of Client Billing

- Most clients pay their bills begrudgingly. Rarely is a client thrilled to pay his legal bills, even when the results obtained are better than he could have expected or anticipated. If the outcome is a good one for your client, he will likely pay the bill sooner, but you will still have to listen to complaints about the bill. No matter how much or how little it is, it's still too much.

- It is more difficult to collect two months of billable hours than it is to collect one. You have a much better chance of collecting $500 than you do of collecting $1,000 or more.

- Establish a protocol of regular billing cycles every 30 days, on or very close to the same date each month. This practice will help the client know when to expect your statement every month. This does not mean that he will pay any faster, but at least he will know to expect the statement. Some clients do actually plan their finances.

- Some clients try to plan their finances around their income depending on pay periods when they have income coming. Work out an agreement with the client to wait for payment until the 15th or the 20th of the month, or whenever he has the income available to pay you. Waiting a few extra days to get your bill paid but working with the client will build goodwill with the client, and you will know when to expect his payment.

- Confirm that all timekeepers have entered their time for each billing period. Clients are always looking for reasons to dispute bills and ask questions to delay payment. A red flag goes up when a client receives a bill in May for April work with March time on it. In these (hopefully) rare instances, it is sometimes easier and more cost efficient to write off that time than it is to respond to a client dispute.

- Clients always want to know, "What happened to my money?" Make sure that your billing statement not only includes the balance that is owed but also any funds left on retainer in trust for fees and costs and any disbursements made from those monies. Don't make your client try to decipher invoices. It should be simple to determine what is in trust and what remains in unapplied funds. If it is too confusing, she will put it aside and tell herself she will deal with it later. If later never comes, neither does your payment. See a sample invoice in Appendix Three.

- Sometimes the only money you will see from a client is the fee retainer paid at the commencement of a matter. Be sure to estimate as accurately as possible a retainer that will cover the services to be rendered. Be sure to secure a cost retainer, as well, unless you plan to advance costs, such as expenses for court reporters, process servers, filing, and the like.

  Vendors do not care that your client has not paid you. The vendor's agreement to provide a service to your client is with you, not with your client. Therefore, the vendor will hold you responsible. Make sure you have the client's money to pay these vendor bills as they come due. This will avoid problems with the vendors that you depend on to continue to provide services, and the client will know up front what costs are involved so that he can plan for these expenditures.

  It is important for your firm to maintain a good relationship with your vendors. Do not risk your business relationship with them, or you will end up having to pay in advance before they will work with your firm.

- Carefully track the balance of the fee and cost retainers the client paid you. When those retainers are nearly exhausted, request a replenishment retainer. Be sure to include language in your retainer agreement that a replenishment retainer for fees and costs is due within a specific number of days after your request. Your firm administrator should check the balances every time a billing cycle occurs. If you request replenishment funds before fee and cost retainers are exhausted, this should give you sufficient time to ask for and receive replenishment monies before you go into the red with a client.

- Clients are not impressed by the number of billable hours that you worked on their case. The number of billable hours does not relate in their mind to hard how you worked—this only represents how much you are charging them. No matter how successful the result you achieved for a client, the number of hours that you billed is always too many. In the client's mind, you should have been able to get the same result in less time. Essentially it comes with the territory.

We cannot stress enough the importance of billing each and every client every single month without fail. This practice will avoid a telephone call the following month when there is billable time and trust monies have been exhausted. We guarantee that the client will call wanting to know what happened to his money, even if he is holding the bill that details the time that was spent on his case and how retainer monies or unapplied fees were applied.

HOW TO REDUCE CLIENT COMPLAINTS ABOUT BILLING

So now that you know the realities of client billing, come to terms with the fact that clients will never be totally satisfied with their bills regardless of the outcome of their case. Call the outcome satisfactory, exceptional, outstanding, or superb. It does not matter. The client will still be unhappy because they have to pay.

Having worked as a law firm administrator for almost 20 years, Liz can tell you firsthand that having billing procedures in place, with rare exception, can make all the difference in generating regular collection of fees and costs from your clients.

There is a lot to do in law firms, and for smaller and medium firms especially, there arc sometimes not enough hours in the day to accomplish everything. But there is nothing more important than generating those precious billable hours.

Following a close second is actually preparing the bills. If bills are not prepared and sent timely in such a way that clients actually pay their bills, then the billable hours mean nothing. For some firms, there are no hard and fast rules about client billing. Even if there is a general billing protocol that the firm follows, the billing may be delayed by something seemingly more important on the agenda. Liz once worked for a firm in which the senior partner reviewed the client list to decide which clients were to be billed that month. Haphazard billing procedures like this equate to haphazard collection of fees. It's that simple.

Take these steps to reduce and/or prevent client complaints about their bills.

1. ESTABLISH A REGULAR BILLING CYCLE OF EVERY 30 DAYS. Then, bill every client *every* month. Tell the client when they retain your services that you will do that in your retainer agreement.

Cut off time by the close of business for the prior month on the last day of each month. Give your timekeepers until the close of business on the first of the month to have all their time in. Because they should be entering their time contemporaneously, their time entries should be current. If you are consistent, your staff will know every month what the cut-off date is and they will work with it.

On the second or third day of the month, run your pre-bills. Circulate the pre-bills for review to the attorneys and paralegals so they can make necessary edits to the description of services or the time billed. Afterward, present them to the managing partner for final edits

225

and revisions. Allow two days for the return of the edited pre-bills.

If everyone is timely in meeting deadlines to return the edited pre-bills, you should be able to establish a final date for the actual bills to be sent to the client. The tenth of the month would be a good day as it will allow for edits from attorneys who might be in trial, on vacation, or otherwise unavailable or away from the office.

In smaller or solo firms, the process can go more quickly. With one of Liz's clients, she runs pre-bills at 5:01 pm on the last day of the month. She does the initial review for grammar, punctuation, duplicate entries (never send a client a bill with a duplicate time entry), and the time billed. Having actual legal experience, she can recognize that preparing a memorandum of law should not be billed at .2 hours and will bring it to the attorney's attention.

The next day the attorney reviews the pre-bills and makes appropriate edits. The bills are finalized that same day and are emailed to the clients. Ledgers are updated and trust transfers are made from clients who have fees or costs in trust. If replenishment retainers are required, Liz includes the request for cost or fee replenishment retainers in her billing email. The firm's bills are efficiently prepared in one day.

It is important to develop and adhere to the billing cycle schedule. After a few months, clients will know when to expect statements. Consistency is critical. Clients will respect that your law firm is run as a business with professionalism.

2. THE RETAINER AGREEMENT IS WHERE YOU MUST OUTLINE THE BILLING ARRANGEMENTS WITH SPECIFICITY. If the case is an hourly rate billing, be sure to specify the individual hourly rates for partners, associates, paralegal, legal assistants, and administrative staff. This is a bulletproof way in which to avoid any questions or confusion down the line when a client claims that he was unaware of a particular timekeeper's hourly rate.

3. OCCASIONALLY THE FIRM INCREASES FEE RATES. Your retainer agreement should notify the client of this possibility. When this happens, clients must be notified in writing 30 days before the increase is implemented that rates are being adjusted and to what amounts. It is inappropriate to raise the hourly fees of any of the timekeepers without written notice in advance to the client; and it will likely create client discontent. Ensure this doesn't happen by having set procedures and following them. (See *Rate Increase Notice* in Appendix Four.)

4. YOUR BILLING STATEMENT MUST REFLECT TRUST MONIES, UNAPPLIED FUNDS, AND COSTS HELD IN TRUST. It should also state what clients' monies were disbursed and to whom they were paid. If monies were deducted to pay fees, that should be reflected as well. Clients are less likely to question how their funds were disbursed or what is remaining if it is plainly and clearly laid out in the billing statement.

Of primary importance is the continuity and consistency of billing procedures. It does not matter what day you choose to generate pre-bills and finalize and send your bills to your clients. What matters is the consistency of sending bills every month at the same time so your clients will know to expect the bills. This is the reason why your mortgage and car payments are due on the same day every month. You know when these bills must be paid every month and you plan accordingly. It helps your clients to know what to expect so they can budget their finances and, in turn, will help your firm collect its revenues on a more consistent basis.

You cannot control your revenues or your collections so that the firm generates the same income every month. Billing procedures like these can help your firm to collect a larger percentage of its monthly billable hours and help stabilize the finances of your firm. This will make it easier to prepare and adhere to your firm's budget.

Remember, clients are sometimes unwilling participants in litigation for reasons that are beyond their control. For many, hiring an attorney is an almost unaffordable necessity. They have limited funds and see the expenditure for attorneys' services as an unavoidable expense when they would rather spend their money elsewhere.

Clearly, that is something over which you as the lawyer have no control. Certainly, you are entitled to be paid for your work, and the client knows that. In an effort to alleviate some of the client's anxiety and apprehension, and to reduce the stress on your firm and the person who does your billing, approach billing with the foregoing in mind to pave the way towards a smoother billing process for the client and your firm.

The collection of fees can be an uncomfortable but necessary evil. No one likes to ask for money or to be paid, even when she works hard and is entitled to be paid. When a client refuses to pay his bill month after month, you may feel compelled to do less work for him. But, as long as you are his attorney, you must represent him to the fullest, with zealous advocacy. You cannot simply ignore deadlines or hearings because he hasn't paid his bill.

If you feel that your work product and dedication for a client has waned because he refuses to pay you for your services, you must withdraw rather than work at a diminished level. The non-payment of fees can create a conflict of interest between you and your client. You will each begin to resent one another. In this type of scenario, it is better to cut your losses and withdraw than to end up with a client who owes you six figures or who files a bar grievance against you because you have lowered your standards.

Finally, if you haven't withdrawn quickly enough, and you let the client get too far ahead, consider asking the client to sign a promissory note for the total amount he owes you while you are still on good terms. While it is not a pleasant experience, the reality is that you might eventually have to file a lawsuit to collect monies due your firm for work performed for him. If you have already obtained that note, and the client does not abide by its terms (of a promissory note he voluntarily signed), your collection attorney can sue on the note instead of or in addition to suing for fees owed or for breach of contract. (See Appendix Five for a sample promissory note.)

You might be wondering what difference that will make. If you sue for breach of contract or for account owed, the client will use that opportunity to question all of your billable time. Even if you ultimately succeed (and, the few times Joryn has had to do this, she has), this is a huge timewaster. You can spend a couple of hours defending your billable time sitting in the witness chair.

If, on the other hand, the client has signed a promissory note, the basis of the lawsuit will be failure to pay on the note. This avoids empowering the client to argue about services rendered, the terms of the retainer agreement, the time that you billed, and the monies owed, as it is the promissory note on which you are suing. Either way, this will not be a pleasant experience, but with the promissory note in hand, you dodge the extra headache of listening to the client trying to pick apart your bill and to convince the judge to second guess all the work that you performed for the client.

It becomes financially counterproductive to render services and bill the client for the work and costs expended and then to spend almost as much time justifying the fees and costs incurred. When you reach the point at which the work and the collection process take the same amount of time, your time is actually better spent sitting on the beach.

REVIEW QUESTIONS THIRTEEN

Lawyers:

1. Do you use billing software to manage your client billing? What kind? List the software.
2. Are you confident that you know how to use it as efficiently as possible? Have you been trained to use it? If not, register for a training.
3. If you do not use software, what kind of system do you have in place for client billing? Explain it in writing.
4. Would adding a software program save you time and money? List the advantages and disadvantages.
5. What do you do when a client refuses or is unable to pay a bill? Do you immediately withdraw from representation? If not, how long do you wait until you withdraw? Write down your firm's policy. Revise it, if necessary, and inform your staff.
6. How do you collect on your unpaid bills? Sue the clients? Send them to collections? Cut deals with them? Place liens on their property? List the advantages and disadvantages of each of these options.

Law Students:

1. Has anyone ever owed you money and refused to pay it? What did you do to try to collect the debt? Journal that experience.
2. Once you open your practice, have you thought about what your policy will be regarding clients who don't pay their bills? How long will you give them before you withdraw? What if you really like the client and feel bad for their situation? Would you wait longer to withdraw? Write down the policy that you believe you will implement, and confer with a lawyer friend to see if it is reasonable. Discuss the advantages and disadvantages of same.

CHAPTER FORTY-FIVE
HOW TO DETERMINE THE FINANCIAL REPORTS THAT YOUR FIRM NEEDS

Every business revolves around its financials. Profit and loss statements are not sufficient for law firms because they do not tell the whole story. Law firms sell time. Lawyers must capture time, and they should not overlook any opportunity to generate revenues or recoup costs.

Whether you are preparing an annual budget or just reviewing the firm's revenues for the previous month, financial reports generated by your accounting and billing programs are crucial to understanding where your firm is financially.

Ignorance is not bliss. Ignore the importance of staying on top of, or better yet, ahead of your financials and you will discover too late that the revenues are not covering the monthly expenses. Financial reports are *essential* to the survival of your firm.

There are billing and accounting software programs developed specifically for the legal profession that will generate the reports you need to manage the finances of your firm. It is important to analyze client billing to identify the clients in good standing as well as to identify and analyze the reasons for habitually late paying clients. The following reports will help you manage your law firm's finances so that they don't manage you.

1. TIMEKEEPER REPORTS. This report should be part of your billing program. At the end of the month, you can generate timekeeper reports showing the number of billable and non-billable hours each attorney and paralegal generated for the month. Timekeeper reports allow you to track whether your timekeepers are meeting their monthly or annual billable hour quotas. You can also calculate the revenue lost to the firm for every timekeeper who did not meet his monthly requirement. Don't just look at the number of hours a timekeeper's billables are short, but also multiply the shortage by his billable rate. Somehow a 23-hour billing shortage by an associate does not have the same impact as a loss of $6,325 in a month.

2. FEES COLLECTED REPORT. Your billing program should be able to generate a report of how much each client has paid versus the balance that was due. This will determine what percentage of billables are actually being collected. It will show you which clients need more encouragement to pay their invoices. The purpose of this report is not to track the firm's income. If you require clients to post replenishment retainers when their fee retainers fall below a specific amount, this report, in tandem with your trust balance report, will tell you which clients need to replenish their fee retainers. If a client's billables run consistently higher every month than the replenishment retainer you requested, you need to ask for a

larger replenishment retainer.

3. MONTHLY EXPENSE REPORTS. This is part of your accounting program and should be tied to your operating account. Journal entries should be made every time a payment is issued from your firm's operating account identifying the expense category. You will know what you are spending on office supplies, rent, equipment, utilities, meals, and other expenses. This is *the* opportunity to learn where unnecessary spending, or overspending on necessary expenses, is occurring. It does not make sense to spend $21 for one highlighter when you can purchase a whole pack for $12. Prices of copy paper vary from supplier to supplier. We know it is not cost effective to have an administrator spend ten hours to find the best deal on paper. If you have an experienced law firm administrator, she already knows where to get the best deals, and she will negotiate with your vendors for the best deal.

4. DEPARTMENT INCOME REPORT. Some firms have different departments for areas of specialties such as real estate, probate, and business litigation. It is a good idea to break down the income that each area of the firm's specialties is generating. If the real estate department is not covering the overhead for that department, while business litigation is extremely lucrative and carrying the real estate department, consider moving staff to business litigation. Support the areas of the practice that are performing or create a plan to make sure that each department is not only carrying its own overhead but also generating a profit for the firm. Perhaps consider reviewing your marketing strategy to focus additional revenues on real estate work.

5. ACCOUNTS RECEIVABLE REPORTS. Review your accounts receivable every 30 days, without fail. The longer you wait to review and act on your accounts receivable, the longer it will take to collect. If a case has concluded and you do not promptly follow up with the client to get paid, the client will let it go until he is ready to pay, if ever. Some clients believe that if they wait long enough to pay your bill, then they will receive a discount because the firm wants to get paid and get the debt off their books. You did not perform discount work, so you should not offer or accept a discount payment. After 120 days or more of not receiving payment, many firms will take what they can get, causing the firm to take a financial hit. Don't put yourself or your firm in this position. Stay on top of your accounts receivable.

6. FEE TRUST BALANCE REPORTS. Many firms take upfront fee retainers that are deposited into trust for future billables. When a client's bill is generated, the firm will pay the bill out of the monies on retainer in trust. Your law firm should generate a monthly fee trust balance report to ascertain how much money each client has available in trust each billing cycle. Set a limit, and when a client's fee trust balance falls below that limit, ask for a replenishment retainer. *Do not wait until the balance is zero.* You will end up trying to collect on an invoice from the client because the client has no more fee money in trust. Had you approached the client when the fee trust balance was $1,000, you would have funds available to pay the client's bill. If a client does not replenish the fee retainer when there is a $1,000 balance in trust, you will have sufficient time to withdraw from representation before your

firm goes into the red.

7. CLIENT COSTS ADVANCED REPORT. If your law firm advances client costs, make sure the journal entries are accurately reflected as "client costs advanced" with the name of each client. These client costs must be entered on the client ledger every time an expense is paid and needs to be included on the billing statement to ensure that the firm recovers the costs from the client. To avoid having to seek reimbursement from a client for costs advanced by the firm, request a cost retainer at the time when the client retains the firm. Cost retainers should be replenished the same as fee retainers. When they fall below a nominal amount of $100, request that the cost retainer be replenished by the client.

These are reports that you will want to share with a select few individuals in your firm: partner, administrator, and bookkeeper. We do not recommend sharing these reports with timekeepers or other employees in your firm. Business owners understand the concept that generation of revenues does not equate profit to the firm. There are expenses involved in running any business, and the revenues collected pay the overhead to run the firm, including employees' salaries.

Several years ago, Liz was an administrator for a law firm in New Port Richey. The firm had a few areas of law that it practiced and was set up in departments. No matter how much you pay employees, they always want more: more compensation, more benefits, or a bigger bonus. In this particular firm, the founding partner was becoming unnerved with the continuous complaints of employees wanting more of something. One month, he told Liz that he was considering sharing the income and expense report for the firm with the employees for the past month. He thought this was a good way to make employees realize how much the overhead was to maintain the firm so they would all have jobs.

Flabbergasted would be a good word to describe Liz's reaction to this suggestion. Her immediate thought was that employees were going to look at the revenues the firm generated that month and *only* the revenues. They would not see the other half of the equation of income and expenses—*the expenses*. Although the firm was generating income of about three million dollars a year, the operating expenses for the firm were significant. Never share more financial information with employees than you absolutely must. Doing so will actually cause more resentment among the staff because it will reinforce their opinions that they are underpaid.

When revenues are not sufficient to cover your firm's overhead expenses, the solution is not always that the firm is not generating sufficient revenues. Mismanagement of revenues, or perhaps, *the lack of management of revenues*, is often the problem. These reports will help your law firm manage its income and expenses and ensure that receivables are collected promptly.

Collections don't fall under either category. When you discount a bill or send a client account to collections, thereby losing a percentage of the monies owed to the collection agency, your law firm is losing money. No one is in business to lose money. Utilizing these reports will help keep your firm operating in the green.

CHAPTER FORTY-SIX
HOW TO PREPARE YOUR LAW FIRM FOR YEAR-END

Somehow the end of the year always seems to creep up on us before we are ready for it. Suddenly, you look up from your work and realize it is the fourth quarter of the year. You find yourself in the midst of tying up loose ends on client cases before the court, judges, opposing counsel, and experts take time off for the holidays. You may be planning a holiday lunch, dinner, or party. It's December, and your employees are talking about Christmas bonuses. You are likely grappling with what to do about Christmas bonuses.

When the end of the year approaches, there are some things that you can do to prepare for success in the coming year. As the saying goes, "People don't plan to fail, they fail to plan."

1.   PREPARE YOUR BUDGET. You will need this as a footprint for where your firm is going in the coming year and how you will get there. Excess spending in a law firm happens most often when something is needed in a hurry because no one has planned for it. Suddenly your printer is out of toner, and there is not a spare one in the office. You need to get one somewhere, and because you need it right then and there, no one cares about what it costs. The budget is all about planning. Cut unnecessary spending. There is always a way to save a dollar. Remember, money matters.

2.   REVIEW TIMEKEEPER BILLABLES FOR THE YEAR. Ideally, you should have reviewed these every quarter to track productivity, as well as discussed billing quotas with timekeepers who did not perform as well as they should have. If there are issues with billable hours, you need to address these now before the new year brings more of the same.

3.   REVIEW YOUR STAFFING. With a billable hours report, review your staffing needs and determine whether changes are in order. If the last six months have shown a decrease in billables because the work isn't there, consider downsizing or rightsizing the firm. While it is never a pleasant task, it certainly is necessary unless your firm can afford to carry the extra overhead in spite of a lack of profitability. Alternatively, consider a redistribution of the work or a reassignment of staff to different tasks or departments.

4.   PREPARE FOR TAX TIME. Corporate taxes will be due soon. Have your firm administrator or bookkeeper begin assembling the documents you will need to provide to your accountant to prepare your corporate taxes. She will be able to use your billing or

accounting software to generate some of the reports needed to prepare your corporate taxes. If you are a sub-chapter S corporation, your law firm's corporate taxes will need to be prepared before you will be able to prepare your personal income taxes.

5. W-2S AND 1099S ARE DUE BY JANUARY 31. Make sure you meet this deadline. Some employees file their income taxes the minute they receive their W-2 forms to get their refund as soon as possible. If you use a payroll company, you should be able to download and distribute W-2 forms to your employees by the first week of January. Some accounting programs have the ability to allow you to generate 1099 information, provided that journal entries accurately reflect when payment is made to a 1099 employee.

6. CALENDAR DEADLINES FOR THE COMING YEAR. Know when your leases, your contracts with credit card providers, and other contracts are set to expire. Do not let these dates sneak up on you without planning to shop around to negotiate a better deal than the one you have. Even if you want to stay where you are and keep your current space and other services, remember that everything is negotiable. So negotiate.

7. REVIEW YOUR WEBSITE. Make sure the message of "what we can do for you" is coming through on your site. A potential client should understand how you can help them within 30 seconds of looking at your website. Update bios, photos, and blogs. It is important that your website information is up-to-date, that it loads quickly, and that all links are functioning.

8. REVIEW YOUR TRUST ACCOUNTING PROCEDURES EVERY YEAR. Evaluate the procedures being followed by the individual responsible for reconciling the trust account. Ensure that procedures are being followed to the letter. Implement any changes to your trust account procedures to make sure you are in compliance with local bar rules. With the help of your law firm administrator or bookkeeper and accounting program, this is not as difficult as it sounds. In the event of a trust account audit, you can be confident that your firm's reconciliation is in compliance with the guidelines.

9. PERFORM ANNUAL PERFORMANCE AND COMPENSATION REVIEWS. It is a good practice to perform a peripheral performance review of employees every 90 days. It is easier to address issues as they arise rather than waiting months until the next performance review. January is a good time to perform annual reviews and performance evaluations of your staff. This is much easier than doing anniversary reviews throughout the year, which can sometimes be disruptive to schedules and result in delays. Be sure to ask the following questions: "How do you think you are doing?" and "What do you need help with and how can I assist you?" Do not make a performance evaluation adversarial. There is no benefit, and it will accomplish nothing.

10. TRACK THE ROI (RETURN ON INVESTMENT) OF YOUR MARKETING DOLLARS. You should review the money spent to bring in new business, as well as the conversion of potential

clients to new business, every three months. But now that year-end is almost here, do not spend another penny on marketing before you know whether your marketing strategy is even paying for itself. If it isn't, get help from someone who knows how to implement a marketing strategy that works for your law firm business model, and dedicate the monies you were spending to a plan that will bring results.

11. GO PAPERLESS. This sounds like a more daunting task than it really is. Follow three simple steps: choose a document management system; start your paperless protocol with the next file you open; and set up your paperless files the same way you would set up a paper file. Make sure you get buy-in from your staff. It will make the process much easier. If you do go paperless, be sure to ensure that a backup protocol is in place to automatically backup files in a secure fashion.

You may feel you already have plenty to do without adding these tasks to the list. But don't overlook these important issues. Managing the business of practicing law is an important facet of the practice of law. You cannot build a house without a solid foundation. Your law firm is no different.

CHAPTER FORTY-SEVEN
HOW TO DETERMINE WHETHER CHRISTMAS BONUSES ARE APPROPRIATE

One of the most popular Christmas movies showcasing the dilemma of a bonus at the holidays has to be *National Lampoon's Christmas Vacation*. The protagonist Clark Griswold is the corporate grunt who is so sure he will get a Christmas bonus, he puts a non-refundable deposit on an in-ground swimming pool for his family.

However, Griswold discovers on Christmas Eve—when his bonus arrives a few days later than usual—that instead of giving him money, his employer has enrolled him in the Jelly-of-the-Month Club. It's quite the letdown, and Griswold lets his disappointment be known in no uncertain terms.

As Clark Griswold points out in the movie, many employees, especially those with children, depend on the Christmas/year-end bonus as part of their compensation or for holiday shopping. Unless a year-end or holiday bonus is negotiated or offered as part of the compensation package, however, bonuses are discretionary. There is no obligation by the firm, nor should there be any expectation by an employee, to give or receive a bonus. Yet, there is often an expectation—and sometimes apprehension—by the employee wondering if they will receive a bonus from the firm.

There is no one-size-fits-all formula for giving your law firm employees a Christmas bonus. The economy has affected law firms large and small. Reduced revenues affected by alternate billing practices stemming from clients demanding value for their money has affected the year-end Christmas bonus to a great extent. Plainly put, law firms are really feeling the pinch in recent years.

The precedent that exists in many firms, especially for timekeepers, is that Christmas bonuses have gone the way of pay-for-performance bonuses. The equation for calculating these bonuses is based on the revenues generated by the billing timekeeper. Many law firms can no longer afford to reach into the coffers and give bonuses that are not tied to some kind of performance review. When this type of bonus is the one offered by a firm, funds are often not distributed until February or March of the following year as calculations of income, expense, and profit/loss are involved in these types of bonuses.

No matter what the circumstances of your firm, don't totally be a Scrooge and ignore the holiday season or the contributions that your employees have made to the success of your law firm. Here are some options that will let your employees know their work is appreciated, regardless of what your budget is:

1. GIVE A GIFT CARD. This can be especially thoughtful if you give a card to a store or a

website that you know your employee frequents or one that can be used anywhere and is the equivalent of cash.

2. GIVE A WEEK'S SALARY. Even if the budget is tight, a week's salary for each employee is something you can make part of your annual budget, avoiding the last-minute scramble to come up with a week's salary for each employee.

3. CLOSE THE FIRM FOR THE WEEK BETWEEN CHRISTMAS AND NEW YEAR'S. Unless there is an emergency, usually by the 22nd or 23rd of December things have slowed down as your clients are on focused on their own families. You can either arrange for a skeleton crew of one or two on a rotating basis one day during the holiday or forward the phones and have someone check emails.

4. HAVE A HOLIDAY LUNCH AND THEN GIVE EMPLOYEES THE REST OF THE DAY OFF TO FINISH THEIR SHOPPING AND OTHER HOLIDAY PREPARATIONS. Things get so hectic at this time of the year. Everyone will appreciate a few extra hours to get things done.

Finally, if your firm does distribute any kind of cash or pay-for-performance bonus, try to distribute it a week before Christmas. With the economy being what it is, many employees wait to do their Christmas shopping until they get a bonus (hoping that they will get one), so if possible, distribute it a week before December 25th. Your employees will appreciate it.

CONCLUSION

We have written this book with the understanding that buying furniture or opening a bank account is basic business that we do not need to address. Neither Joryn nor Liz can make recommendations to help a lawyer or firm decide on what billing or accounting software to purchase without knowing more about your firm and your clients. There are too many variables that would affect our recommendation.

This book was written addressing the fundamentals of law firm administration that can and will increase your firm's profitability, success and ultimately its survival.

Liz and Joryn have both seen first-hand how mismanagement of a law firm's business can be detrimental to a firm's success. We have also seen how a firm heading on a downward spiral, due to mismanagement or perhaps, better-phrased, *lack of management,* can be turned around within three to six months of active, hands-on management of the firm.

This book was not written as a textbook or in the style of a guidebook. We did not want it to be boring. We hate boring books and we do not learn well from them. We wrote this book to be interesting and informative. The purpose is to provide you with valuable and practical information that you can apply to real life situations in your own office. We have given real life examples of Liz's experiences as an administrator and Joryn's experiences as an attorney to show you how the outcome of a situation can be affected by the way it is addressed. Fortunately for Liz, much of her success in managing the business of law firms comes from a foundation in the legal profession that precedes and serves as a foundation for her work as a professional law firm administrator.

Every situation has its own nuances. Circumstances that arise will be affected by the culture of your law firm and so you will have to tailor our information and guides to your own firm.

As attorneys, we know that there is no way that you can handle the administrative functions, tend to the business of practicing law, actually practice law, and bill those hours to keep those revenues coming in. If you think you can, you are only fooling yourself. Do not go it alone. There are many ways to get help with the administration of your firm that will not impose a 25-hour workday on you. You cannot possibly wear every hat in the office and do a good job. *Jack of all Trades, Master of None* does not work when you are trying to run a successful law firm.

Working in the legal profession is the only career path Liz has ever pursued. She loves her work and is passionate about it. It is her personal goal to make attorneys and their offices function at maximum efficiency, productively and profitably. You can be a success!

We know this book may not have all the answers you might need. We intended it as a guide and a resource. If you have a question, a problem, or a comment, or perhaps you just want to chat with us, we look forward to hearing from you. You can get in touch with Joryn at Joryn@OpenPalmLaw.com and e-mail Liz at Liz.ManagementConsultant@gmail.com.

We make it our personal goal to respond to every email that is sent to us. We want you and your firm to achieve its goals. Thanks for reading!

APPENDIX

APPENDIX ONE
CONTRACT FOR LEGAL SERVICES

I, _____ ("the client"), the undersigned, do hereby retain and employ LAW FIRM ("the firm") as my attorneys to provide legal services with respect only to _____. This representation does NOT include any related tort, civil, or criminal claims not expressly described above. I hereby acknowledge that I understand there may be a limitations period that applies to any such related matter(s). Therefore, time may be of the essence, and I understand that I should contact another attorney soon to ensure that I do not lose valuable legal rights if I wish to pursue any such matter.

I understand and agree that I employ the firm, and that the firm may associate other attorneys at its discretion, as long as the association is timely disclosed to me, and I do not timely object, and that employment is accepted by the firm, upon the following terms and conditions.

1.   **Cancellation:** This contract is made and entered into this ___ day of _____, _____. It may be canceled by written notification to the firm at any time within three business days of the date of signature. If canceled within three days, there is no fee due, other than for the initial consultation, and for any services already performed by the firm. The client is obligated to repay any money reasonably spent by the firm on his/her behalf upon such cancellation.

2.   **Non-refundable retainer:** Receipt from the client of an initial non-refundable retainer and minimum fee of $10,000. This retainer will be applied to the final invoice. The client hereby acknowledges and agrees that this non-refundable retainer is reasonable.

3.   **Refurbishing retainer:** There is no additional retainer. The client will pay the invoiced amount monthly within thirty days of being invoiced.

4.   **Attorney's fees based upon time expended:** Employment of the firm to handle this matter is on an hourly basis. The client will pay the firm a reasonable attorney's fee based principally upon the time involved and at a rate of $450 per hour for partners, $200-300 per hour for associates, $300 per hour for consulting attorneys, and $150 per hour for law clerks, paralegals, and other legal assistants. The client understands and agrees that this is an hourly

rate that includes time spent on, among other things: phone calls; preparation of letters, e-mails, and pleadings; discovery; client and other office conferences; and travel to, preparation for, and attendance at court hearings, mediations, and settlement conferences. The client understands that it is the firm's practice to compute not less than one-tenth of an hour for each service rendered, including each telephone call, no matter how short its duration.

These rates change periodically. If the rates increase during the course of representation, the firm will so advise the client in writing, and this contract will be governed by the new hourly rates.

The client acknowledges that the firm has fully explained the basis of computing its compensation, and that the firm's compensation is based upon, among other factors: the time and labor involved; the novelty or difficulty of the issues presented; the results obtained; the time limitations imposed by this representation; and the reputation, experience, and ability of the firm in performing this type of service. The client understands that the primary factor in determining the cost of a case is both parties' willingness to compromise and to settle issues. Based upon information provided by the client at the initial consultation, the firm may have estimated the fees necessary to conclude this matter; however, this estimate may vary greatly from the final total and is in no way a limitation on the potential charges.

CREDIT CARD

The client will pay the firm's monthly invoice for legal services and costs by credit card:

___ Visa   ___ MasterCard

_____   _____
Printed Name on Card   Authorized Signature

_____   _____
Account Number   Expiration Date

_____
CVT2 Code (last three digits on back of card, by signature)

Cardholder Billing Address _____

If the credit card identified above is denied for any reason, the client will provide another valid credit card to which the firm may bill its invoices, or this agreement is deemed breached.

5.   **Costs**: The client agrees to pay all costs expended by the firm on the client's behalf,

including but not limited to office costs, court costs, costs of experts, transcripts, and travel expenses.

The client agrees to pay all costs, necessary disbursements, and reasonable personal and travel expenses that are expended by the firm for or on behalf of the client, and in connection with the client's cause. In the event that the firm advances such funds, the client shall reimburse the firm, and such funds will not be credited against the initial non-refundable retainer, if any. The client and the firm will confer to evaluate and assess what, if any, cost deposit is necessary to proceed. Should the client decline to advance any additional costs and the firm is thereby required to withdraw, the firm shall be entitled to retain fees from any monies received from the client. In the event that there exists an unpaid charge for legal services rendered by the firm to the client by the affixation of signature(s) hereto, the client expressly agrees to the application of any unexpended amounts in the firm's trust account (cost deposit account) to the payment of unpaid legal fees.

The client agrees to pay necessary expenses and disbursements separately as they are incurred and/or made by the firm. Expenses and disbursements may include, but shall not be limited to: fees for private investigators, expert witnesses, and court reporter transcripts; travel expenses for attorneys and investigators; and any and all other expenses that the firm considers reasonable and necessary for the proper litigation of this action. The firm will charge a periodic administrative overhead fee, in lieu of billing for in-house copies, regular postage, incoming/outgoing facsimiles, long distance phone charges, and other minor incidentals.

6. **Bills**: Invoices are usually prepared on a monthly basis. The client agrees to review bills and promptly state, within fifteen days, in writing, any objections or dispute as to the fees or costs charged and the amount owed. All unpaid bills for costs and/or for professional fees shall bear interest at a rate of 18% per annum after thirty days.

7. **Unpaid fees**: It is clearly understood that all outstanding fees must be paid 30 days prior to the final hearing in the client's cause. In the event that fees are not paid within 30 days of being invoiced, and a mutually agreeable payment schedule is not made, in writing, and thereafter adhered to, the client agrees to bear the costs of collection, including reasonable attorney's fees, costs, and any other expenses, losses, charges, and damages incurred in the protection and enforcement of this agreement, whether or not a civil action is actually filed, and up through and including appeal. In the event of a legal action or other proceeding arising under this agreement or a dispute regarding any alleged breach, default, claim, or misrepresentation arising out of this agreement, whether or not a lawsuit or other proceeding is filed, the prevailing party shall be entitled to recover its reasonable attorneys' fees and costs incurred in litigating the entitlement to attorneys' fees and costs due to it.

The parties recognize that the firm shall be entitled to an attorney's fee under this paragraph whether or not the firm retains an attorney outside the firm to represent it, because of the opportunity costs that will be involved in having to enforce this agreement, and hereby agree that a reasonable fee is the fee which would be due under the terms set out in ¶ 4, above.

Further, the reasonable costs that the prevailing party shall be entitled to recover shall include any costs that are taxable pursuant to any applicable statute, rule, or guideline (including, but not limited to, the Statewide Uniform Guidelines for Taxation of Costs), as well as costs not taxable thereunder. Such recoverable costs shall specifically include, but not be limited to, 1) costs of investigation; 2) costs of copying documents and other materials whether for discovery, filing with the court, internal review, or any other purpose; 3) costs for electronic discovery; 4) Westlaw, Lexis Nexis, or other electronic research service charges; 5) telephone charges; 6) mailing, commercial delivery service, and courier charges; 7) travel expenses, whether for investigation, depositions, hearings, trial, or any other purpose; 8) information technology support charges; 9) any and all consultant or expert witness fees, whether or not such fees are incurred in connection with a court-ordered report or testimony at a deposition, trial, or an evidentiary or non-evidentiary hearing; 11) mediator fees; and 12) any other reasonable cost incurred by the prevailing party in connection with the dispute.

The client and the firm waive the right to a jury trial in any action related to either collection of payments due or services rendered under this agreement.

CHARGING LIEN

The client specifically agrees that the firm shall have and is hereby granted all general, possessory, and retaining liens, and all equitable, special, and attorney's charging liens as permitted by law upon the client's interest in all real, personal, and intangible property, monies, including lump sum or periodic alimony, assets, and other things of value that are recovered, obtained, preserved, or protected for the client in this litigation, for any balance due, owing, and unpaid. Such lien(s) shall relate back to the date hereof and shall be superior in dignity to any other lien subsequent to the date hereof, and are subject to statutory interest. The client expressly acknowledges that s/he intends to waive any homeowner's exemption in such property to which s/he might otherwise be entitled, by execution of a separate mortgage agreement in favor of the firm, and expressly consents to this lien on any such property, and on any other equitable distribution to which s/he may be entitled. Furthermore, the client expressly agrees that s/he is hereby waiving any objection or defense s/he may have, including but not limited to "head of family" under Florida Statute § 222.11, to the enforcement of such a charging lien, or any other judgment for fees in favor of the firm, against any payment of alimony, of future wages, and/or of disposable earnings to which s/he may be entitled.

Especially in the event that the firm is discharged or withdraws as the client's counsel before completion of this litigation, the client confirms that the firm is entitled to file a *lis pendens*, to obtain an order protecting its right to a charging lien, and to have the amount of its fee and the costs incurred, including any fees and costs expended in withdrawing and enforcing this agreement, determined in the same action before the suit is dismissed or otherwise concluded.

The firm confirms that it shall not seek an order confirming its right to a charging lien unless and until the client has failed to make a payment as required under this agreement. The client acknowledges that s/he has received timely notice of the firm's intent to pursue the charging lien upon the client's delinquency in payment or the firm's withdrawal from representation.

The client hereby agrees that the charging lien will follow any property recovered, obtained, preserved, or protected for the client in this litigation, whether the dispute is settled or tried by the parties. In the event of a settlement, however, the client acknowledges that s/he is obliged to notify the firm of any proposed settlement agreement.

WAGE ASSIGNMENT

If the client executes a voluntary wage assignment in favor of the firm, the client acknowledges that such assignment does not constitute an election of remedies and that the firm continues to be entitled to any and all of its legal and contractual rights to pursue payment, including its right to impose a charging lien on the client's assets.

RETAINING LIEN

The client agrees that, so long as the client owes the firm payment, the firm is entitled to retain possession of the client's papers, money, or other property of the client in the firm's possession, until the fees and/or costs are paid. Should the client request that the firm release possession of the file or other property, then the client shall make adequate arrangements for payment of the fees and/or costs owed or for the posting of adequate security, and the firm shall have absolute discretion to determine the adequacy of the arrangements or security.

INSOLVENCY

The client acknowledges that s/he is insolvent at this time, i.e. that his/her debts are greater than his/her assets, and/or that his/her monthly income is greater than his/her monthly expenses. Therefore, in exchange for the firm's agreement to undertake his/her legal representation, the client agrees that any and all monies that shall be owed to the firm shall not be dischargeable in any bankruptcy proceeding or otherwise, and specifically that such a debt is non-dischargeable under Bankruptcy Code § 523. For this reason, the client hereby waives the dischargeability of any outstanding fees and/or costs. The client agrees that the firm may file a copy of this

retainer contract as evidence of that waiver, in the event that the client is involved as a debtor in any bankruptcy proceeding.

8.   **Collaborative Process**. In the event that the representation becomes collaborative, the provisions in this subsection (the "Collaborative Section") will apply. If there is a conflict between the other terms of this agreement and the terms of the collaborative section, the terms of this Collaborative Section will govern.

Upon the execution of the collaborative participation agreement (a separate document from this agreement), the firm's representation will be limited to the collaborative process. Accordingly, no court hearings will be set other than those necessary to enter agreed orders and final judgments. If you and the other party are unable to reach an agreement, or one of you files a contested pleading or motion with the court, then the firm must withdraw from this representation pursuant to the terms of the collaborative participation agreement.

Moreover, you acknowledge that the firm reserves the right to withdraw for the following reasons, which are in addition to the reasons for withdrawal outlined elsewhere in this agreement: (i) you use delay to gain an advantage in the collaborative process; (ii) you persistently refuse to follow through on commitments; or (iii) you insist on using direct or implicit threats to gain advantage in the collaborative process.

You acknowledge that the firm has a right and potentially a duty to terminate the collaborative process if you engage in any of the following behaviors and persist in doing so after counseling by the firm: (i) you refuse to disclose information, including the existence of documents, which in the firm's judgment must be provided to the other party or any member of the collaborative team; (ii) you answer dishonestly to any inquiry made by the other party or member of the collaborative team; (iii) you take an action that results in compromising the integrity of the process; or (iv) you fail or refuse to take an action which failure or refusal compromises the integrity of the process.

Under any of these circumstances, if you refuse to terminate the collaborative process, you authorize the firm to terminate the collaborative process on your behalf by written notice to the other party, the collaborative team, and the Court. The firm's right and/or duty to terminate the collaborative process and notify the other participants and the Court survives your request that the firm withdraw and/or your termination of the firm's services.

9.   **Disclaimer**. From time to time during the course of the client's representation, the firm may express an opinion concerning the outcome of the litigation or a particular claim, defense, or course of action. Client acknowledges, however, that litigation is an uncertain business, that the firm does not and cannot assure or warrant any particular result, and that any statement made by an employee of the firm regarding an anticipated outcome is merely an opinion based on information available at the time and not a promise of the outcome.

WE CAN NEVER GUARANTEE AN OUTCOME!

Therefore, nothing in this agreement or in the firm's statements shall be construed as a promise or guarantee of the result of the case. The outcome of litigation is dependent upon the decisions of other parties, changing discovery of facts or opinions, and countless other variables. The client also understands that, in the event of losing the case, or in a suit for dissolution of marriage, there may be a judgment against the client for the opposing party's court costs and/or attorney's fees.

The client understands that the firm will not take a legal position that is not supported by material fact, and that any material fact provided by the client must be supported by testimony or other independent evidence. In the event that the client wishes the firm to argue for an extension, modification, or reversal of existing law or any other similar attempt to establish new law, the client agrees to indemnify and hold the firm harmless for any attorney's fees that may be awarded to the opposing party, pursuant to Florida Statute § 57.105 or otherwise.

DISSOLUTION OF MARRIAGE

In a suit for dissolution of marriage, this acknowledges that the firm has advised the client that s/he may wish to consider changing his/her last will and testament, as well as any trust instruments. This will also acknowledge that, because any settlement in this matter will likely include the exchange of general releases, the firm has suggested that the client have an AIDS or other STD test, should s/he believe that the opposing party has committed any marital infidelity, and that the client has agreed to bring any positive results to the firm's attention.

Further, should the client question whether he is the biological father of the child(ren) born during this marriage, under current law, he acknowledges that he must raise that claim during the dissolution of marriage. Failure to do so will bar a future challenge of paternity.

The firm has also recommended that the client discuss with his/her tax specialist whether it is advisable to file an "Innocent Spouse" election, in the event that s/he has filed a joint return with the opposing party, as well as any other tax issues relevant to payment or receipt of alimony, child support, and/or equitable distribution.

Finally, although it may seem far-fetched, because the opposing party may go through the client's garbage looking for information, the firm has advised the client to take care not to discard documents at his/her home that s/he does not wish the opposing party to see.

LEGAL MALPRACTICE

In a legal malpractice case, the client agrees and understands that it is not cost effective to pursue uninsured or underinsured lawyer-defendants with small "self-liquidating" insurance policies. Thus, to the extent that this is a problem, then the client agrees to settle within the insurance limits projected to be available after trial, or for a nominal amount, if any, with a lawyer-defendant who is or becomes uninsured.

10.   **Documents**: The firm will copy the client with all documents received or produced by the firm with respect to the client's case. The client agrees to review these documents as they are received and to ask any questions s/he may have promptly. In this manner, the firm ensures that the client is aware of the status of his/her case, and that the client has a duplicate file to that which the firm maintains. The firm will always copy any original documents and return them to the client. The firm never retains originals. When the client's matter is resolved and closed, the firm's file will be scanned and shredded.

11.   **Payment by opposing party**: In the event that payment of all or part of the reasonable attorney's fee or costs is made by the adverse party pursuant to agreement or court order, such payment shall be credited to any outstanding amount due, and any balance shall thereafter be reimbursed to the client. However, this clause is not to be construed as a waiver of the client's obligation to pay the attorney's fees and/or costs him or herself.

The client hereby assigns to the firm any right to proceed against the opposing party, whether before or after final judgment, to recover attorney's fees to the extent that the client would be entitled to recover same from the opposing party, and to the extent that the client owes fees and costs to the firm.

12.   **Withdrawal**: The client understands and agrees that if the firm determines at some later date that his/her claim or defense should not or cannot reasonably be pursued by the firm, the firm may notify the client of this decision in writing and withdraw as his/her attorneys. The firm shall have the right to withdraw from the client's cause if client fails to, among other things, 1) make payments as required by this agreement; 2) disclose material facts; 3) follow advice rendered; and/or 4) attend conferences, depositions, and/or hearings.

13.   **Termination**: In the event that the services of the firm are terminated, no earned part of the fee paid at the time of termination shall be returned. If it develops that the firm cannot represent the client because of an ethical consideration or some other reason, the firm will return such portion of the fee already paid that exceeds the services rendered. The client understands that the scope of representation excludes objectives or means that the firm regards as repugnant or imprudent.

14.   **Warranties**: The firm makes no representations or warranties concerning the successful termination of the client's cause. The client understands that any statement of the firm on these matters is a statement of opinion only. It is further understood and agreed that the firm has made no promises to the client or to any other person with regard to the outcome of this case, except that it has promised to render its best professional skill in the

matter.

15.   **Personal Guaranty**: The undersigned, signing as the client, or on behalf of the client, personally guarantees the performance of the client's obligations under the terms of this agreement.

16.   **Fee indemnification**: The client hereby agrees to indemnify the firm for any and all attorney's fee and/or cost awards issued against the firm and/or an individual attorney employed by the firm that arise from the firm's representation of the client. In the event that the firm is assessed monetary sanctions for the client's failure to cooperate and/or comply with the requirements of mandatory disclosure, the client agrees that such sanctions shall be added to client's invoice as a billable cost, collectible by any means, as set forth herein.

17.   **Appeals**. Appeals are subject to a separate fee arrangement. Any appeal, post judgment, or enforcement proceeding subsequent to the final judgment shall be the subject of a separate fee agreement.

18.   **Cooperation**: The client shall not discuss the subject matter of the cause described above with anyone, other than employees of the firm, without the firm's express permission. The firm is the chief legal counsel in this matter and has the final decision on all legal questions pertaining to it. The client shall: 1) follow the advice and instructions of the firm; 2) cooperate fully with the firm in the handling of the case; 3) act in connection with the cause only through the firm; and 4) avoid all acts that are illegal, immoral, or unethical, or that might jeopardize the cause.

19.   **Failure to comply**: The client consents to the firm's withdrawal from the client's cause, as described in the opening paragraph of this contract, and from all services in connection with this contract, in the event that the client fails to comply with any of the terms of this contract. Thus, the client's failure to comply with any term of this agreement is tantamount to termination of it.

20.   **Other matters**: Payment of the above-mentioned fees does not obligate the firm to represent the client or any other party or entity in any other matter or case other than the matters described in the opening paragraph of this contract.

21.   **Conflicts**: The firm represents to the client that its professional loyalty and legal duty is to no person, entity, or cause other than the client; the client represents to the firm that he/she is fully satisfied with the firm's independence as stated herein and is aware of no conflict of interest, actual or perceived, which may impair that independence.

22.   **Whole agreement**: This contract, including any addenda hereto (e.g., a mortgage agreement; a voluntary wage assignment agreement; and/or a waiver of the head-of-household exemption) represents the entire agreement between the firm and the client.

There are no promises, terms, conditions, or obligations, other than those contained herein; this contract supersedes all previous communications, representations, or agreements, either verbal or written, between the firm and the client.

This is a binding contract. Before signing, please read it carefully and ensure that you understand it. If there is anything that you do not understand, ask us to explain it or consult with another lawyer before signing it.

The client has read and understands all conditions of this agreement and agrees to all of its terms. The client subscribes to and is liable to the firm to comply with the terms of this contract. The client's signature below represents his/her consent to its terms. Please return the signed original and retain a copy for your records.

DATED this __ day of _____, _____ at Tampa, Florida.

_____
Client (signature)

_____
Client (printed name)

PAYOR EXECUTION
DO NOT SIGN BELOW IF YOU ARE THE CLIENT

I agree to be bound by the terms of this agreement, and to pay for the legal services described herein. In addition, I acknowledge that I am NOT the client described herein, and that the firm will resolve any conflicting instructions received from the client and myself in favor of the client.

_____
Payor (signature)

_____
Payor (printed name)

_____
Payor's Social Security Number

_____
Payor's Driver's License Number

LAW FIRM EXECUTION

I accept this cause for representation and the client named, with the express understanding that this contract is conditioned upon receipt of any retainer fee set out above, and upon the client's express waiver of the dischargeability of any fees and/or costs s/he may owe the firm in the event that s/he becomes a debtor in any bankruptcy proceeding.

_____
Esquire
LAW FIRM

ADDENDA TO CONTRACT FOR LEGAL SERVICES

WAIVER OF HEAD-OF-HOUSEHOLD EXEMPTION

IF YOU PROVIDE MORE THAN ONE-HALF OF THE SUPPORT FOR A CHILD OR OTHER DEPENDENT, ALL OR PART OF YOUR INCOME IS EXEMPT FROM GARNISHMENT UNDER FLORIDA LAW. YOU CAN WAIVE THIS PROTECTION ONLY BY SIGNING THIS DOCUMENT. BY SIGNING BELOW, YOU AGREE TO WAIVE THE PROTECTION FROM GARNISHMENT.

_____

Consumer's Signature

_____

Date Signed

I have fully explained this document to the consumer.

_____

Creditor's Signature

_____

Date Signed

Appendix Two
Not Retained Form

PLEASE READ CAREFULLY AND SIGN BELOW.

I understand that I have consulted with an attorney from Open Palm Law regarding certain legal issues, **but I have not retained the law firm at this time.** If I do decide to retain Open Palm Law, I understand that I will be required to execute a retainer agreement, and to provide a fee retainer. I understand that Open Palm Law does not represent me regarding any matters discussed during our consultation, **unless and until both I and a representative from Open Palm Law execute a written agreement for representation.**

I understand that I may have important deadlines approaching. I understand that, if my legal problem involves a lawsuit, or a potential lawsuit, certain lawsuits must be filed within a certain period of time called a statute of limitation.

I understand that Open Palm Law has urged me to schedule a second appointment with the firm at the earliest possible time or to consult with other legal counsel immediately in order to protect my rights.

_____

Name

_____

Signature

_____

Date

APPENDIX THREE
SAMPLE INVOICE

Law Firm Letterhead

To: Client
        Email

April 25, 2017

Date	Description	Time Spent	Rate	Amount Billed
4/1/2017	Open and set up electronic file	1.0	130.00	$130.00
4/2/2017	Telephone call with client regarding upcoming deposition of non party witnesses	0.2	275.00	$ 55.00
4/10/2017	Prepare for deposition of non-party Witnesses	0.5	350.00	$175.00
4/12/2017	Attend deposition of non-party Witnesses	1.5	350.00	$525.00
	Totals:	3.2		$885.00

Trust funds
Fee retainer received - 4/1/2017 $2500.00
Cost retainer received - 4/1/2017 $ 500.00

        Total default as of 4/25/2017 $3,000.00

Disbursements:
Attorneys' fees   (885.00)
Costs (court reporter)   (350.00)

        Total disbursements: $1,235.00
        Total default balance: $1,765.00

Appendix Four
Rate Increase Notice Form

(Letterhead)

Important Notice

FROM: JORYN JENKINS

TO: ALL CLIENTS

EFFECTIVE MAY 1, 2017, THE HOURLY BILLING RATE FOR JORYN JENKINS HAS INCREASED FROM $400 PER HOUR TO $450 PER HOUR. THE BILLING RATE FOR PARALEGALS, LEGAL ASSISTANTS, AND LAW CLERKS WILL REMAIN AT $150.00 PER HOUR, AND FOR ASSOCIATES AND OF COUNSELS, WILL REMAIN AT $250.00 TO $300.00 PER HOUR, DEPENDING ON THEIR EXPERIENCE LEVELS.

SHOULD YOU HAVE ANY QUESTIONS OR CONCERNS, PLEASE DO NOT HESITATE TO CONTACT ME OR MY ASSISTANT, NANCY RODRIGUEZ.

Return to: Name of Law Firm

This Instrument Prepared by Holder:

Name of Law Firm
Address
Telephone #

Borrower: **[Borrower's name in bold]**

PROMISSORY NOTE

Total Amount Due: Six Thousand Dollars ($6,000.00)

Jurisdiction: _____County   Date:
_____City, State

    FOR VALUE RECEIVED, the undersigned promises to pay the Holder, [Name of Law Firm], in the manner hereinafter specified, the principal sum of Six Thousand Dollars ($6,000.00) with interest beginning July 1, 2017 at the rate of twelve (12%) percent per annum on the balance until the principal amount is paid in full and satisfied. The said principal and interest shall be payable in lawful money of the United States of America at [Address of Law Firm] or at such place as may hereafter be designed by written notice from the Holder to the Borrower hereof, on the date and in the manner following:

1. At the rate of $500.00 per month continuing on the 1st day of each month and beginning July 1, 2017, until the principal sum and all accrued interest is paid in full.

2. The principal sum of $6,000.00, along with the 12% interest, shall be paid in full upon default of the Borrower. Default shall be defined as Borrower being more than five (5) days late.

This note with interest is made by the Borrower hereof in favor of the said Holder, and shall be construed and enforced according to the laws of the State of [State].

If default be made in payment of any of the sums or interest mentioned herein or in said note, or in performance of any of the agreements contained herein or in said note, then the entire principal sum and accrued interest shall at the option of the Holder hereof become at once due and collectable without notice, time being of the essence; and said principal sum and accrued interest shall both bear interest from such time until paid at the highest rate allowable under the laws of the State of [State]. Failure to exercise this option shall not constitute a waiver of the right to exercise the same in the event of any subsequent default.

Each person liable hereon, whether maker or endorser, hereby waives presentment, protest, notice, notice of protest and notice of dishonor and agrees to pay all costs, including a reasonable attorney's fee, whether suit be brought or not, if, after maturity of this note or default hereunder, or under said mortgage, counsel shall be employed to collect this note or to protect the security of said mortgage.

Whenever used herein the terms "Holder" and "Borrower" shall be construed in the singular or plural as the context may require or admit.

Witness: Borrower:

_____   _____
Name: Name:
Address: Address:

STATE OF
COUNTY OF

I HEREBY CERTIFY that on this day personally appeared before me, an officer duly authorized to administer oaths and take acknowledgments, [name of client in bold] to me well known to be the person described herein and who executed the foregoing instrument, or who has produced _____ as identification, and who acknowledged before me that she executed the same freely and voluntarily for the purposes therein expressed, and with regard to penalties under perjury of the law.

WITNESS MY HAND AND SEAL this _____ day of _____, 2017

                          _____
                          NOTARY PUBLIC
                          State of [Name of State] at Large
                          My Commission Expires:

ABOUT THE AUTHORS

Liz Miller is a law firm administrator with 38 years of experience working in law firms. In January of 1979, three days after graduating from high school in an accelerated three-and-a-half-year program, Liz began her career as a legal secretary. Two years later, she obtained her paralegal degree from the Paralegal Institute of New York. In 1985, Liz and her husband moved to Tampa where she continued her legal career as a paralegal for several years.

In 1988, Liz opened Paralegal Professionals, working as an independent paralegal for attorneys who specialized in personal injury, medical malpractice, and general trial work. Offered an opportunity to segue her career into law office administration by one of her clients, in 1997, Liz turned her focus to managing law firms. She subsequently finished her education, earning a Bachelor's Degree in Business Administration and then her MBA with a specialty in finance. Through a series of career transitions between 1997 and 2015, Liz now works as an independent/contract law firm administrator.

Liz is a member of the editorial advisory board of *Law Office Manager* magazine. She writes and blogs for the magazine. Her professional associations include the National Association of Legal Administrators, the Suncoast Association of Legal Administrators, the American Bar Association, the Hillsborough County Bar Association, and the Society of Human Resources Managers.

Liz believes that attorneys sacrifice billable client hours when they handle administrative functions. She helps attorneys focus their time and energy on practicing law and taking care of their clients to build attorney/client relationships, while she manages the "*business*" of practicing law.

***

Joryn Jenkins is an attorney with 37 years of experience in the courtroom. She focuses her practice on courtless divorce at *Open Palm Law* in Tampa, Florida, and has made changing the way the world gets divorced® her mission. Ms. Jenkins received her B.A. from Yale University and her J.D. from Georgetown University Law Center. She is a former editor of *The Family Law Commentator* and the former editor-in-chief of both *The Federal Lawyer* and *The Bencher*, magazines with national circulations. She is the author of five books on the collaborative divorce process: *War or Peace (Avoid the Destruction of Divorce Court)*; *I Never Saw My Father Again (The Divorce Court Effect)*; *A Free Divorce Handbook (How to Organize a Pro Bono Collaborative Divorce Project)*; *Open for Business (Managing Your Collaborative*

Practice for Passion & Profit); and *Open for Business (Changing the Way the World Gets Divorced),* all OPEN PALM PRESS publications. She also has authored *From Rookie to Rainmaker, How to Grow Your Law Business, The Stepmother's Cookbook* (OPEN PALM PRESS), and *Florida Civil Practice Motions* (LEXIS LAW PUBLISHING).

Joryn assembled the collaborative team and represented one of the spouses in the first *pro bono* collaborative divorce completed in Florida. She has appeared on Fox 13, ABC Action News, NBC 8, and Bay News 9, as well as on radio on *The Sam Sorbo Show, Legally Speaking, The Jamie Meloni Show, Ask the Dom,* and *Social Media Today.* She has also been featured in *The Tampa Bay Times, The Tampa Tribune,* and *The World of Collaborative Practice* e-zine, all on the subject of collaborative practice and divorce. She has also been featured in *Real Simple, Redbook,* and *Good Housekeeping* magazines, as well as published in *Huffington Post.*

Joryn founded the Cheatwood American Inn of Court in 1988 and served in its leadership until after her presidency in 2001. She co-founded the Coordinating Council of Florida Inns in 1989 and served on the American Inns of Court Board of Trustees from 1991 until 1997.

In 2001, Joryn received the *A. Sherman Christensen Award,* an award bestowed in the courtroom of the United States Supreme Court annually for her work improving ethics, professionalism, and civility in the legal profession.

The Federal Bar Association also bestowed its highest honor, *The President's Award,* on Joryn in 1997.

Made in the USA
Middletown, DE
15 August 2020

14755987R00163